WILD
COUNTRY
The man who mad

WILD
COUNTRY
The man who made Friends

MARK
VALLANCE

Vertebrate Publishing, Sheffield
www.v-publishing.co.uk

For Jan

WILD COUNTRY
Mark Vallance

First published in 2016 by Vertebrate Publishing.

Vertebrate Publishing
Crescent House, 228 Psalter Lane, Sheffield S11 8UT, UK.
www.v-publishing.co.uk

A CIP catalogue record for this book is available from the British Library.

ISBN 978-1-910240-81-6 (Paperback)
ISBN 978-1-910240-82-3 (Ebook)

10 9 8 7 6 5 4 3 2 1

Design and production by Jane Beagley, Vertebrate Publishing.
www.v-publishing.co.uk

Vertebrate Publishing is committed to printing on paper from sustainable sources.

Printed and bound in Scotland by Bell & Bain Ltd.

CONTENTS

PROLOGUE DIAGNOSIS

Balanced at the limit of friction, calves aching, I tried to rest. Around me stretched vast slabs of granite lashed by a million rainstorms and baked in the Spanish sun, smoothing the rock so that its crystals of feldspar were too slick to use. The rope snaked down for thirty feet beneath me, electric green against the pink rock, to the last, distant bolt. That's the hallmark of climbing at La Pedriza, long stretches without protection. If I fell here, I would scrape horribly down the rock for seventy feet or so. I shifted my feet on the sloping, almost non-existent holds.

The climb, *Caballo Blanco*, had started easily enough with two pitches of grade five, but on the third each move seemed harder than the last and I had climbed forty feet before I could clip a bolt. The slab steepened fractionally and I hesitated; what I really needed was the confidence to make the moves in a continuous flow. The route linked blankness to blankness, moving first left then back right to glean the benefit of what was often less a hold and more of a change in texture. Each time I thought I saw a hold above me it turned out to be worse than it looked. I could feel myself becoming anxious.

One hundred and thirty feet below, Roger, my climbing partner of twenty-five years, was trying to find protection from the sun. The ledge at the top of the second pitch was good but small, yet the Corsican pine growing straight out of the granite, more like a bonsai than a real tree, offered little shade for Roger's substantial frame. I could feel my feet sweating inside my boots as I stood on smears. Retreat was not an option. I could only go up. But a small mistake, the slightest misjudgement, and I would discover how inhospitable granite could be. If I fell,

I would try to control the fall by sliding, but at some point, inevitably, I would start to tumble down the slab.

I needed to move. Lactic acid was building up in my leg muscles. The next bolt was close, three metres up to the left. If I could clip it, I would be safe. I could see a small flake that I could reach with my right hand, not much more than a crystal, but enough to give me the confidence to move up. I dipped my right hand into my chalk bag and rubbed the block with my fingers. Then I got two fingertips of my right hand on the crystal and made two steps up, one very precise and controlled, the second, more of a fumble, wondering if the rubber of my boots would stick. But the bolt was still out of reach. I was losing control. Panic was welling up inside me.

I judged that with one long stretch I would be able to clip the bolt, but in stretching upward I would flex the sole of my shoe, reducing its contact with the rock and changing the angle of my push. Would it stay there? I began taking deep breaths, forcing my respiration under control, as I tried to burn off the adrenaline flooding my system. Then I made the move and the bolt was in range. My quickdraws were racked on the left-hand side of my harness and I gingerly reached for one to clip the rope to the bolt and make myself safe. Then I clipped the bolt and with my left hand dragged the rope up to the karabiner, on the brink of safety and not a moment too soon.

Then I dropped the rope. It slapped on to my thigh. I felt my heart start thumping inside my chest. I tried a second time. The rope flopped back down on to the slab again. I tried once more. The same thing happened. I was starting to tire and again felt myself panicking. Clipping the rope was routine, something I could do with my eyes shut. But my fingers weren't doing what I was telling them. 'This is stupid,' I thought, 'just grab the quickdraw.' I could have, but I didn't. I hadn't come all this way to fail on a technicality. Carefully and very deliberately I reached down and took the rope between two fingers and my thumb. Reaching out I caught the lower karabiner with my index finger, twisted it so the weight of the rope depressed its gate, and breathed a sigh of relief as the rope dropped into the opening and I heard the gate click shut.

Safe.

I raced up the final ten metres to the belay bolts at the end of the pitch without further drama. Not until we were walking down the rocky track back to our campsite did Roger ask the question.

'What was that all about?'

I knew exactly what he meant but just shrugged. It sounded silly but I told him I didn't seem able to use my fingers properly. Roger said something about going to see a specialist. I pushed it to the back of my mind and forgot about it. The rest of our climbing trip went well. My fingers seemed fine and the problem didn't recur.

There was no reason to connect not clipping the rope with how I swung my arms when I was out walking. Jan, my wife, mentioned how my left arm stayed by my side. I hadn't noticed.

'Swing your arms', she would tell me, and I would do so, only to realise a few minutes later that I was back to swinging just the right one. Whatever was causing this, it didn't hurt, nor did it seem debilitating, or even very important, but it seemed to be progressing. It was enough to sow the first seeds of concern.

My GP, Peter Jackson, was a personal friend. He wasn't a climber but had been to the Karakoram as doctor on a small expedition to Latok; I had lent him some bits of equipment and specialised clothing. Two months after getting back from my climbing trip to Spain, in August 1998, I went to see him. He must have known then and there what was wrong with me but he picked up the phone, dialled a number and spoke to someone for a few minutes. Then he looked at me. Was I able to see a neurologist tomorrow afternoon? Getting an appointment so quickly got me worried.

Dr Gwilym Davies-Jones is a neurologist at Sheffield's Royal Hallamshire Hospital. He asked me to do a number of simple tasks like unbuttoning my shirt and then doing it up again. I had to open my hand and touch my thumb and middle finger together as fast as I could for about twenty seconds, then do the same with the other hand. He asked me to walk up and down the corridor outside his consulting room. Within ten minutes he told me I had Parkinson's disease.

I didn't know much about Parkinson's beyond clichéd images of old people shaking or making sudden, jerky movements. I was fifty-four, a little young to be developing the disease. Like most people diagnosed at my age I didn't know what it might mean for me right then, or what it would mean in the future, and I didn't want to know either. I was a fit ambitious climber not long retired from running Wild Country, the equipment company I founded to make Friends. Now I had a bunch of brain cells that weren't working properly. There was no cure. It was only going to get worse.

It would probably kill me.

Bugger.

Robin Hodgkin *(left)*, Nick Longland *(centre)* and me returning from our ascent of *Longland's Climb* on Clogwyn Du'r Arddu, June 1963. *Photo: John Coates.*

1 FIRST MOVES

Many people have suggested I write the history of Wild Country, the company I founded in 1977 to manufacture Ray Jardine's design for a climbing camming-device. I kept putting it off and it's now over thirty-five years since I started to assemble Friends, as they were called, on the kitchen table of our cottage in the Peak District. The people who used to be my customers are the parents and now grandparents of a new generation of climbers. When I eventually started writing, partly in response to suffering from Parkinson's, I found it difficult to separate myself from the company I created. My life is inextricably linked to the development of climbing equipment; what used to be my job is now my story. It is the story of a chance I was given and grasped with both hands.

I was born towards the end of the Second World War, on 17 September 1944, the same day as Reinhold Messner, arguably the greatest mountaineer of all time. His castle in the Dolomites overlooks the headquarters of Salewa, the new owners of Wild Country. My father, Arthur Woolley Vallance, was a Unitarian minister, so too was my mother Elspeth. Both read history at Oxford. The Vallance household, with several thousand books in bookcases that filled whole walls, had an air of academic seriousness that was, to a large extent, wasted on me.

My father was the second of five children. He was born in 1902 and brought up in Manchester. His father had been a successful builder in Mansfield. On his mother's side, the Woolley side, were the manufacturing chemists James Woolley, Sons and Co., based in Manchester. My mother was born in August 1915, the youngest of a family of seven children living in Sheffield. Her oldest brother, Morley, died from septicaemia in Oxford at the age of twenty-one, and there was a sister, Betty, who died of diphtheria aged eight. Both my mother and her other brother, Martin, went to Oxford and became Unitarian ministers. Another sister, Joan, graduated from Oxford and married a Unitarian minister. Her two other sisters became artists and teachers.

We lived on the outskirts of Altrincham, a pleasant market town sandwiched between rural Cheshire to the south and Manchester to the north-east. I had a younger brother, Stephen, and then there was Rachel, my older sister. Rachel had Down's syndrome and died from meningitis when she was four. My mother says that we played together and got on very well but I have no memory of her. I even forgot to mention her when I wrote the first draft of these pages, which makes me feel guilty.

The Parsonage on Dunham Road was a large, red-brick Edwardian house with some mock half-timbering, separated from the main A56 road to Chester by a grass tennis court, a high privet hedge and a big oak tree. To the side were vegetable gardens, mature fruit trees and trees I could climb. It was a garden made for small boys and my younger brother Stephen and I revelled in it. It was also a big draw for our friends. On the inside, the house was more Gothic Revival than mock Tudor, with passages, staircases and landings all on different levels. The Unitarian chapel where my father preached every week was just a stone's throw away on the other side of Sylvan Grove, an unadopted cul-de-sac with potholes big enough to drown in.

My maternal grandparents, Alfred and Amy Hall, lived with us. Alfred was a much-loved and respected elder statesman of Unitarianism and the author of an important book, *The Beliefs of a Unitarian*. He had put himself through school and, apparently like everyone else in my family, graduated from Oxford. Later, he received an honorary doctorate of divinity from Harvard. On his visit to the United States to receive his doctorate, he was given tickets for Buffalo Bill Cody's Wild West Show. I would quiz him for hours about cowboys, buffalo, Annie Oakley and the different tribes of what we used to call Red Indians. I remember him as a benign old man with a wealth of stories.

When asked what Unitarians believe, they often make a list of those things Unitarians don't believe. The name comes from their belief that God is not a trinity. This sets Unitarians apart, and the consequence is a belief that Jesus is not God but a man whose birth obeyed the rules of biology just like the rest of us. So: no virgin birth either and no resurrection. Historically, the rejection of these articles of faith often guaranteed a

Unitarian a very direct passage to the fires of hell, something else they don't believe in. At this point questions about the accuracy of the Bible tend to crop up. Is the Bible wrong? Unitarians think that to lead a good life as defined by Jesus in the Sermon on the Mount is more important than to believe certain rather unlikely ideas introduced many centuries after the crucifixion. If you find yourself in an Anglican church, waiting for the bride or the coffin to arrive, look up the creed for Trinity Sunday in the Book of Common Prayer: for Unitarians, a classic example of gobbledygook.

My grandfather explained in his book: 'Unitarianism is not a set of creeds or beliefs. It is more than anything else an attitude of mind. It lays the stress on the reliability of the human mind to judge for itself. Its method is one of appeal to reason, conscience and experience.' Unsurprisingly, Unitarians have close links with Quakers and there are many Quaker meeting houses that double as Unitarian chapels. When my parents eventually chose the progressive Abbotsholme School for my education there was a lot of common ground between Robin Hodgkin, the headmaster and an active Quaker, and my parents. All three had been at Oxford.

My early childhood was spent in an era of austerity and ration books but if there was any hardship I was oblivious to it, having never known otherwise. Though I didn't lack for anything, my parents were parsimonious. There was no extravagance, no foreign holidays, no parties or alcohol. My father worked hard and gave away much of the money that was bequeathed to him, though my brother and I benefited most; that money enabled him to educate us privately, assuming you consider private education to be a benefit. He would not have been able to do that on a minister's stipend.

I have been privileged in a number of ways, but none more so than in getting a second chance after failing my 'eleven-plus'. Growing up as a duffer in an intellectual and academic atmosphere did not, as it might have done, inhibit my development. Both my parents believed passionately in Unitarianism, and believed that what they were doing, the way they led their lives, was morally right. My father spent most of his time in his study, visiting his parishioners or going to meetings, which he did on a racy pushbike with fancy derailleur gears. He was out most evenings. When my mother became the minister of Urmston Unitarian Chapel my parents employed Dutch au pairs to look after my brother and me. Later, as Stephen and I grew up, this lack of closeness made me wonder if my mother understood the simple fact that if you devote your life to a cause, which she did, you have to make time for those with whom you want to become or remain close. As a consequence, we were not a well-knit family. I don't think we suffered in any serious way, and I was at least able to follow my own path.

My brother Stephen was soon on the side of the angels, becoming a surgeon, a profession, in my parents' eyes, on a par with the clergy: a little lower than Nobel laureates and a little higher than teachers. We were never particularly close, but we frequently did things together and sometimes came to blows, as brothers will. I have no idea what I'd done when he attacked me with a tennis racket and nearly broke my ribs, but I'm sure it was well deserved. Stephen was a lot brighter than me and passed all his exams. We went to the same schools, but though I was two years older than him, I was only a year behind. We also climbed together quite a bit. He joined the Climbers' Club and led routes like *Cenotaph Corner*. He studied medicine at Birmingham, became a surgeon and spent a year as a medic with the British Antarctic Survey at Adelaide Island the year after I left Antarctica. Eventually, in 1985, he emigrated, moving to New Zealand. Now we are 12,000 miles apart, we get on very well.

My mother would have liked me to continue the family tradition and become a Unitarian minister. But by the time I was sixteen I was a committed atheist, the final nail driven home with my discovery of Albert Camus, the French existential philosopher. His novel, *L'Étranger*, 'The Outsider', had a profound impact on me. My rejection of God was based on the belief that we are responsible for our own destiny. To suggest there is a benign force out there looking out for us is not only far-fetched but also irresponsible. The profligate way we are burning through the resources of our beautiful planet may cost us the earth. If we don't take responsibility, nothing else will.

My mother would sometimes say she didn't know where I got my instinct for business. She had that left-wing mistrust of the world of commerce, choosing to forget that two of my father's brothers were very successful businessmen, Alec being the owner of a chain of electrical white-goods shops stretching up the east side of England while George had a substantial photographic film-processing business in Mansfield. My parents were both committed socialists but their politics were theoretical, not practical; party politics was not often on the menu at meal times. Even so, conversation around the Vallance dining table tended to the serious. The 1960s was an era when nuclear war seemed all too likely and both my parents were members of the Campaign for Nuclear Disarmament.

———————

I had a bumpy start at primary school. At the age of five, before I was settled in, I endured a year of illness which set me back and which I can, and frequently do, blame for my poor academic performance. I had the usual children's illnesses, chicken pox, mumps and measles and the less usual scarlet fever. I was also suspected of having rheumatic fever, although it was never confirmed and I have no memory of it. What I do remember is being rushed into an isolation hospital in Manchester with polio. I was extremely fortunate; our family doctor not only came on a house visit as soon as my mother called him, but he also made a quick diagnosis. I don't think I had any idea about how serious my condition might have been.

For the next three weeks I lived in a glass box and I received presents from everyone I knew and also from people I didn't know. To my bitter disappointment, none of these came home with me. For reasons of hygiene, they were all burned. For a five-year-old, that was a bitter blow. My parents were allowed to visit, but weren't allowed inside the glass box to touch me. I remember in particular the thick needle used to take samples from my spine. It took three nurses to hold me in a curled-up position so the doctor could drive it between my vertebrae to draw off cerebro-spinal fluid: the so-called 'spinal tap'. I was lucky to get away without any lasting paralysis but I did spend eighteen months wearing callipers on both legs and was slightly knock-kneed until a surgeon gave me full knee replacements in 2008 and 2013.

That summer I survived another brush with death. The family went on holiday to Abergele in North Wales, staying at a bed and breakfast run by the kindly Mrs Patterson. Excited to be at the coast, we immediately rushed down to the beach to go swimming in the grey murk of the Irish Sea. I had watched people swimming and felt I had the hang of it, so while my father played with my brother, I set out for the Isle of Man. I didn't get far. When my father looked to see what I was doing, he found me floating face down in the water, apparently lifeless. He carried me to the beach and performed artificial respiration until my lungs were empty and I had started breathing again – more missing brain cells.

School was a little over a mile away from The Parsonage, up a hill, along leafy roads and through pleasant countryside. At weekends I could play with my friends in Dunham Woods, an area of several hundred acres of mature woodland and countryside. It had been the site of a prisoner-of-war camp and there were a couple of old, single-skin brick buildings still standing and dotted around the woods rectangular concrete bases for the wooden huts that housed the prisoners. There were miles of dirt tracks to cycle on and then, so it seemed, a vast wood that gave way to a walled deer-park. In the summer my friends and I went on great adventures, sometimes taking picnics, occasionally staying away all day. Go there now and you'll find a beautiful golf course. There is a pleasant footpath through to the deer park, but the magic of the overgrown jungle has gone.

Adventure was a strong presence in my life from early on. There was a glass-fronted bookcase at The Parsonage, which is now in my office. In it was – is – a two-volume edition of *Scott's Last Expedition*. They are attractive books, leather bound with an inscription on the marbled fly-leaf which explains it was awarded to my father at Sedbergh School as the history essay prize for 1918. It contains Herbert Ponting's photographs and Edward Wilson's watercolours, and maps and panoramic photographs which fold out. In the winter when it snowed – and it always did – I would be Scott of the Antarctic, pulling my sledge, fighting blizzards and enduring great hardships.

Such heroism ran in the family. My father had a great uncle called Hermann Woolley, a director of James Woolley, Sons and Co., the Manchester-based pharmaceutical manufacturer. Hermann was big and very strong and was well known in Manchester as a sportsman. He had been a gentleman boxer, a champion gymnast and played football for Manchester. He took up mountaineering at the age of forty-six and made important first ascents in the Caucasus and the Canadian Rockies; with Norman Collie he made the first ascent of Mount Athabasca. At the summit they became the first westerners to see the Columbia Icefield. Uncle Hermann has two mountains named after him, Pic Woolley, in the Caucasus and the grand Mount Woolley in the Rockies' Sunwapta valley. He made first ascents in the European Alps, Arctic Norway and the Lofoten Islands and was also a skilled mountain photographer. I wonder what he would have made of my Rollei 35, a camera I have used all over the world and which weighs a fraction of the full-size plate camera that he carried. Hermann was elected president of the Alpine Club in 1908 and never missed a meeting throughout his three years. He was a founder member of the Climbers' Club, the Manchester-based Rucksack Club and was an honorary member of the Fell and Rock Climbing Club.

Like many youngsters of my generation, I was taken to see the film of the first ascent of Mount Everest in 1953, when Ed Hillary and Tenzing Norgay reached the summit as part of the British expedition led by Colonel John Hunt. Going to the cinema was a big deal in those days, at least for me. I had seen fewer than ten films in my entire life, but this was a school trip in which I had a personal interest. After all, my great, great uncle was Hermann Woolley. We went to the Odeon cinema on Manchester Road on a bus hired for the occasion. I remember being impatient, having to wait outside for our turn as other school groups filed into the cinema. The film made a huge impression on me; to this day I can remember much of the detail, porters struggling with, of all things, a piano, the climbers packing supplies.

Seeing the Everest film was a life-changing event. From that moment I wanted to be a climber. I prevailed on my father, an experienced fell-walker, to take the family to the Lake District the following summer. That first Lakeland holiday, inspired by our reading of *Swallows and Amazons* and suffused with the influence of other people's adventures, was my first experience of the mountains. Our base was a secluded campsite at Baysbrown Farm in Langdale, on the flank of Lingmoor Fell. Stephen, then aged nine, and I, climbed Lingmoor as our very first summit.

Having been educated at Sedbergh School, known for its rugby team and its ten-mile annual fell race, Dad was used to a lightweight approach to hillwalking. We wore shirts and sweaters, shorts and gym shoes with no socks. Sometimes we would carry lightweight oiled cotton cycling capes, which were good for keeping dry. Otherwise, if it rained, we got wet. We climbed the Langdale Pikes, Bowfell, Crinkle Crags and Esk Pike, Wetherlam and Great Carrs in the Coniston Fells, Helvellyn and the ultimate prize Scafell Pike. If Hillary and Tenzing had flags, then it was obvious that they were an important part of a mountaineer's kit. I had made my own Union Jack for the occasion.

On our third trip to the Lake District in 1955, aged eleven, I did my first rock climb on a small friendly cliff in Langdale called Scout Crag. It might so easily have been my last climb too. Ever since our first few weeks on the fells, I had been nagging my father to find a way for me to go rock climbing. As luck would have it, a friend of my father, Len Mason, was on holiday with his family, staying at a cottage in Elterwater, just down the road. Len was a Unitarian minister, his claim to fame being that he officiated at the wedding of Richard Burton and Elizabeth Taylor. He was also an experienced climber.

Staying with Len was his fifteen-year-old son, Hugh, who would lead our chosen route while his father watched me and told me what to do. It was a sunny day, the rock dry and warm to the touch, the angle mostly off the vertical. Hugh gained height quickly but when he was about thirty feet up I heard a crash and a startled cry of 'Below!' I looked up to see a rock about the size of a shoebox, along with a shower of smaller stones, heading straight for me. Len grabbed my sweater and pulled me under the shelter of a small overhang and the stones hammered into the ground where we'd been standing. Hugh had pulled on what he thought was a good hold and the whole lot had come away. That he managed to recover and not fall was amazing. He didn't seem to be at all fazed by the incident and was soon on his way again. When he was about halfway up the cliff, he stopped on a good ledge. Pulling up some slack rope he used it to form a loop, which he placed over a large spike of rock. He made a few adjustments, and then called 'Taking in!' and started pulling up the rope I was attached to by a loop round my waist tied with a bowline. Soon the rope was tight and he called again: 'Climb when you're ready.' Immediately I sprang into action, pulling on anything and everything I could get my hands or fingers on.

'No, no, no!' Len said. 'Take your time, but first you need to tell Hugh that you are about to climb. When you are ready, just shout up "Climbing!"' Having warned Hugh, I started battling with the rock again, thinking that it seemed much harder than Hugh had made it look.

'Use your feet and legs to gain height and only use your hands to steady yourself and balance,' Len told me. That was good advice. Soon I was ten feet off the ground, then twenty. Here the rope passed through a karabiner, a steel link attached to a loop of rope, which had been threaded behind a small stone jammed in the crack. Hugh had clipped the climbing rope into the steel link and, peering down at me from his ledge, explained how this would limit the length of a leader fall. It was my first experience of protecting a rock climb. I couldn't possibly know that I would revolutionise the ease of use and security this little rock jammed into the crack offered.

Later that holiday, my parents took me to visit Cressbrook School in Kirkby Lonsdale, a beautiful market town on the banks of the River Lune, nestling under the shadow of Casterton Fell on the edge of the Yorkshire Dales. Cressbrook was a small school with sixty pupils. I was introduced to the headmaster David A. Donald, or 'Dad' as the boys called him. Donald was handsome and athletic, a pillar of society in his mid forties. He taught Latin and games. Most students at Cressbrook, including me, were expected to go on to Sedbergh School, where both my father and David Donald had been head boy. Donald had been the only ever double winner of the ten-mile fell race, the Wilson Run, an event held in early spring every year, usually in atrocious weather.

It was a surprise to me when I discovered I was going to boarding school. It was really my father's wish. My father had been one of the first students to go to Cressbrook, which was founded in 1913 by Felix Dowson, a lovely old man who was in his eighties when I met him. My mother was less enthusiastic. It was usual for those educated privately to start 'prep school' at the age of eight, to study a curriculum that included French and Latin which led inexorably to the common entrance exam at the age of thirteen, for which each public school set its own standard. If I was to go to Cressbrook when I was eleven, I would have a lot of catching up to do. Having been to a state school, I had not done the three years of French and Latin that my peers had. I was not an academic child and never did catch up with my Latin and French.

It got worse. Private schools had no need of the eleven-plus exam, which, at the time, divided sheep from goats in the state sector. Public schools, that is 'private schools', tended not to take the eleven-plus very seriously. I failed it and because I never did catch up with my French and Latin, I would go on to fail common entrance too. At least my late start meant I didn't suffer the singularly English middle-class tradition of being torn from home and family at the outlandishly young age of eight. I wasn't bullied nor was I ever homesick. Once I accepted the strange prospect of leaving home, I not only adjusted to life at Cressbrook, I actively relished it. To begin with, I was mentored by a boy called Christopher Darwin, a talented violinist who became leader of the National Youth Orchestra and was later an experimental psychologist. I played the violin in the school orchestra, and occasionally sang solo in St Mary's, Kirkby Lonsdale's magnificent parish church. Another friend was Mark Crompton, who lived quite close to my home in Cheshire; Mark was a good linguist and an outstanding sportsman, particularly as a distance runner. The headmaster's daughter Kate was also in my class. She played cricket with us in the summer term and of course I fell deeply in love with her.

I was quite good at sports, or 'games' as they're called at private school. I played tennis and was in the first team for cricket and rugby. Two captains of England, John Spencer and Bill Beaumont, learned to play at Cressbrook. I played at full back, could kick long and accurately and was considered a safe pair of hands when it came to catching high balls. I could tackle and had I been a faster sprinter I might have gone further, but my true interest lay elsewhere. Various cups were awarded every year for the best sportsman in the various games we played, but there was an unusual trophy that I coveted more than any other: the Dowson Mountain Cup, established by Felix Dowson to honour the school's best climber. It was awarded to me in my final year.

Two factors conspired to fan the flames of my climbing passion. My desire to climb was strong, but opportunities to do so were few and far between. The summer after I started I cycled to Stanage Edge with Hugh Mason, the boy who had taken me on my first rock climb, from his holiday cottage in Tideswell. We climbed *Robin Hood's Crack Left Hand*, *Flying Buttress* and on Grey Wall. On another occasion I went with my father. Such was my introduction to climbing and though limited in scope and frequency, it taught me the basics: how to tie a bowline, choose a suitable belay and make myself safe. I learned rope management and how to provide a waist and shoulder belay. I was taught to use my feet, not to use my knees and to keep my heels low, although to this day I don't know why.

I did not cover myself in academic glory at Cressbrook. I was good at maths and art and not too bad at English, although I couldn't spell to save my life, which should have been a clue. I was bottom of the class in Latin, French and history. The only achievement I can remember being praised for was winning a prize for italic handwriting in a boring publication called the *Children's Newspaper*, bought by parents who did not approve of comics for children who would, in a later era, be absolved with the label 'dyslexic'.

Looking back, perhaps it was good fortune that I failed my common entrance and ended up at Abbotsholme rather than my father's old school. If, by some miracle, I had got into Sedbergh, I would have spent my whole school career trying to catch up. The door on which I had been knocking remained shut. There is nothing to be gained from asking 'what if?' The sense of failure stayed with me for some time but what lay behind the door that did open was beyond my imagination. I attended an assessment weekend at Abbotsholme during the Easter holidays and, much to my surprise, was awarded a £60 annual bursary, enough to cover about a fifth of my school fees, on the strength of scoring well in their internal intelligence test. My parents were delighted that at long last I had demonstrated some ability with my brain cells. Until then, I had never won, or come first, in any academic arena.

Abbotsholme was a 'progressive' school, sometimes a euphemism for one that lacked the traditions of more famous schools. But Abbotsholme, located on the banks of the River Dove seven miles from Ashbourne, did benefit pupils with its alternative approach to education. It didn't fit easily into the hierarchy of English public schools. It was a member of the Headmasters' Conference, but was not long established. It was informal in style and had none of the pretentions or questionable initiation rites that many public schools then fostered.

Outdoor education and recreation held a significant place in the curriculum with regular camping and youth hostel trips, expeditions to Snowdonia and Scotland and even to the Alps, the Pyrenees and the Atlas mountains. These trips probably marked out the school as much as anything, although Abbotsholme was also the first school in Britain to teach biology, a subject not considered fit for the sons of gentlemen. The school's founder, Cecil Reddie, was an influential educationalist; a German teacher, Hermann Lietz, who worked at Abbotsholme, would go on to found several schools in Germany. Another visitor was Kurt Hahn, who as a refugee from the Nazis founded Gordonstoun and the Outward Bound movement.

I would not be the first to blame lack of academic success on dyslexia, but the talents I possessed were well hidden and needed to be dug out, scrubbed and polished. I don't remember hearing or using the word dyslexia until I was in the fifth form at Abbotsholme, and it wasn't a term I would dream of applying to myself; it seemed far too sophisticated a word for that. As the word achieved common usage I began to realise it might describe some of my difficulties. I don't know how the severity of my affliction was measured, but as with polio I seem to have got off lightly. I read slowly and read aloud badly. My spelling is imaginative. I am also inclined to blame dyslexia for my poor language skills and my extremely poor ability to read music on sight. And yet, while it could be embarrassing, it has not, so far, proved fatal.

My new headmaster, Robin Hodgkin, not only understood what I needed, but accepted the challenge, for which I will forever be in his debt.

I think, at the start, that he thought of me as a project and he was an inspirational teacher, one of the leading educationalists of his generation. He was a one-off, radical, always pushing boundaries, stretching brain cells, opening closed minds and encouraging experimentation. He was a sort of pedagogical Pan, with a broad smile and sharp eyes, a slight figure at five foot eight, light on his feet, amazingly so considering he had no toes. I immediately recognised Hodgkin in John Fowles's description of Maurice Conchis in his iconic book, *The Magus*: the intelligence, the slightly simian features, although his straightforward manner and ready smile soon dispelled any sense of enigma.

Robin Hodgkin was born into a talented Quaker family in 1916. His father died in Baghdad in 1918, when he was just two. His elder brother Alan won the Nobel Prize for medicine; Dorothy Hodgkin, his cousin by marriage, was the chemistry Nobel laureate that pioneered the science of X-ray crystallography. Robin was also a well-known and respected mountaineer. While an undergraduate at Oxford he was the driving force in a rejuvenated mountaineering club and as a young man he was considered by some to be the best rock climber in England. With George Mallory's daughters Clare and Beridge, Hodgkin and David Cox climbed all the routes on Clogwyn Du'r Arddu in Snowdonia during a summer week in 1937 spent camping by the lake beneath the cliff. Hodgkin and Cox made excellent first ascents of the Wall Finish on *Pigott's Climb* on the East Buttress, and the Top Traverse of *Great Slab,* a challenge that had defeated Colin Kirkus. It was the first time anyone had ventured out of the cracks and chimneys on to blank rock; Hodgkin said Cloggy gave him the confidence to do the face climbing required on his new route on Ushba later that year. (Ken Wilson once asked him outright about the sleeping arrangements that week with the Mallory girls by the lake. Hodgkin responded that they were total innocents. They had separate tents and spent the time reading Jane Austen's *Emma* to each other.)

Hodgkin did much of his climbing in the two years that culminated in his attempt to climb Masherbrum in 1938, a mountain that just fails to make it into the 8,000-metre club. Helping a Sherpa to descend from a high camp during a storm, he was badly frostbitten and lost all his toes, the last joint of both index fingers and retained only one joint of the rest of his fingers of both hands. He still had his thumbs. Despite this he continued to lead climbs up to Hard Severe. Later, in semi-retirement after Abbotsholme, he became reader in education at Oxford and wrote several books, influenced by his intellectual mentor Michael Polanyi.

I had just turned fourteen when I arrived at Abbotsholme at the end of September 1958 and went straight into the third year. The pecking order in boarding schools is well developed. Length of tenure is important, intellectual prowess is suspect, but acceptable if seen to be effortless. Sporting prowess was of supreme importance. I was the only new student in my year group and settled in quickly.

On one occasion I was carrying a large armful of books and papers to the geography room. As I entered I tripped, spilling books and papers all over the place. I was not aware of any one else in the room, and as I picked myself off the floor I said in a loud voice: 'Oh bother!'

Hodgkin, who taught geography and geology, was sorting out some books in the library area behind a large bookcase that acted as a partition. He popped his head round the corner and said with a chuckle: 'Very restrained, Vallance.'

There was one incident that might have ended my relationship with Robin Hodgkin and almost got me expelled. I had signed out for a weekend of climbing and also signed out for another boy who had decided to run away. He said he was going to go to Australia. I don't think we believed him, but it was a good story. When we got back on Sunday evening, without Billy, there was all hell to pay. Billy got to Toulouse and did not come back to school. Several of the teaching staff thought that I should go too, and I would have if Hodgkin hadn't given me his support.

One of my classmates was a boy called Nick Longland. Nick was three months younger than me but had started at Abbotsholme the previous year. He was near the top of the class in most subjects along with John Coates, later treasurer of the Fell and Rock Climbing Club. I don't remember any particular time or occasion when I started to think of Nick as a friend. We were both aware the other was interested in climbing. Nick was lucky to come from a climbing family; his father and his elder brother John were able to teach him. I didn't have anyone I could ask to take me climbing. At this point I had only managed roped climbing on five occasions. At Abbotsholme I was reliant on Robin Hodgkin to take me out. The first time I climbed with him was at the Roaches where we climbed *Jeffcoat's Chimney* and several other routes. Such trips became a regular feature of school life. Before we left Abbotsholme in July 1963, Robin drove Nick, John Coates and myself up to Snowdonia to make a memorable ascent of *Longland's Climb* on Clogwyn Du'r Arddu.

Learning to climb at school was surprisingly unstructured, even casual, especially if one compares what happened then to how it is done now. One Wednesday afternoon, Hodgkin took a group of us to Rainster Rocks near Brassington, an outcrop of dolomitic limestone only ten miles from school. The climbing was on a series of steps, about twenty to thirty feet high, most of it relatively easy. The rock had hundreds of holes, like Emmental cheese, a great place to climb for beginners who might easily get into trouble on a more serious crag.

On the way back to Abbotsholme, we stopped in Crich at the house of a friend of Hodgkin's. It turned out that this was also Nick's family home. I suddenly realised that Nick's father Jack was more than just a climber. He was an influential and respected mountaineer who had made first ascents of what were, at the time, considered to be some of the hardest climbs rock climbs in Britain: *Longland's Climb* on Cloggy and *Javelin Blade* in the Ogwen Valley. He had been a member of the 1933 Mount Everest expedition and climbed to over 27,000 feet. Being fifteen, I was inevitably impressed, but I couldn't possibly know the huge influence Jack would have on me.

He was very different not just from my father but also from the fathers of my other friends. Jack treated me like an adult. Even when I was fifteen he listened to what I had to say. He was also very generous to me and in a number of ways. On one occasion Nick and I had been climbing together and arrived back at Nick's house as the family were getting ready to go out to a restaurant for dinner. I was about to cycle home when Jack invited me to join the family. It was done in such a way that I was made to feel that my being there was assumed. I was simply being treated as one of the family. Nick's mother, Peggy was a superb cook. I never once saw her fazed when Nick or his brother John turned up with a couple of car loads of climbing friends, all expecting to be fed and watered.

What happened next didn't seem a big deal at the time but it would have a lasting impact on my life. Nick's family moved to Bakewell from Crich, and my family moved to Chesterfield from Altrincham. The combination of living within cycling distance of suitable crags, and close enough to each other to be able to climb together during the school holidays, provided the catalyst for some strong alchemy. When I cycled over from Chesterfield to Bakewell, I entered another world, an enchanted world, a world of intellect and conversation and humour, of exotic food and fine wine. A world where there were no limits.

Brown's Eliminate, on Froggatt Edge in the Peak District, June 1960. Originally graded HVS, it is now E2 5b. Note the gym shoes and no runners.

2 LESSONS FROM JACK

Chesterfield has two things going for it, the iconic twisted spire of St Mary and All Saints, its parish church, and its proximity to the Peak District. There used to be a sign on the main road into town that read: 'Chesterfield: centre of industrial England.' It was never clear to me if this was a warning or a recommendation. When my family moved there from Altrincham, I didn't know anyone. Our new family home was smaller in every respect to The Parsonage in Altrincham, being an end-of-terrace three-bedroom red-brick house with a tiny garden and no character. To a fifteen-year-old public schoolboy it was not only an unwanted wrench from the familiar but also a social disaster. I didn't immediately realise that our new home was on the edge of the Peak District, and that I could now cycle up to the Robin Hood Inn near Baslow in half an hour and fifteen minutes later could be climbing on the best rock on the planet. I also had friends in Bakewell from school, and could now get there on my bike in under an hour.

Today, Bakewell is clogged with day trippers shuffling about aimlessly or buying ordinary stuff in equally ordinary shops. In the early 1960s it was still a pleasant farming market town. The Longlands' family home, close to the thirteenth-century bridge over the River Wye, became the hub for a group of teenagers for whom climbing was increasingly important. Living in Chesterfield, I was on the fringe of this emerging social scene, but it still offered me a sense of spontaneity I found exciting and altogether new. To call Jack a role model wouldn't be accurate; the idea I could or should aspire to be like him, with his double first and athletics 'blue' at Cambridge, was not achievable. What Jack did was to open a window that looked out on to a much bigger world than I had previously known existed. If the Longland family hadn't befriended me, I would never have known such a world existed, let alone been part of it.

He was never 'Mr Longland', always Jack. I never heard anyone who knew him call him anything else. Radicalised during a spell lecturing at Durham University, where he came to know the local mining community, he was an enthusiastic supporter of comprehensive education, despite his establishment upbringing. As director of education for Derbyshire Jack had established the first local authority outdoor education centre at White Hall near Buxton, which predated the national centre at Plas y Brenin by two years. He was a vice-chairman of the Sports Council, president of the British Mountaineering Council, a persuasive advocate for national parks as board member of the Countryside Commission, a member of two royal commissions – the exemplary public servant. There were nights when I was staying over in Bakewell, having spent the day climbing with Nick, when Jack would clear away the plates and replace them with stacks of files that he'd work through, often into the early hours.

He was understated, though his entry in *Who's Who* mischievously included 'broadcasting' under 'Pastimes', a reference to the radio programme *My Word!*, the popular semi-intellectual quiz show Jack presented for twenty years with team captains Denis Norden and Frank Muir. It was Frank Muir who, in an after-dinner speech to the Alpine Club, came out with the oft-repeated line: 'The Alpine Club did not start with a bang, but with a Whymper!' Jack also presented *Round Britain Quiz* and was a regular on *Any Questions?*.

Their door was always open and, having entered, a mug of coffee would shortly follow and the conversation would start. Without needing an excuse, Jack would host a party for climbers and invite friends from Bakewell who would mingle with the best of the climbing world. Every May bank holiday, Jack invited what seemed to be the total membership of the Climbers' Club for drinks prior to the club's 'gritstone' dinner. I remember arriving in Bakewell one day, just in time to get a lift to Stanage in Jack's car. As we set off, and introductions were made, I discovered I was sitting next to two climbing legends from the 1920s and 1930s, A.B. Hargreaves and Ivan Waller. I still feel privileged. I'm not sure younger and older climbers integrate now in the way they did then.

Apart from the Longland household, Bakewell held another attraction for me. Her name was Sue, daughter of a local businessman. She had two older brothers who sometimes came climbing with us but they weren't as naturally gifted or as enthusiastic as Sue. A common attitude in the 1960s was a chauvinistic disinclination among male climbers to let girls lead let alone encourage them to do so. But Sue was talented and without any apparent effort or commitment was able to lead VS after a few years. We climbed together a good deal until I left for Antarctica. Sue went to an art college and married an old school friend of mine, Tony Maufe, a keen glider pilot. I didn't see either Sue or Tony for many years, until they turned up unexpectedly late one December afternoon at my house in Foolow. When Sue took off her coat, I realised she was heavily pregnant and we discovered that both she and my wife Jan were due to give birth in the New Year. Their daughter Hannah was born two days before our daughter Jody arrived. The girls became good friends and shared many adventures. They had the strange knack of meeting in far-flung places unexpectedly, arriving on the same day in the New Zealand resort of Wanaka to look for skiing work without knowing the other was in the country.

In September 1959, Robin Hodgkin led a climbing trip to Glencoe. Nine of us camped at Gunpowder Green below Buachaille Etive Mor. That long dry summer regular climbers had begun to climb the routes of Joe Brown and Don Whillans. Our group climbed some classics, *The Bow*, on the east face of Aonach Dubh, and *Crypt Route* on Bidean nam Bian, a route that finishes right on the summit. We traversed Aonach Eagach. Yet the highlight of the trip was unexpected. On the evening before our last full day, a gaunt Scotsman walked on to the campsite as we were cooking dinner. He asked how old we were and who was in charge. Hodgkin stuck his head out of his tent and asked the Scot if he could help. The man introduced himself as Hamish MacInnes. This was a visit from royalty. Hamish explained he wanted to make a film of youngsters learning to climb and planned to use a route on Buachaille Etive Mor. We learned later why he was keen to know our ages: had we been over sixteen, Hamish would have had to pay us.

If it were done, then 'twere well it were done quickly, since the following day was our last. The morning was fine and we hiked up the now familiar path that spirals round the conical peak of the Buachaille, bringing us to the start of *D Gully Buttress*. The film was titled *Up the Wall with Hamish MacInnes*, part of an ITV series called *Out and About*; it was only the second time a television programme had been dedicated to rock climbing. (The first, made two years earlier, had featured Joe Brown climbing *Suicide Wall* in North Wales.) After we had finished filming,

Hamish took Nick and myself to Rannoch Wall and we climbed the classic *Agag's Groove*. The next day we would be driving home but that evening after dinner I listened to MacInnes and Hodgkin talking about climbing Ushba, in the Caucasus. Hamish reminisced about his ascent of the *Bonatti Pillar* on the Dru; Robin asked Hamish why there had not yet been a British ascent of the Eiger's north wall. We sat there and listened, spellbound. It had been a great day, and a great week. Apart from the climbing, I had started ticking off the Munros, a project I am unlikely to complete, having only done about half of them; at my present rate it's going to take a hundred and thirty years.

The first half of Hamish MacInnes' half-hour programme featured Robin Hodgkin, Nick Longland and myself climbing in Glencoe. For the second half, Nick and I were asked to go down to London on the train to demonstrate rope-work and other technical aspects of climbing in the studio. Wooden boxes had been cobbled together and painted grey to represent a rock face. It all had to be done in one fifteen-minute take. Our interviewer was a veteran actor called Larry Payne, who was there to ask all the usual how-do-you-get-the-rope-to-the-top questions. Larry had worked on the film *The Mountain*, released in 1956, with Spencer Tracy and Robert Wagner but it was obvious not much of that experience had rubbed off on him.

There is a postscript. In June 2015, Bill Supple and his wife Jennifer came over from America to stay with Jan and me. Bill had been CEO of Wild Country USA and was now performing the same function for Mammut in the USA. They wanted to climb Ben Nevis and I said I would do it with them. It was a glorious day with acres of deep snow on the summit plateau, but thanks to Parkinson's, it took five and a half hours to do what I would have done in two hours a few years earlier. I was very tired by the end and lost my balance half an hour from the car. I managed to hurt myself quite badly, and so we went to hospital in Fort William, where I was stitched up. The nurses were very friendly, and learning I was a climber, one of them mentioned that Hamish had been in for a long visit the previous winter. There was a bad forecast for the next day, so I asked the nurse if she thought that Hamish would appreciate a visit. She encouraged us to go and so next day we turned up at his house to find him directing the placement of a new gatepost in the pouring rain outside his house on the back road to the Clachaig Inn. We hadn't seen each other for fifty-five years.

During the summer holiday of 1960, when we were fifteen, Nick and I started to climb together regularly, cycling out to the gritstone edges. As our climbing developed, we encouraged each other and kept up with each other. If Nick climbed a hard route, I would do it at the next opportunity, and vice versa. Sometimes we would climb twenty routes or more. If there was a particular day that I can point to as the real start of our climbing partnership, it was 22 July 1960. It was the beginning of the summer holidays and we went to Birchen Edge, a great place to develop our skills. The rock is near-perfect gritstone; it's clean, faces south-west and consequently gets the afternoon and evening sun. It also has a friendly atmosphere and most of the climbing is off vertical.

We stashed our bikes over a wall – you could do that in those days – and walked up to the crag. A stone memorial sits on top of the cliff, erected in 1810 to the memory of Horatio Nelson; three distinctive boulders were also carved with the names of prominent ships: *Victory*, *Defiance* and *Royal Sovereign* (carved as 'Soverin'). Not surprisingly, many of the routes have a nautical theme. I led *Horatio's Horror* and followed Nick up *Nelson's Nemesis*. Today these climbs are almost completely hidden by birch trees, but then they were exposed to the elements, a consequence of a great moorland fire the previous year. On the main crag we climbed *Nelson's Slab*, *Victory Crack*, *Emma's Dilemma* and, best of all, *Topsail*, finishing with *The Crow's Nest*, a delicate, unprotected fifty-foot VS both of us had been attempting for ages, but climbed on a top rope.

After that, Nick suggested we go back to Bakewell where his mother Peggy asked me to stay for dinner. Nick's younger sister Vicky was busy with homework, but his older sister Jo had a friend staying. These two older girls took great delight in putting Nick and me in our place, the way only older girls can. War was about to break out when I had the idea of locking them in the spare bedroom. Having done so, I worried that things would get out of control, and the longer we left them locked up the greater would be the repercussions. In the end we unlocked the door a few minutes before dinner, giving the girls enough time to change but not enough to cause a fuss.

Over dinner, Jack quizzed us about our day. He asked me a lot of questions about where and what I had climbed before. I felt I was having some sort of test; if it was a test, I think I passed. Jack was roughly the same age as my father but I had never before come across someone of his generation who engendered both respect and friendship: one or the other, but never both simultaneously. Right from the start I was treated as a member of the family. On one occasion he opened a bottle of Château d'Yquem – a sophisticated, very expensive Sauternes – and poured me a glass. Jack could so easily not have included me. As a sixteen-year-old, I didn't expect to be. But I was.

Our climbing now seems very parochial. Nick and I tended to keep to the Eastern Edges for no better reason than there was so much quality climbing on them and there was a limit to how far we could cycle: Birchen, Gardom's and Chatsworth were nearest, followed by Froggatt. Stanage Edge was at the limit of our range. I once cycled from school to Stanage Edge and soloed *Robin Hood's Cave Innominate* and *Leaning Buttress Direct* and cycled back, a round trip of eighty miles. Curbar Edge had a fierce reputation and overawed us. We led or soloed up to Severe. As relative beginners, we had a healthy respect not just for routes we couldn't climb but those we could. We would do routes again and again, and never lost regard for them, not surprising given we were still climbing in gym shoes. I've always thought gritstone was the best rock to learn on. Start on gritstone and you can move on to anything else; it doesn't always work the other way round.

We tied the hawser-laid rope around our waists with a bowline. Protection came from the careful use of rope slings of various diameters, spliced or knotted to form a loop that could be placed over a spike of rock, or doubled behind a chockstone to form a lark's foot or doubled around a tree trunk. The prospect of a serious fall on this gear was not inviting. Manufactured chockstones had not yet been introduced commercially, pitons were not acceptable, and the guiding principle was that the leader should not fall.

Before the introduction of kernmantle ropes there was a fashion to tie in with a Tarbuck knot, which slides, supposedly absorbing the energy of a serious fall. This sliding knot would be attached to a length of quarter-inch hemp rope, tied round the waist several times. The Americans would have called it a swami belt. The climber used a large screwgate karabiner to link the Tarbuck loop to the swami belt. I used a large twelve-millimetre steel karabiner, the strongest I had then, as my tie-in point for several years. Years later, when I made my own rather crude testing-machine, I decided to try out my now redundant steel krab as the attachment for slings I was testing. I was expecting a result of 2.2 kN so was left a little shaken when the steel karabiner I had assumed would deal with any fall snapped clean in two at 650 N.

Nick and I had a code that dated from this time. I can't remember ever discussing it, but we took it seriously. The code was we should never top-rope. We would climb only from the ground up; the only exceptions were routes we never intended to lead. If we were climbing multi-pitch routes we would lead through, which meant we seconded every other pitch. If the climb had an important crux pitch we would either arrange to climb with someone else, or, as we did when we climbed *Cenotaph Corner*, toss a coin for it. Whoever won the toss would lead the route first and when he had completed the route would pull the ropes and the other one would lead the pitch. I think our ethic was inspired by that first day together at Birchen in July 1960. We both agreed that top-roping *The Crow's Nest* was a cop-out. The other exception was *Great Slab* on Froggatt Edge. When I was fifteen I fell from the crux, quite a way off the ground, while climbing alone. I finally soloed it on my twenty-first birthday after top-roping it.

If there had been a few more Very Severe climbs on Birchen Edge, other than *The Crow's Nest* and *Orpheus Wall*, we might have broken through the barrier sooner. *Orpheus Wall* was a very technical climb. Nick had been shown its trick move by someone and, after watching me fail repeatedly, showed me how to do it. A thin finger-crack and small finger-holds get you off the ground to a six-inch-wide shelf. Above this the wall overhangs. With both hands on the edge of the shelf, you pad up with your right foot and swing your left leg up on to the ledge like a high jumper doing a western roll. At the left end of the ledge, the rock juts out allowing you to twist the toe of your shoe against it, and get a lot of purchase. Between your left foot and your right hand, you can rotate your body upwards and reach good handholds.

Nick and I had a long apprenticeship from which we emerged strong, confident and ready for greater things. Between October 1959 and October 1962, according to my diary, I went climbing ninety-eight times, including eighteen visits to Gardom's Edge, thirteen to Froggatt, and eleven to Birchen Edge. I don't remember ever having a fall that resulted in injury, though ironically Nick fell from his father's route *Birch Tree Wall* at Black Rocks, which resulted in a badly bruised heel. We did many hundreds of routes during these visits without an accident. Nick and I kept up with each other as we worked through the grades. We both lead *Crow's Nest* on the same day, and soon after Nick climbed it, I led *Orpheus Wall*. If one of us climbed a difficult route, the other would usually have bagged it within a week or two. *Lone Tree Groove* at Black Rocks and *Brown's*

Eliminate were two examples. This continued until we left school: Nick for Bristol University to study geology and me for India.

My first leader fall was from *The Dangler*, a strenuous and serious roof crack on Stanage. I was feeling good and quickly climbed the first twenty-five feet to where the crack splits a six-foot overhang. Here I placed a runner, a cast-iron wedge about the size of a MOAC but made by my school friend Richard Johnson. The runner looked good where I had set it at the back of the overhang and on painful hand jams I climbed quickly to the lip of the overhang, jamming my left foot into a constriction. From here the route becomes very strenuous so speed is important. Not seeing another runner, I pulled up and then locked off my left hand to reach up into the continuation of the crack with my right. I could see a good jam but couldn't quite reach it. I needed to get my whole body just a little bit higher. I cranked on both arms but as I reached for the jam my foot came out of the constriction and I found myself hanging from my left hand, surprised I hadn't fallen. I found a poor hold for my right hand, tried to pull up, but there was no strength left. I tried to climb back to where I'd placed the runner. Nick was holding the rope quite tight, and as I moved back, I thought I saw the steel wedge move. If that came out I'd be in for a nasty fall. Now I was hanging from both hands at the lip of the overhang, unable to go up or get back. I was going to fall and the only runner I had was loose. I hung there getting progressively more tired. I looked about for a miracle. I didn't have to wait for very long to confirm miracles weren't currently available. I was going to fall. My fingers were opening.

I fell.

As I dropped, I twisted to get my shoulder facing the rock, knowing that if the runner held, I would swing inwards and slam hard against the lower part of the climb. I also tried to remain upright so that if the runner came out I could try and land on my feet. My shoulder thumped into the rock. Then nothing. No pain. No more falling. The runner had held.

Although I attempted harder routes from time to time, I had a mental block about leading routes of Very Severe, in those days still a grade of consequence. Today it would be the equivalent of breaking the Extreme barrier. I spent 1960 leading Severes, gaining experience, confidence, strength and judgement. I learned that gaining physical skill requires the participant to repeat movements over and over again so the movement becomes 'hard wired'. That repetition applies to all the moves you can think of so that you build up a repertoire to draw on without needing to think. When climbing at one's limit, the body must perform subconsciously, leaving your conscious mind free to concentrate on any new or unexpected situations you find yourself in.

Robin Hodgkin drew on the educational theories of Michael Polanyi to suggest that when one learns a new skill, rehearsing it again and again, a network of remembered actions develops, stretching back in time, that one can bring to bear on the present moment. (Modern advances in neuroscience rather back him up on this.) Each new climbing experience not only increases one's database of experience, it also opens up new opportunities in the future. Following this theory, Nick and I had not only amassed a wealth of experience, we primed ourselves for future success.

In the Easter holidays of 1961 I cycled out to Gardom's Edge to meet Nick. My diary entry starts: 'Today I beat the VS barrier.' I soloed a route called *Cider*, then led *Capillary Crack*, *Undertaker's Buttress* and *Traction*, all of them Very Severe. The next day we went to Froggatt Edge and I climbed four more: *Sunset Slab*, *Sunset Crack*, *Janker's Groove* and *Janker's Crack* – the last three of which I soloed. Back at school I had an afternoon at Black Rocks and added *Lone Tree Groove*, *Lean Man's Climb* and *Birch Tree Wall*. On the weekend before my O levels, Hodgkin took a group of us to Stanage Edge where we had a great weekend romping up many climbs. A few days later I soloed twenty routes at Birchen Edge, including *The Crow's Nest*. Suddenly it all seemed so easy.

At that time, the early sixties, it was considered naff to buy expensive rock climbing boots, known as PAs, if you didn't have the ability to justify the purchase. You learned to climb in Vibram-soled boots and climbed the harder routes in gym shoes. I had set myself the target of climbing *Brown's Eliminate* at Froggatt Edge before considering myself worthy of buying a pair of rock boots. First climbed by Joe Brown in 1948, the route was graded Hard VS. There was no protection and it had a reputation for being dangerous. My friend Clive Jones had broken both wrists and severed one of his optic nerves in a fall from below the crux; many years later another friend, Paul Williams, was killed when a handhold broke off near the top. Today *Brown's Eliminate* is graded Extreme, or E2 5b to be precise.

Having finished my exams, I spent five days on a course at White Hall just outside Buxton, the outdoor centre Jack Longland had established in 1950. My diary entry for 13 July reads:

We walked from Bakewell and climbed several routes on Birchen Edge then walked to the Bob Downes Hut at Froggatt, which had only recently been opened. After a good supper Adrian Holgate and I went up to the edge. I left Adrian at the top and went down to look at my chosen climb. I was looking up at forty-five feet of not quite vertical rock. A six-inch wide ledge bisected it at fifteen feet after which a few fingertip flakes indicated the line I had to take to reach good holds about ten feet from the top. I climbed up as far as the ledge without difficulty and edged along it till I was under the line of flakes. I placed my fingertips on the top edge of the first flake. It was square edged, positive, but very narrow – maybe a centimetre at the most. I worked out the next few moves up a series of similar thin flakes, which provided narrow, spaced, but positive holds and led to the good holds below the top. I placed the tip of my gym shoe on to a small edge on the side of the first flake, straightened my leg and lifted my right foot and placed it sideways on the top of the flake. From here I could reach the top of the next flake with my right hand. If anything this flake was narrower than the first. I waited, not feeling at all comfortable. My legs began to shake and I climbed carefully back down to the big ledge. Joe had been wearing a pair of Tricouni nailed boots when he made the first ascent, which would have enabled him to stand on the small flakes with confidence. I rested for a few minutes and had another go, this time feeling a sloping flake with my left hand. I waited there, poised, getting used to the feel of the rock, the balance, trying to feel comfortable. My feet began to 'sewing-machine' again and I climbed back down. I felt better for being able to climb down in control. Next time I'd get it. I rested for five minutes, shouted up to Adrian who was watching from the top that I was going to go for it. I climbed quickly up to my high point. The first joint of the fingers of my left hand were on the sloping hold and I found that by using my thumb I could hold myself in balance. There was a faint scoop about three feet below the left handhold. I lifted my left foot and placed it in the scoop, trying to get the maximum of smear from my gym shoes. This was it. I relaxed and felt myself rise as I pulled with my left hand, pushed with my left foot against the scoop and placed my right foot on the top flake. It was a long reach but I was able to get my fingers on to the good hold and in no time I was pulling over the top with a huge grin on my face.

My efforts at Froggatt did not go unnoticed. One of the White Hall staff, unbeknownst to me, had been watching from a distance and mentioned it to Eric Langmuir, White Hall's principal. Before going home Eric took me aside and asked me if I would like to become a voluntary instructor. I was flattered; sixteen was very young to be a 'VI'. I had some free time before joining Nick and Jack in the Dauphiné Alps, so I joined a course doing a range of outdoor activities with a group of German exchange students. Three of them wanted to climb, and so were allocated. The two boys were older, but Inga, a stunningly beautiful gymnast from Darmstadt, was the same age as me. She was very impressed that someone of her own age would be instructing her and she turned out to be a very good climber. We stayed in touch for several years until she went to America to study and I left for India.

Eric made another introduction some years later that had a significant influence on my life. In the spring of 1968 I was skiing in the Cairngorms and had a chance meeting with Eric, who had moved on from White Hall to become the principal at Glenmore Lodge, the Scottish National Mountaineering Centre near Loch Morlich. Eric asked if I would like to help out on a winter survival course that was due to start that weekend. In those days, this was the most prestigious course in the British mountaineering calendar and I was very excited at being involved. When I arrived, Glenmore Lodge was buzzing. I found Eric in the equipment store; he pointed to an athletic-looking bloke on the other side of the room.

'That's John. Tell him I sent you. You'll be his gopher.'

John, it turned out, was John Cunningham, one of the best and most experienced ice climbers in the world. I couldn't have wished for a better mentor. I learnt more about winter climbing in that week than in any other before or since. Scotland was at its most beautiful, covered with snow, basking in sunshine by day and freezing hard at night. We spent a night in a big snow hole close to the north summit of Ben Macdui, at sunset walking up to the brass plaque on the summit that shows the location of the main summits of Scotland. It was very cold, twenty below, and crystal clear. We could see every peak from Ben Lomond in the south to Ben Hope in the north, and everything in between. Only over Skye was there a little cloud to obscure the view.

In 1960, when I was sixteen, my parents took me to Switzerland; they were planning to attend an interdenominational conference in Davos. Robin asked if I would like to join him in Zermatt to climb 'one of the major peaks'. I didn't need to be asked twice. With my parents and brother, I walked up the valley to the Gornergrat and we had dinner at the Bahnhof in Zermatt. We rarely ate out as a family, but with twelve francs to the pound, Switzerland was incredibly cheap in those days. Next morning my family left for Davos and I spent the day on my own, feeling very grown up, before Robin arrived. We walked up to the Rothorn hut with three days of food.

My first Alpine climb was the Trifthorn, a nice little peak where I was introduced to the use of crampons, in this case a very heavy pair made for Robin by a blacksmith in the Sudan, where Robin had worked as a teacher. Next day we climbed the Zinalrothorn by the Rothorngrat – a classic route with some serious climbing and my first 4,000-metre peak. My introduction to Alpine climbing by a mountaineer of Robin's standing was a fabulous opportunity and an experience without equal. At the time I took it for granted as only the young can do. Robin Hodgkin's philosophy of education centred on the importance of exploration and consequently to adventure and this suited me very well. He was never a typical headmaster, but by then our relationship was more like that between nephew and favourite uncle.

In the summer of 1962, it was Nick's turn to go to Zermatt, with his brother. I would have liked to go to the Alps too, but how, and with whom and where? My father helped out by introducing me to a member of the Manchester-based Rucksack Club, a fellow Unitarian minister called Keith Treacher who was leading a small group of young climbers on an expedition to Norway. I met Keith at Birchen Edge and we had a really good day's climbing at the end of which he invited me to come too. 'Expedition' is a rather grand name for a summer holiday in Norway, but at the age of seventeen a trip to Norway sounded like a journey to the North Pole. In six days, plagued by breakdowns, we drove from Manchester via Dover to Norway and the remote village of Øye, deep in Hjørundfjord south of Ålesund and below the Sunnmøre Alps made famous by William Cecil Slingsby. Having discovered there was no campsite, we took over the top floor of the Union Hotel, once a haunt of European royalty, now available for ten shillings a night each.

Øye is dominated by the dark rock pyramid of Slogen (1,564 metres), which we climbed in early August via a new route up the north ridge. Then we moved to other peaks with beautiful names like Smørskredtind and the Velleseterhornet. It was a wild area with many 5,000-foot mountains offering good ridge climbing, some of it scrambling, some of that roped. The worst thing was the difficult approaches, bushwhacking through miniature willow for 2,000 feet before getting on to rock. On the way home, we stopped in Oslo to visit the city's historic ship museums including the Fram, the ship Fridtjof Nansen designed to drift through the pack ice around the North Pole.

The following year I left Abbotsholme after taking my A levels and embarked on my course at White Hall. That summer, Jack was planning to visit to La Bérarde in the Dauphiné with A.B. Hargreaves and a group of friends. It was no problem to tag along. I left Chesterfield early one July morning to hitch-hike to France but it took four days to reach the mountains and, by the time I reached the outskirts of Grenoble, I was exhausted from lack of sleep. A Renault 4 pulled over and I climbed in. The driver introduced himself as Louis Lambert, also on his way to the Dauphiné. Louis wanted to climb La Meije, hopefully doing the traverse, one of the classic routes of the Alps. I was also keen, but totally unacclimatised. I didn't want to let my new friend down, so I told him my misgivings but we agreed to give it a go.

I assumed we would spend the night in La Bérarde and go up to the Promontoire hut the following day, but Louis had other ideas. The hut is a long walk north from the village up a valley with a steep scramble up rocks, which we climbed in the last of the daylight. We arrived at 10 p.m. It was too late to cook a meal and all the beds were taken, but within minutes of stretching out on the floor I was asleep, only to be shaken awake at 3 a.m. by Louis amid the usual noise and clatter of climbers getting ready for a long day. The only light came from climbers' headlamps and across the table I glimpsed a familiar face, that of Eric Langmuir, for whom I had recently worked as a volunteer instructor at White Hall.

Louis and I were first out of the hut and set off up the classic route with several other parties hard on our heels. The first part took a blunt arête on mainly good rock but as dawn brightened we stopped to put on crampons, ready for the diagonal climb across the *névé* of the Glacier Carré where Eric and his climbing partner Geoff Sutton caught us up. The final steep pyramid of the main summit provided interesting climbing on good rock and slowly the sun began to warm us. La Meije is shy of being a four-thousander by just thirteen metres. Here we had to make the decision to descend or continue with the traverse. Most of the other parties seemed to be heading down, back to the hut, but Geoff's car was in La Grave on the other side of the range and he and Eric were keen to do the full traverse. We had made good time, the weather was good, and having had a rest I felt ready for whatever was ahead. We continued with Eric and Geoff, first down to the Brèche Zsigmondy, now much bigger and deeper following a monumental rockfall a year later. The ridge beyond was absorbing and technical but we eventually reached the Pic Oriental and then made a 300-foot abseil from the summit. Continuing down steep ice and snow on the north face, the angle eased and we were soon on the glacier at the start of one of the longest descents I have ever done, 10,000 feet down to La Grave.

The sun had gone down when we eventually reached Geoff's car, a handsome Facel Vega. Louis invited us to stay at a chalet belonging to his university. I was not only tired, I hadn't had a proper meal since leaving Chesterfield five days before and I was desperately hungry. Judging by the amount of beer that slid down I was dehydrated too. Large bowls of soup appeared from nowhere, followed by a large platter of thinly sliced meat and pickles. Next was a rich casserole that had clearly absorbed a lot of red wine. There was a different wine with each course and after we'd made a large hole in the cheese board, we finished with a liqueur, *Noisettes des Alpes*, and coffee. I then slept for twelve hours, waking refreshed and ready for a late breakfast. Eric and Geoff were gone already, and Louis was trying to organise a lift to La Bérarde.

Back at the village, I said goodbye to Louis and retrieved my tent from his car. Most of our group had arrived, and when I met Jack later that day, he asked me what I had been doing. When I told him I had traversed La Meije, he was very complimentary and insisted on buying me a drink at the bar, where he quizzed me further. It was only later I realised he had been a little sceptical. Lucky for me I'd been with Geoff and Eric – unimpeachable witnesses.

Age was never a barrier when climbing with Jack, even though he was almost forty years older than me, of my father's generation. Our party was not as fast as it should have been. We were benighted after a ludicrously late start and casual ascent of the Grande Aiguille de la Bérarde and had to spend the night out with inadequate gear. I listened to Jack, A.B. Hargreaves and Tony Moulam bemoaning the fact they were suffering their first forced bivouac, as though it was our fault. The galling thing was that my partner Martin Sinker and I could have been back in the village before dark spending the night in the comfort of our sleeping bags had we not made the decision to stick with the old men. At the end of the week, after some easier routes, I hitched home and went to Wales with Nick Longland, climbing some hard classics on Dinas Cromlech.

We tossed a coin to see who would go first on *Cenotaph Corner* and Nick won. When he got to the top he fixed up a rappel and came down to belay me. This was more like it.

Knowing Jack meant I could get some impressive references when it came to job applications. A few years later, when I applied to the British Antarctic Survey, the personnel officer Bill Sloman called me in for an interview. His first question was: 'How the hell did you get references from both Jack Longland and John Cunningham?'

More than ten years after I climbed with Jack in the French Alps, I was nominated by the British Mountaineering Council to become a member of the Mountain Leader Training Board, then one of the biggest sporting training organisations in Britain, having been established in 1964 with Jack as chair. My fellow nominees were Dennis Gray, then the BMC's first professional officer, and the well-known rock climber Pete Livesey. The BMC had recently tabled a motion of no confidence in Jack, part of a long and agonising feud that split amateur climbers and professional outdoor educators. The inciting incident was a terrible accident in the Cairngorms. Over the course of two days in November 1971, five schoolchildren and one eighteen-year-old trainee instructor perished from hypothermia during a school winter mountaineering expedition. The fatal accident enquiry heard evidence from some of the most experienced guides working in Scotland, including Eric Langmuir. Inevitably, the tragedy prompted calls for new restrictions on climbers and there was a fierce and longrunning debate about whether educationalists should be the ultimate arbiters of safety, or grassroots mountaineering's representative body, the BMC. Many ordinary climbers felt the lessons of the accident had not been learned and the consequences might damage the sport.

I told Jack I thought that the issue was a mountaineering matter, not an educational one and that I would have to vote with the BMC at the no-confidence vote. Jack said I could abstain but that was not an option I could take. I was representing the BMC and I thought that Jack was wrong. Jack told me that we would have to do what we thought was right. The BMC duly lost the vote, as was expected. It was a lost cause from the start, but if we lost the battle, we would eventually win the war. The Sports Council, founded in 1972 with Jack and John Disley as influential vice-chairmen, then withdrew its funding from the BMC, but it transpired that not only was the Sports Council not within its rights to withdraw funding from the legal governing body of mountaineering, the MLTB itself was not legally constituted. In a nutshell, the Sports Council had acted unconstitutionally in taking funding from the BMC and transferring it to a self-appointed group that had no legal status. It took the intervention of Lord Hunt as an independent arbitrator to sort the mess out.

I had thought that by forewarning Jack about my decision I had done enough but he took my vote against him very personally and very hard. I was surprised that I had the capability to hurt him like that. For several years he didn't speak to me. With Nick's help, I eventually made my peace with Jack, inviting him and Peggy to dinner where I served the best red wine I know – a Château de Beaucastel. But our relationship was never quite the same again. I don't know how I would handle such a situation today, but I find myself thinking that I should have abstained. Had I done so then the result would have been the same. Then I reflect that I did the right thing after all.

Jack was knighted for his services to education and mountaineering following his retirement in 1970, before our crisis. I heard the news in Antarctica and sent him a congratulatory telegram, which I was told he was particularly pleased to receive. It is only now, writing this memoir, and many years after his death in 1993, that I realise just how generous Jack was to me personally. Jack was the consummate committee chairman. He could make an agenda dance to his tune. He was always way ahead of those who might try to outwit him. Without his example, I would not have understood the work the BMC does, or what it takes to change such an institution. Without our friendship and the time I spent with him, I would not have had the confidence to be president of the BMC or to take on the senior mountaineering clubs, persuading them to do away with their block vote. It was a privilege to have worked and climbed with him.

An ornately carved wheel at the Konark Sun Temple, India.

3 INDIA

Leaving Abbotsholme, I knew I wanted to travel and I thought I wanted to be a teacher. My A-level results were less than spectacular so I was surprised when Goldsmiths at the University of London offered me an interview. At Goldsmiths, unlike many colleges of education, students were treated like adults; lectures were optional and the syllabus was broadly based. Students were encouraged to read outside their chosen subject and there were many more opportunities to gain experience both academic and practical. I thought I might be pushing my luck telling the panel I wanted to spend a year doing voluntary work in a developing country, but it seemed to go down well and we spent most of the allotted time discussing the merits of various countries. The dean of studies told me, barring an unexpected eventuality, there would be a place for me on the education course the following year and asked me to get in touch in good time when I returned.

Today, my time in India would be called a gap year, but in the early 1960s it was an unusual way for a school-leaver to broaden his horizons. Perhaps it wouldn't have mattered much where I spent my year off, but India was a good choice, challenging me constantly with the privations of what was then called a third-world country, an old and complex culture, the opportunities of low-cost travel and a constant barrage of different ideas. By then I had grown tired of expedition books, the formulaic sequence of picking the team, the trek to base camp, and so on. I was more influenced by Howard Somervell's autobiography *After Everest*. Somervell had been a member of the Everest expeditions in 1922 and 1924, the latter when George Mallory and Sandy Irvine disappeared. Somervell climbed to over 27,000 feet with Edward Norton, higher than anyone ever before, but on his return from Everest he gave up high-altitude mountaineering and a promising medical career in England to spend the next forty years as a missionary surgeon in what was then the kingdom of Travancore and is now Kerala in southern India.

So in the autumn of 1963, aged nineteen, I travelled 6,000 miles under the illusion that I was going to help other people even though, in truth, I was the person, possibly the only person, who was going to benefit. Having grown up in a household where the pursuit of 'goodness' was assumed, I regarded myself as someone who could easily make judgements about what was good and what was not. I had yet to learn that in the real world, the law of unintended consequences applies, and those who would bring 'goodness' need a large slice of humility, something a nineteen-year-old former public schoolboy can sometimes lack.

I travelled out on the SS *Cilicia* on her last voyage from Liverpool, an old ship with a charm that only years of waxing and polishing can bestow. The voyage took three weeks and I enjoyed every minute of it. There were fifteen different types of marmalade to choose from at breakfast. Steaming south along the coast of Western Europe, the ship turned east towards the Mediterranean Sea and the Suez Canal at Port Said. The passengers were offered an excursion to see the pyramids, but I couldn't afford it, and anyway, the itinerary seemed rushed. I felt confident the pyramids would still be there next time I passed through.

Leaving the Suez Canal for the Red Sea, I fell into conversation with a young agricultural engineer going out to an Anglican farm and training school in Bihar. Alec Morris had seen David Lean's film *Lawrence of Arabia* and wanted to go for a ride on a camel and asked me if I'd join him. We spent an afternoon riding camels in Aden, and later, when we got to Karachi, explored the souk together. We agreed we would meet up in the summer for a trip to Darjeeling to see how far we could get along the ridge that leads north towards Kangchenjunga.

I had the offer of a job at the Ramakrishna mission school in Narendrapur near Calcutta. The Hindu saint Sri Narendra Ramakrishna was born in 1836 and died in 1883; his disciple, Swami Vivekananda, developed his guru's philosophy through the Ramakrishna Movement, which acknowledged and admired the best principles of the world's great religions, cultures and traditions, their wisdom and teachers. The main emphasis of the mission remains educational but they work in other fields too, like healthcare. My role, at the mission's secondary school, was to interact with the pupils, play sports, referee and umpire games and generally take every opportunity to promote a high standard of spoken English.

My new job was due to start in a few weeks, so to fill the time I took up an invitation to visit Margaret Barr, an old friend of my father's, in the Khasi Hills of what was then part of Assam, a lovely high plateau between Bangladesh and the Brahmaputra. Margaret was an extraordinary woman, joining the Unitarians while a student at Cambridge and becoming one of their most outstanding women ministers. She applied to serve the small Unitarian community in Assam in 1932 but was turned down. The role was deemed too demanding for a woman. So she got a job teaching English in Calcutta and began making short visits to Assam. Eventually she was given charge of the Unitarian churches in the Khasi Hills and there she remained, more or less, until her death in 1973, first running the churches at Shillong, and then establishing a rural school at the remote village of Kharang, a fifteen-mile walk down a rough track. She was not just a teacher but a nurse, midwife, counsellor and friend to the surrounding community. I found her formidable, while also glad she was not my mother, but felt she too readily assumed she knew what was best for local people. It was while staying with Margaret that I heard John F. Kennedy had been assassinated. The news was five days old by the time it reached us.

A day's walk from Kharang is the village of Cherrapunji, noted for having the highest rainfall in the world, with an average rainfall of almost forty feet a year, most of it falling in the months of June, July and August. The monsoon sweeps in from the Bay of Bengal and the first thing it hits is the barrier of the Assam hills rising 6,000 feet from Bangladesh's northern border. Luckily for me, in December every day is like a perfect summer's day in England. As I walked I would reach up to pick oranges off the trees. The Cherrapunji orange is one of the most delectable fruits I have ever tasted. Peeling them is easy. The skin is quite loose and comes away with a single pull; the orange itself is quite large and sweet, like a Jaffa.

Narendrapur is on the south side of Calcutta, in those days at the end of a bus route. The grounds at the Ramakrishna monastery were extensive and included a farm, a junior school, a secondary school and a college linked to Calcutta University. I was invited to events at the college from time to time and was flattered to be asked to help in their production of Shakespeare's *Julius Caesar*. It was a strange situation. I was over forty before I started to appreciate Shakespeare, but because I was English the college students assumed that not only would I be familiar with all the plays and have informed opinions about them, but I would also be able to quote important speeches. When the student who was playing the part of Mark Antony was hospitalised two weeks before the performance, I was told I would have to stand in for him. The task felt wholly beyond me. At school I was always the second soldier, or someone's servant.

'Why me?' I asked.

'Because your name is Mark.' Fortunately it was only one performance.

My accommodation at the monastery was basic but pleasant. I lived in a small, skimmed brick house, in reality just a room. At the back there was a walled enclosure with a cold shower and toilet. I had an electric light, a desk, a fan, a chair, a small wardrobe and a bed with a mosquito net. It was situated at the edge of a large garden in which there stood the guesthouse, about a hundred yards from my house across a lawn that was mown using an industrial-sized mowing machine pulled by a team of six workers with ropes. The guesthouse was a pleasant bungalow with bougainvillea cascading over one end, hibiscus growing in profusion around it, and occasional papaya trees. It had three bedrooms and a dining room, which gave access to a large terrace. At the back was the kitchen. It was here that I had my meals with any guests who happened to be staying in the bungalow and occasionally an American aspirant monk.

During most of my time there the guesthouse was used only occasionally although sometimes it got quite busy. Two Fulbright Scholars were staying there later in my stay, one from Harvard and the other from Yale, and also at the start of my visit, during the centenary celebrations for the birth of Swami Vivekananda, the disciple of Sri Ramakrishna who founded his movement, it was in constant use. Sometimes it was used for meetings or to host meals for important guests. I looked forward to these the most, because the variety of the food, if not the quality, was better.

―――――――

I had spent the morning at school minding a class of twelve-year-olds and then, after break, took an art class. Clearing up after that took me longer than expected, which meant I was late for lunch. When I arrived at the guest bungalow and hurried into the dining room, I was out of breath and suddenly confronted with a large party already eating. Usually I would be told in advance if guests were expected. I saw there were no extra places at the table and backing away started to apologise for my interruption.

'Come in Mark,' said Swami Lokeswerananda, the head monk, getting to his feet. 'We'll make some room for you.' He indicated for Narendra, the cook's assistant, to fetch a chair, which he put at the head of the table, the only space available. Swamiji remained standing while he made the introductions. There were eight men and two women and they all seemed to be Americans. There was no way that I could remember what all of them were called but the man opposite Swamiji was called Chester Carlson. He was a big man with an air of authority dressed in a well-cut cream suit. Later I learned he was the inventor of the Xerox machine. I forget the names of the others apart from another monk, or rather, a *brahmachari*, an aspirant monk identifiable by his white dhoti and his *tiki*, the little tail of hair growing from the crown of his head. He was sitting on my left and was introduced to me as John Yale. He was very thin, which was accentuated by his shaved head. Yale, a successful publisher from Chicago, was now known as Prema Chaitanya and had published the story of his first trip to Ramakrishna as *A Yankee and the Swamis*. He was part of a well-known Vedanta centre in Hollywood.

The last person to be introduced was the man on my right who I guessed was in his late fifties, dressed in grey flannels and a crumpled linen jacket. His name was Christopher Isherwood.

'The writer?' I asked, shaking his proffered hand before sitting down. I was furiously trying to think of something, anything, he had written, and recalled he had, with Swami Prabhavananda, translated an Indian classic, the Bhagavad Gita. This was years before his book *Goodbye to Berlin* was turned into the musical *Cabaret*. My headmaster had given me a copy. 'I'll have to get you to sign my copy of the Gita,' I finally added. Isherwood was obviously pleased that I recognised who he was, and said so. A bowl of hot soup was placed in front of me while the rest of the soup bowls were removed. I realised this must be a party of delegates for the centenary celebrations of Swami Vivekananda's birth which were being held all over India, but particularly here in Bengal, his birthplace.

By the time a large bowl of fruit was placed on the table I had managed to catch up with the rest of the diners. Conversation had been wide-ranging and animated. I had been trying to remember what I knew about Isherwood, so if he asked me what else of his I had read, I would be ready. This brought me on to *The Ascent of F6*, the play he had collaborated on with W.H. Auden. We had a paperback copy at home and while I hadn't read it, I had dipped into it because of its subject matter. That is how the conversation got round to a discussion of mountaineering and the merits of outdoor recreation. Some of the guests had to get back to Calcutta, but John Yale, Isherwood and three others went out on to the patio where coffee was being served and we continued the conversation outside.

Because it was Friday, I had no duties in the afternoon and by the time the remaining guests and Isherwood left to go back to Calcutta it was getting on for four o'clock. I was quite flattered that he had wanted to talk at such length. It was not till several years later that I became aware of Isherwood's sexual orientation. Some time ago a writer who had been retained by the Isherwood family to write his biography got in touch. She had wanted to know who else was present that lunchtime, having gotten my name from Isherwood's diaries. I wondered if his diary reflected that my intellect had fuelled our conversation or if his interest was less high-minded. Unbeknownst to me, Isherwood was in the middle of a fractious period with his partner Don Bachardy, thirty years younger than Isherwood, and also writing his best novel, *A Single Man*, later a successful movie starring Colin Firth.

The entry for that day, 31 December 1963, reveals Isherwood was recovering from a night of the 'gripes and shits', struggling to square the way he lived in California and his public support for the Ramakrishna Movement. 'As long as I quite unashamedly get drunk, have sex and write books like *A Single Man*, I simply cannot appear before people as a sort of lay minister.' Then he was brought to Narendrapur to look over the mission. 'Sick as I was and groggy from the hot sun, I was hugely impressed. It makes you feel India isn't in such a bad way after all.' As for our lunch:

> I very much liked Swami Lokeswerananda, who runs the place;
> he reminded me of Dore Schary [president of Metro-Goldwyn-Mayer
> and Oscar-winning writer]. Also, there was a nice solid young bra[h]
> mapachari from Pavitrananda's centre in New York, called Amul
> (his name is Clare Street) who has been here three years already. Also a
> handsome and sexy nineteen-year-old boy from Cheshire, named Mark
> Vallance, who isn't a devotee yet but has come here to teach English
> – or rather, his very no-shit Midlands accent. He plans to start reading
> Vivekananda's works as soon as he has finished *For Whom the Bell Tolls*!

I did read some of Vivekananda, but it wasn't really for me. But I read the Hemingway twice.

Talking of sex, I had a fascinating trip to Puri in what is now the state of Odisha, on the east coast of India south of Calcutta. This is the home of the god Jagannath, a form of Vishnu from whom we get the word juggernaut. In the distant past, or at least so the rather unreliable legend goes, devotees would throw themselves under the gigantic wheels of the god's chariot, a sure-fire way of going straight to heaven. While in Puri, I visited the Konark Sun Temple, with its erotic carvings. Many years later I was able to catch up with some of the other obligatory sights I had missed as a student, including the Taj Mahal, which didn't disappoint, but also the erotic temples at Khajuraho in Madhya Pradesh. Every conceivable sexual position for up to four people is carved in fine detail, but while I found them interesting, the carvings didn't strike me as being in the least bit erotic.

After the summer term, I met up with Alec again in Calcutta. Our assault on the mighty ramparts of the Himalaya was less successful than that of John Hunt and co eleven years before. We took the train to Siliguri and then changed for the picturesque small-gauge railway to Darjeeling, the toy train. We visited the Indian Mountaineering Institute where Tenzing Norgay was principal, though we didn't get to meet the great man. Darjeeling is not well provided with campsites but arriving after dark we were given permission to pitch our tent on the small hill behind the institute. Nobody thought to mention that this area contained a small zoo. The noise a tiger makes when it can smell breakfast concentrates the mind quite quickly, especially if you're emerging from a deep sleep. For a moment, both of us thought that all that separated us from our doom were the few square feet of our Egyptian cotton flysheet.

The Chinese had tried to invade India across the border and through Sikkim in 1960. Four years later the hills north of Darjeeling were still considered a militarily sensitive area. We hiked up the Singalila Ridge that runs north from Darjeeling towards Sandakphu, the highest hill in West Bengal and a great vantage point from which to observe not just Kangchenjunga but Everest and Makalu as well. I don't think we were particularly threatening, but the further north we walked, the greater interest we seemed to generate. Eventually three very smartly dressed military policemen arrived in a pair of equally smart jeeps. They were very polite and the captain spoke better English than I do. But they were adamant.

We would have to turn around. We told them we had no intention of invading either India or China but they must have thought we were a significant danger. We asked that if we couldn't go on, could we have a lift back down the trail? This request was met with a certain amount of mirth. Maybe it was just as well, because later one of the jeeps was reported as having driven off the road with fatal consequences for one of the drivers.

Both of us had a standing invitation to visit an English couple who we had met on the voyage out, Jim and Barbara Lyness. They owned a tea garden in Assam. We had arranged to visit them after our Kangchenjunga trek and when we got back to Darjeeling we sent them a telegram asking if we could come earlier. We then took a train to Guwahati, the capital of Assam, where a Land Rover was waiting to whisk us sixty miles to the middle of nowhere for twelve days of five-star luxury.

Jim Lyness had been a conscripted soldier in India during the war and had stayed on. By dint of hard work, he had built up a tea garden of which he was justly proud. In Assam, most of the tea bushes are trimmed and shaped like a large orchestral drum with a flat top so the workers can harvest the leaves easily. Some of the leaves are left in the sun to dry out and shrivel up to make a lighter green tea. Most of them are crushed and start to ferment, going a dark brown. Then the leaves are dried and broken up to produce black tea. A lot of dust is created by this process, which is mixed with leaf for use in teabags. While staying with Jim, a tiny gyrocopter, like a gizmo from a Bond movie, buzzed the verandah where we were sitting and then landed on the tennis court in front of the house. Out stepped Gareth, the local tea-taster who advised planters how to achieve the sort of product their customers wanted to buy. He took over a long bench and made twenty small pots of tea using different samples from different parts of the garden. When the tea was cold he poured a small quantity into clear glass tumblers and then sniffed, slurped and spat like a wine taster.

We started our return journey to Calcutta by spending a couple of days on a paddle steamer transporting tea down the Brahmaputra before catching the train to Calcutta. Recalling our journey, fifty years later, I found that I could no longer remember Alec's surname; we had lost contact after India, when I returned home and he continued on to Australia. I checked it in my diary and thought no more about it, but was amazed two days later to get a call from a friend in the Derbyshire village of Elton, where I used to live. He told me a chap had turned up asking after me. 'Have you

ever been to India?' It was Alec, or Alex as he now called himself, and we
had great fun catching up over dinner.

As the son and grandson of Unitarian ministers, it was a natural assumption for me that rational thought was superior to blind faith or unques-
tioning belief in dogma. So experiencing a religious culture that seemed
to revel in both was too good an opportunity to miss. When one day
some of my kids turned up at the guesthouse and asked if I would like
to go to the puja with them, I leapt at the chance. I had been to various
pujas, or prayer ceremonies, and found them fascinating. The Hindu temple
at Narendrapur was only a few hundred yards away but it was not until
I was inside that I realised today was special. It was Kali Puja, the day late
in the year when Hindus, particularly in Bengal, worship Kali, an incar-
nation of Durga, or Parvati, the wife of Shiva. Animal sacrifice is a major
part of the ceremony. The usual banging of sticks and drums, chanting,
and general mayhem went on for a good half hour with a number of priests
coming and going and the volume getting more and more frantic. Then a
wooden framework was carried in. The wood was old and almost black.
I did not have to be told what it was for. There was something about the
way it looked and articulated that was distinctly medieval.

A goat was brought into the central part of the temple and placed astride
the frame's central wooden shaft. Its horns were fixed to a slab of wood
carved into a 'Y' shape through drilled holes. Its two front legs were lifted
and pulled up and backwards. This swiftly immobilised the animal. Then
one of the priests lifted an ornate blade about three feet long. The blade
came down, cleanly severing the head, which fell to the floor. A huge pulse
of arterial blood travelled twenty feet across the central part of the temple
followed by several more spurts, each weaker than the one before. Then
the next goat was brought in. I was aware that I was being watched by my
students and stuck it out for a few more goats before making my apolo-
gies. The floor of the temple was by then a bloodbath. I recalled some lines
of Emerson: 'If the red slayer thinks he slays,/Or if the slain think he is
slain,/They know not well the subtle ways/I keep, and pass, and turn
again.' I think it likely Emerson would think differently had he witnessed
what I just had.

I eventually went home in January 1965. I had suggested to the headmaster that the charity Voluntary Service Overseas might be willing to find

a suitable replacement and sure enough a volunteer arrived six weeks before I was due to leave. I was able to show him the ropes, although it wasn't really necessary. VSO continued to supply volunteers for several years after until all Western charity workers got kicked out in a spat between congress and Henry Kissinger over the civil war in what was then East Pakistan. I travelled to Delhi in the luxury of an air-conditioned train and stayed for two days at the Ramakrishna headquarters before flying home. My fourteen months in India, arriving as a teenager, was an education in its own right. I would find it difficult to make a comprehensive list of what it was exactly that I learned, but it certainly taught me to be patient, something that made me better able to cope with Parkinson's.

Thirty-five years later I found myself sitting next to the American climber and Harvard-educated doctor Charles Houston at the centenary dinner of the Climbers' Club. He had been part of the Anglo-American expedition that made the first ascent of Nanda Devi in 1936 and led two attempts on K2 in 1938 and 1953. Houston was then in his mid eighties and I was exhausted after a day of meetings; I found it quite hard to keep the conversation going. Then we discovered we had India in common. Charlie had been based in Delhi as director of the Peace Corps in India when I was living in Narendrapur. Having been in India at the same time, with a similar store of memories, we were soon locked in fond reminiscences.

The north face of the Aiguille de Triolet, June 1964. The route takes the line of slanting ice from the bottom left to the top right of the photo. *Photo: Richard Hale.*

4 NEW SCHOOLS

I arrived home in January 1965, eight months before starting at Goldsmiths College. Needing money for my summer's climbing in the Alps, I looked for work, which in the mid sixties was readily available. My first job was 'pop driller' at Darlton Quarry in Stoney Middleton. My task was to bore a one-inch-diameter hole into the centre of any boulder too big to go through the crusher. We then had to estimate how much dynamite would be needed to reduce each block of limestone to manageable proportions. I was paid four shillings and five pence an hour but most weeks got a bonus of up to eighty per cent.

The day I started, an aging Irish navvy, the caricature of a leprechaun, was given notice to quit at the end of the week. His reaction was carefully considered. In the middle of one of the quarry bays was a large brick-shaped boulder, and by large I mean the size of a single-decker bus. It must have weighed fifty tons and had sat there, like an unwelcome guest, for some time. Nobody knew what to do with it.

The soon to be unemployed leprechaun took it upon himself to solve the problem. He began drilling holes up to two metres deep into the middle of it. Methodically, quietly, he got on with his task with a fervour that was almost religious in its intensity. Fifteen minutes before we were due to light the blue touch paper on our little boulders, he showed us what he had done to his. The bus now had more holes than a Swiss cheese. The Irishman then asked us to make sure that nobody, especially not management, came into that part of the quarry before he had launched his Parthian shot.

The bang, when it came, was a little disappointing, but when we went back to look at his handiwork, the boulder was gone. It had ceased to be.

There was no stone there at all. Where the boulder had sat, there was now a shallow depression in the quarry floor. Whatever was left was now somewhere else and eventually we found it. Eyam parish council wasn't pleased that there were now thousands of small bits of limestone covering the lane up to the village. The county surveyor almost had a seizure when he saw how much was littering the busy main road through the dale.

I was assigned to the cleaning-up operation, which took the best part of five days, and I didn't see a single bit of limestone bigger than my fist. We didn't get a bonus that week, but I was given responsibility for dishing out the high explosives. I thought this was in recognition of my reliability and maturity but discovered later it was because I could read, write and do the simple arithmetic the job demanded.

My next job was pouring concrete for a new dam being built in the Goyt Valley. One afternoon a lorry load of the stuff was mistakenly poured down into a works tunnel. The site manager asked for volunteers to dig out the hundred or so tons of concrete before it hardened. We worked till midnight. Next day I was dead on my feet but the hardened Irish navvies alongside me were still at it, as hard as ever. The foreman, who had marked my card as a weak link, sacked me, telling me to collect my cards. On the way up the hill I saw the site manager who asked me why I had such a long face. Explaining I'd been fired, he directed me to the tool shop where I was given a cushier job at the same rate of pay as I had been getting in the tunnels – eight shillings an hour plus bonus.

One of my new responsibilities was to take the site manager's car to fetch small items as the need arose. He drove a souped-up Lotus Cortina but I found it a disappointing drive. The roads I was driving were exciting and twisty, but however hard I pushed it, I never seemed to be able to get over fifty miles an hour. On my last day on the job, the site manager asked me if the car's speedometer had given me any trouble. I didn't like to be critical so I said it was fine.

'That's good because it's knackered. When it says fifty, it's really doing more like eighty.'

'All the same,' I said. 'Nice car.'

When I started climbing in the Alps in the 1960s, gear was still rudimentary, especially ice-climbing equipment. Routes that now seem approachable classics, thanks to decades of technological advance, were in those days technically demanding and absolutely terrifying. Tucked away at the end of the Argentière glacier, the north face of the Aiguille de Triolet is one such challenge. It goes largely unseen by most alpinists, but framed in the big windows of the Argentière hut, it was asking me some demanding questions. It looked steep – incredibly steep.

The north face is 2,500 feet high with a huge, blocky ice cliff halfway up. First climbed in September 1931 after a summer of poor weather by André Roch, later of Everest fame, and Robert Gréloz, it was considered for many years to be the hardest ice climb in the Alps. More than that, it remained for decades the reference point from which other hard ice routes were calibrated. By the time I arrived at the Argentière hut, the north face had been climbed about twenty-five times, with two ascents by British teams.

My early tuition on ice had come directly from the top, from Chris Bonington himself, by way of his Eiger lecture. This was what you did. First, with your ice axe, you cut a hold at full stretch. Next, using your ice axe in your right hand and an ice dagger in your left, you levitated or more likely scrabbled up to stand on this hold. Then it was simply a question of repeating this manoeuvre until you had climbed seventy-five feet. Then you put in an ice screw to give the illusion that you were in charge before climbing the next seventy-five feet. Then you cut a bigger foothold and put in another ice screw. However big you made this hold it was never big enough.

As for protection, everyone agreed that Stubai's ice screws, which we then all used, make for a very good corkscrew. I still keep one in my drinks cabinet. But I never heard any other claims for their reliability. All the same, it was easier to stand in balance on one of those footholds that you wish you had cut bigger and screw in a belay, than endure the destabilising process of hammering in an ice peg only to spend long minutes cutting it out again.

Even so, my confidence was high. I was equipped with the very best equipment of the era, including an unbreakable MacInnes ice axe. (It might not have been very good, but it was reassuringly expensive.) My ice dagger was home-made and my crampons only had ten points. My résumé of Alpine ice routes was as makeshift as my equipment. It included an ascent of the Frendo Spur that took three days, which must qualify me for some kind of record. To get well ahead of the pack we had started up in the afternoon to find a good bivouac ledge but were woken by Frenchmen tripping over us in the dark. Though the rock climbing was straightforward, we never saw them again. Somehow we managed to lose our way on the *rognon* near the summit ridge, resulting in a second bivouac in the tunnels of the cable-car station. My partner for this route never climbed again.

As well as the Frendo, I had also climbed the north face of the Lenzspitze in Switzerland's Pennine Alps with my school friend Richard Johnson, and Al Edmonds, a climber he had met at Leicester University. Al was wonderfully patient and a great second: always reassuring and never complaining. That route went without any drama and in a respectable time. I had led all the way trailing two ropes, so Richard and Al could then both climb together.

Al seemed the perfect partner for the Triolet. We set off early from the hut and arrived at the foot of the face after an hour or so. To begin with we had the advantage of a nearly full moon, but the sky clouded over as we approached the bergschrund and a few flakes of snow started to settle. By the time we stopped to put our crampons on, it was snowing hard, so we turned round and scuttled back to the hut, thankful to have an excuse to delay the moment of commitment. We had a lie-in, got up again at noon, and spent the afternoon watching the Triolet getting steeper and steeper.

Next morning, leaving the hut at three o'clock, we crossed the bergschrund without incident. I ran the rope out before cutting the usual big foothold and belayed. Al led through, but before he reached the next belay point I noticed one of his crampons was hanging down. A steel ring that attached the metal frame to the climbing boot had broken. We made the best job we could of tying the crampon to his boot but it wasn't secure enough for Al to be able to lead. Despite this setback we were already several pitches up the route by daybreak. I was aiming for the right hand of two small rock islands, thinking I might be able to get a decent belay, but the rock was very compact and I had to press on, moving slightly right towards that fearsome barrier of ice cliffs 1,200 feet above the bergschrund.

The start of the climb had been reasonably angled, about fifty-five degrees, but now it steepened and we found ourselves on sixty-degree ice as we neared the ice cliff, reaching it at mid morning. This proved a haven where we could relax for the first time in the comfort of a wind scoop below a vertical, off-width crack in the ice. This we would somehow have to climb to get to the top part of the face. There was a lot of soft snow in the wind scoop but though the crack looked hard, it gave an illusion of safety and I was able to take Al's ice axe and hammer it into a horizontal crack, ferule first. I used this first to pull up, mantel and then finally ended up standing on it. With a bit more grovelling I reached the top of the crack.

I looked up at the next section and my heart sank. It wasn't that the angle was steeper than the first half of the face, which it was; it was more that the ice was grey water-ice covered in patches with thin streaks of snow. It was also very hard, considerably harder than on the first part of the climb, and brittle. Striking the ice with the pick of my axe caused it to shatter or 'dinner-plate'. I was worried that by using too much force I might dislodge myself from the few millimetres of ice that I had managed to penetrate with my crampon points. If, at that moment, there had been a way to escape I would have taken it, but the prospect of retreating was no more appealing than going on. I had climbed myself into this. I would just have to climb myself out of it.

Time now began passing more quickly. Each move was not so much hard as 'thin'. I got into the discipline of kicking my front points just far enough in to take my weight. These weren't front points as they are on modern crampons. I had bent them forward, more than perhaps I should have. But they worked. One mistake though and I'd be testing those ice screws, and I really didn't want to do that. To hurry would be suicide. I recalled Tom Patey's wise words: 'Ice is for pouring whisky over.' I should have paid attention. Those last thousand feet seemed to go on forever. I was trying to link up the snow streaks, constantly aiming for the next one and hoping it would be firm *névé*, but it turned out to be like frozen shaving cream: not weak enough to ignore but not strong enough to give confidence.

The sun was going down and it was getting colder. The pink glow that lit the summits of the surrounding mountains mocked us with the memory of warmth. Then, almost unexpectedly, we arrived at a small crevasse where the ice pulled away from the rock at the top of the face, offering a sheltered, safe and, as these things go, comfortable bivouac. We had been climbing for eighteen hours and I was physically and mentally exhausted, but warmed by a satisfaction that suffused my mind and body. We spread the rope out to make some insulation and sat on it while we ate the remaining food: a few biscuits, some chocolate and some dried apricots. I was desperately thirsty but there was nothing to drink. I pulled my oiled cotton anorak over my head and zipped it up. Then I unlaced my boots and used them as a pillow, thrusting my legs into my rucksack, as far as they would go. Al said, 'This is what they say you should do.' And, looking a little uncomfortable about it, he put his arms round me. Within five minutes he was sleeping like a baby. I knew for certain I wouldn't be able to sleep and then woke up at first light feeling remarkably well rested.

Next day, walking down the main street in Chamonix, we bumped into Bill March. 'Big Bill' had a reputation as an ice climber.

'Hey, guess what I've just done.' He was obviously very pleased with himself. 'The north face of the Plan!' It was quite an impressive achievement; the route he'd climbed varies considerably depending on the state of the séracs and snow conditions. But it's quite short and can't hold a candle to the Triolet.

'Congratulations,' I said pumping his hand and thinking: 'Please, please ask us what we've done.'

'How about you?' Bill asked, as if on cue. 'Where have you been?' We told him. To give Bill his due, he blinked once, then said: 'Bloody hell!' Then he ushered us towards the bar. 'The drinks are on me.'

That winter Al Edmonds sent me a Christmas card with a short extract from André Roch's description of the first ascent:

> There is one situation I hate above all: to be the second man on the
> rope on an ice slope and especially on the ice slopes of the north
> face of the Triolet. I watched intently every one of my companion's
> movements, and I anxiously reckon how long he takes to cut one step.
> How slow he is. The worst moment comes when he moves from one
> step to the next. A succession of tiny moves, a short heave with the
> lower foot. For one second his poise is rather awkward. Is it 'yes',
> or 'no'? It is 'yes'. The crampons, almost all the points of which I can
> see from below, rest again on the ice, and it goes on and on all the time.
> What a grind. Every minute I ask him whether it is okay. And his reply
> is always the same: 'Okay but pure ice!'

Three weeks after our ascent I heard that the Burgess twins, Al and Aid, had climbed the Triolet and in the autumn that Nick Estcourt had also climbed it. It was a classic illustration of the principle of grade drift. Grade drift is what happens when a very hard route starts to be climbed by ordinary climbers. It works like this: there are three climbers, A, B and C. A is the best climber, B is quite good and climber C is competent but not as good as the other two.

Climber A climbs The Hard Route. B hears that A has climbed The Hard Route and thinks, 'If A can do it, then I have a good chance of doing it too.

B attempts to climb The Hard Route and succeeds. If A had failed or not attempted to climb The Hard Route, B would not have attempted to climb it. Climber C hears that A and B have both climbed The Hard Route. C would never have thought about attempting The Hard Route but when he hears that both A and B had succeeded, he starts to think about it. The mystique of the route has been dented; climber C thinks that it can't be that hard and soon everybody – the whole alphabet – is climbing it.

Many years later I climbed the Swiss Route on the north face of the Courtes, also in the Argentière valley and quite close to the Triolet. If anything it is slightly harder and longer than the Triolet, but less sustained. It was Nick Longland's first Alpine ice climb. With the help of twelve-point crampons, a pair of modern ice tools each, and stainless steel tubular ice screws, which were useless as a corkscrew but might actually stop a fall, we cruised up the route in one third of the time the Triolet had required. Today the Triolet is graded *Difficile* and has suffered the indignity of snowboard descents.

The ice axe is the iconic symbol of mountaineers and mountaineering. For someone like me, with a great enthusiasm for the design of climbing equipment, the development of axes is fascinating. The axe used by my great uncle Hermann Woolley in the 1890s was heavy, about three feet long with a hemlock shaft almost as thick as my forearm. The pick was short, straight and square in section, but it is recognisable as an ice axe, and that is the point. It was an axe, designed and manufactured to 'chop' ice.

There was no forerunner of the ice axe. Alpenstocks performed a useful function in the mountains, but they were more hindrance than help on technical ground. They had long shafts and helped the mountaineer by providing a third point of balance. They were suitable for their time, better than today's ice tools when probing for crevasses and they would be useful when improvising a canvas shelter at a time when there were few Alpine huts. The alpenstock was not the forerunner of the ice axe, but of the ski mountaineering stick. Hermann Buhl used ski sticks on his outrageous solo first ascent of Nanga Parbat, and left his ice axe on the summit to prove he'd been there. The axe, made by Stubai, was found a few feet from the top by a Japanese climber in 1999 and presented to Buhl's wife. It took the amalgamation of a woodcutter's axe, sometimes used by guides, and the alpenstock to produce the first proper ice axes.

The design of these ice tools reflected the needs of mountaineers at that time: first, a hiking stick, second, a step-cutting tool, and finally as a climbing tool. As a walking stick it was only good for easy-angled snow or ice. As a step-cutting tool it could be used on ice up to sixty degrees or so. But it was as a handhold that the ice axe came of age, through the development of the modern reversed curved pick, but that was a long time coming.

In the late sixties, when I did the Triolet, climbing steep ice was a very different proposition. Ice climbing was unfashionable and also dangerous. Even now it is a minority activity among mountaineers but modern ice-climbing equipment is much more sophisticated than the equipment available in the sixties: ice screws that hold falls, lightweight boots that keep your feet warm and crampons that don't fall off.

It was a tradition among British alpinists that one used a Willisch ice axe made by hand in the village of Täsch. George Mallory and Sandy Irvine had them on Everest. The break with that tradition came when Hamish MacInnes became the first manufacturer to use aluminium for the shaft of the axe. The adze and the pick were usually forged, often by hand by the local blacksmith, though latterly some axes were fabricated from sheet steel. When two tools were used as a pair, one would have an adze, the other a hammerhead.

With the advent of twelve-point crampons with forward-angled front points came the possibility of climbing on ice steeper than sixty degrees. But there existed a catch-22 in the development of ice climbing. Because the pick was designed for cutting steps it was fairly straight; downward-curving axes like those developed in the late sixties by Yvon Chouinard and the Snowdon Curver made in North Wales were advances. But if the curve of the pick was angled down too much, the pick might pull out. The steeper the ice, the more likely it was this would happen. It wasn't until the seventies that axes developed as a handhold with the steeply angled pick of MacInnes' Terrordactyl.

The biggest breakthrough was the Chacal. The first time I saw its reverse-curve 'banana' pick was visiting the Simond factory in Chamonix to negotiate a distribution deal for Friends, soon after Wild Country started. I took a small swing at a telephone pole outside the factory and the pick went in about half an inch. As I pulled down I could see the pick trying to penetrate deeper into the wood. The Chacal had solved the problem: it could be used as a hook but you could also swing it hard against the ice. The revolution was almost complete. But when I climbed the north face of the Triolet in 1968, it was, without doubt, the hardest ice climb I had ever done and would remain so.

When eventually I got to Goldsmiths during an especially fine autumn I threw myself into student life, joining the climbing club, founding Goldsmiths gymnastics club and signing up to the college orchestra. I had intended to study geography as my main subject but when I came back from India, I was asked if I would join the physical education course, which was undersubscribed. Initially I wasn't happy about this. I did not see myself as a PE teacher. Then it was pointed out to me that were I so inclined, I could bring my skills and interest in outdoor pursuits to the course. This was much more appealing. My final thesis on instructing rock climbing and mountaineering created a lot of interest when, as chair of the Mountain Training Trust, I took it to Plas y Brenin. Robin Hodgkin had sent me a copy of his book *Playing and Exploring* with a covering letter saying that I was the first person who had taken his suggestion regarding the importance of repetition of skilled movements as being fundamental to learning, whether it be multiple twisting somersaults in the gymnasium or rock climbing.

The education department at Goldsmiths had built up an excellent reputation over the years but was eclipsed by the art college whose reputation has been unassailable. A visit to the art school was quite intimidating. You had to run the gauntlet of art students at the extremes of fashion's cutting edge, with the most daunting hairstyles and razor-sharp clothes. At least humanities students could get away with jeans and a T-shirt. We didn't get judged day after day on the brilliance of our wardrobe, or how often it was washed.

In 1964 there were 1,700 students at Goldsmiths of whom 1,200 were women. I was not aware of this statistic when I applied, but when I arrived the imbalance was obvious. I don't know when I first became aware of the very attractive dark-haired girl in the drama department, but it was not till the end of my second year that I actually got the chance to meet her. The drama students were a small, very integrated group; they kept to themselves and were protective of each other.

My chance came before a screening of *The Servant*, a film all about role reversal, at the college film studio. Among those waiting for the doors to open was the diminutive form of the girl from the drama department with her close-cropped black hair. When the doors opened, the seats rapidly filled and I struggled to find a seat. Then I noticed one free beside the drama student and I found myself sitting down next to her. I think she smiled at me. When the film was over, I asked if she'd like a drink and we went to the student union bar, which was mercifully quiet. Her name was Jan and she was clearly highly intelligent. We talked about a hundred different things, but I didn't see Jan again for over a year. I took a year out, and while I was gone, she joined the college climbing club. The first time Jan and I climbed together was at Tremadog: *Meshach*, a pleasant route but not easy. I remember how impressed I was. Over the next year we climbed routes like *The Corner* ('Cloggy Corner'), *The Wasp*, and *Cenotaph Corner*, hard climbs in those days. It proved to be a partnership for life.

The 'Beatles' dog team setting out from Halley Bay in cold conditions.

5 GASH HAND

Before starting at Goldsmiths, I got a letter from Peter Noble, a climbing friend on our trip to Norway in 1962. It was postmarked South Georgia. He wrote that he was working as a mountaineer with the British Antarctic Survey (BAS). I felt irrationally jealous. This had been my ambition too. I knew he had been thinking about applying, as others had, but Pete was the only one who had made the effort. I was pleased for him, and it gave my own desire to do the same a sudden boost. I wrote to BAS asking about the possibility of working for them and received a small dossier, which warned that any employment with them shouldn't conflict with completing one's education. My dream would have to wait until I graduated, but I was eventually hired as a general assistant, a job, as the advert mentioned, requiring mountaineering skills. I was assigned to Halley Bay – also known as Base Z – the biggest, southernmost, coldest and most isolated of the six British bases then in operation.

Every year in September, BAS takes over a Cambridge college to hold a five-day symposium for new recruits, before the BAS ships start their journeys south. This is an intense introduction of lectures, socialising and discussion groups that allows BAS to observe their new employees and judge their ability to cope with stress, and general suitability for living in difficult conditions. It's far more important than the initial interview and the process continues on the journey south.

I was on the last ship to sail from England in December, which left me with the best part of three months without a job. As bad luck would have it – his, not mine – the chief instructor at White Hall had just broken his leg and I got a phone call from the principal Kim Meldrum asking if I was available. It was a beautiful autumn, one I spent climbing in the

Peak District, Snowdonia and the Lake District. Because I had only recently left Goldsmiths my salary was tax free and when I joined the *Perla Dan* in Southampton on the morning of 8 December 1969, I was fit from working in the mountains. I can still feel the excitement, the sense of anticipation, like the last day of the summer term at school. A new life was about to start. Fifteen of us sailed on the tide that evening on a voyage that would last eight weeks and an adventure that would last for three years.

We had an excellent five-course meal, which I assumed would be a one-off to celebrate our departure, but the same lavish fare continued throughout the voyage. Yet the excited atmosphere at dinner that first evening was tinged with an unspoken sadness. We were leaving familiar lives behind. We did not know each other and we did not know where the common ground lay. When someone suggested we had an after-dinner liqueur, everybody chipped in to buy a bottle of Chartreuse, based on the fact that nobody had any idea what it tasted like. During the voyage we continued to work our way through an array of exotic drinks, strictly in the interest of education, and got to know each other better.

Although I was now an employee of the British Antarctic Survey, a holiday atmosphere persisted well into the voyage. I was bunking with Mike Warden, the other mountaineer, or 'gash hand' as we were disparagingly known, 'gash' being naval slang for something that is rubbish or worthless. The mountaineer jobs were always the most sought after, and the nickname was a way of keeping us in our place. All of us were known as 'fids', people who were attached to the BAS, which was formerly known as the Falkland Islands Dependencies Survey.

We were expected to fit in with the routine of the ship and do any jobs that the captain asked us to do, but most of the time we were free to do whatever we liked. One of our regular jobs involved the sled dogs on board, this being before the new Antarctic Treaty of 1994, which banned dogs altogether. The captain had selected six Greenland huskies to help strengthen the bloodlines of the BAS breeding program. Four of the dogs would go to bases on the Antarctic Peninsula and two to Halley Bay. Every morning after breakfast Mike and I cleaned out the six kennels, which were on deck, and generally tried to keep the forward area clean and tidy.

Our first port of call was Montevideo, arriving on New Year's Day 1970. It was good to be able to go for a walk and spend an evening at a pavement restaurant eating the most sumptuous steak I ever tasted with a bottle of Malbec, a grape I had never previously tried. We sailed from Uruguay for the Falkland Islands on 3 January, reaching Port Stanley four days later.

BAS had its logistics headquarters in Stanley and we each collected a kit bag with our Antarctic clothing. Some of this, like the army trousers, was archaic and uncomfortably scratchy. The woollen shirts and Norwegian sweaters were good, but it was the outer layer that really impressed. We were issued a simple smock-style 'Ventile' anorak for working round base and a more sophisticated BAS sledging anorak, with wolverine trim around the hood. Using soft copper wire to form a tunnel, you could work or travel in blizzard conditions without your nose and cheeks freezing. Wolverine, unlike other fur, is too smooth for ice to stick. Ventile is a very tightly woven, hundred-per-cent cotton fabric that is almost waterproof. When the fabric gets wet, the cotton fibres swell, making the fabric even more waterproof. For us getting wet was not a problem. It never rained at Halley Bay. During my two years there the temperature rose above freezing on two occasions, once for a couple of hours on Christmas Eve. I took the opportunity to go for a swim, diving in and diving right out again.

We spent the best part of a week in Stanley and made the most of it, doing some easy solo climbs on Mount Tumbledown, site of one of the fiercest battles twelve years later in the war with Argentina. At a party in our honour at Government House I met Pete Guilding, a teacher from the secondary school, and his wife Jacky, who was the daughter of the superintendent of education. She told me Jan would be arriving in Stanley in February. This was news to me. It was always a source of irritation to Jan, after we left Stanley as husband and wife, when people back home in Britain inferred she had followed me out to the Antarctic. In reality, I was being posted somewhere nearly 2,000 miles away from Port Stanley, with no prospect of us meeting for two years.

The *Perla Dan* sailed for South Georgia on 13 January in conditions that were windy even for the South Atlantic, surfing down huge waves to arrive at Grytviken on the island's north coast in good weather four days later. Here BAS maintained – and still does – a largely biological scientific station. We visited Ernest Shackleton's grave and enjoyed good views of the mountains including the highest, Mount Paget, a mere 2,935 metres high, but with its base at sea level looking Himalayan in scale. Then we got down to the novel if unpleasant task of butchering fifty or so elephant seals that the fids on South Georgia had shot for us over the course of the previous two weeks – meat for the dogs. The carcasses, some of which weighed over a ton, had to be cut into strips to be transported as deck cargo and stacked out in the snow when we arrived. When the temperature dropped to minus thirty, we could use a chainsaw to cut these strips into 'doggy dinners', a doggy dinner being six pounds of red seal meat with any blubber that was attached to it. As a signatory to the Antarctic Treaty, we weren't allowed to kill any animals south of the Antarctic Circle without a licence; feeding dogs was not considered justification for getting one.

The voyage to Halley Bay from South Georgia usually takes four days but thanks to the state of the ice it took us the best part of two weeks. The *Perla Dan* was ice-strengthened as opposed to being an icebreaker, able to nudge its way through heavy pack but not barge its way through thick sea ice. We entered pack ice just at seventy degrees south on 22 January and for the first time I saw the midnight sun. At first we moved quite quickly through light pack, but had to slow down for extensive areas of old fractured sea ice, usually between six and ten feet thick and forming in the winter. Two days later we were back where we started. To get around a large area of quite dense pack, we were forced to sail north-west by west when we really wanted to go in the opposite direction. The captain would drive the ship from the crow's nest high above the foredeck, where he had a great view of the surrounding ocean, frozen or otherwise. After another two days spent testing possible leads, we found ourselves once again at the same place we had first entered the ice. Finally, nine days from Grytviken, we were blessed with clear water and able to sail through flat seas covered, unusually, by a layer of cat ice, less than an inch thick. This we could cut through at full speed.

Halley Bay is located two miles from the northern edge of the Brunt Ice Shelf and forty miles from the edge of the continent to the south. It was chosen in 1956, International Geophysical Year (IGY) 1957–58, because of its proximity to the magnetopause, the imaginary ring on the earth's surface where the lines of magnetic force are at their most intense and enter the great magnet that is our planet. It's also where Joe Farman and his team at Edinburgh University recorded data from which they concluded there was a growing hole in the ozone layer.

The day we arrived was cold, about minus twenty, but bright. There was a thick layer of rime, essentially frozen fog, on exposed surfaces and the rigging, and sea smoke on the surface of the water, caused by relatively warm water coming into contact with cold air. Sailing south-west down the northern edge of the Brunt Ice Shelf, we saw the first sign that our arrival was imminent, a column of black smoke pouring from a forty-five-gallon oil drum perched on top. Here the ice cliffs were a little higher, maybe a hundred feet, and jutting out by as much as 200 feet. This was High Headland.

Shelf ice flows down from the high Antarctic plateau that forms most of the interior of the continent. When it reaches the coast it floats, creating areas of flat ice that can be huge. The Brunt Ice Shelf is medium-sized, about fifty miles long and forty miles wide, and at Halley the ice is about 700 feet thick, though only the top hundred feet is above water level. Every now and then some of the shelf ice breaks off, or 'calves', to form an iceberg. The area where the ice leaves the edge of the continent and starts to float is called the hinge zone – a nasty, dangerous and ever-changing area up to ten miles wide where the ice literally hinges up and down on the tide every day.

The sea at the end of the shelf freezes in winter to form ice between six and ten feet thick. The captain carved out a dock using the bows of the ship to crack sea ice that filled a substantial bay in the ice cliffs, which we came to know as Third Chip. Four railway sleepers were winched over the side and dropped into slots in the sea ice with a strop around them to make 'dead-man' anchors. The boat was tied off to these so the process of unloading, which would take four days, could begin. About two-thirds of the base's crew were out on the ice and they swarmed aboard, confident, brash, not interested in the new boys, not, that is, until we bought a case of beer from the bar and introductions were made.

Before we started work the captain of the *Perla Dan* invited us to his day cabin for a drink to celebrate the end of our voyage. There was a real sense of occasion. Large cut-glass tumblers were laid out neatly in lines on the chart table. Each tumbler held two chunks of ice. As he poured us each a shot of whisky, the captain told us we would remember this drink for a long time. I doubted this. Glenfiddich is not one of my preferred malts. Then he explained how one of the chunks of ice was local, while the other had been transported from the Arctic in the ship's freezer. The whisky might have been poor, but the captain was right; I've never forgotten that drink.

Antarctica is uncompromising, unforgiving and remote. It is huge, as big as the United States and Europe combined and covered in ice with an average thickness of 7,000 feet, reaching 13,000 at its thickest. It is a place of great beauty and great danger. BAS then employed about a hundred people down in the Antarctic at any one time, and it was sober-ing to think that on average one person died each year. A one per cent fatality rate was hardly Russian roulette, but it did concentrate the mind. At Halley, three people were killed when a Muskeg tractor went into a crevasse. When sea ice broke up in a sudden storm, a dog team and driver perished trying to get back. A base commander at Halley died after being hit by an airplane on its landing approach. On Signy Island, a zoologist was attacked and killed by a leopard seal while she was working under the ice.

We watched the two-ton Muskeg tractors nose cautiously on to the sea ice and then pick up speed after fifty yards as confidence grew. There were about 300 yards of sea ice between the edge of the ice cliffs and the *Perla Dan*. The Muskeg stopped well clear of its edge and the driver got out to make an inspection on foot. There would be no calamities today. As soon as he knew the sea ice, which was about six feet thick, was strong enough, load after load of cargo started appearing out of the hold, winched over the side and lowered on to big cargo sledges. Muskegs pulled these across the sea ice and then up a long incline on to the 'bondu', as old hands called the surface of the ice shelf. From the top of the incline it was about two miles to the base.

One of my first jobs was to deal with the seal meat. The first officer was particularly keen to see the back of this, as it was making the deck slippery. Now cut into strips, it was already easier to handle but forty tons of seal meat and blubber is quite a challenge. With the meat stowed on a cargo sled, we set off for the base. A vague mound in the distance was all we could see at first, but after a mile or so, Malcolm Gyatt, known as 'Bloke' and starting his second year on the ice, pointed out two quite large grids of dunnage driven into the snow, dunnage being low-grade planks and stakes used on the ship to stabilise odd-shaped items of cargo.

'Petrol dump,' he said, pointing to the smaller of two quite large grids. 'The red drums are petrol. Next is the fuel oil, Avtur, a bit like diesel but this is aviation fuel. It works in cold weather, unlike diesel.' We were close to the base now and I could see a variety of aerials, the tallest over fifty-foot-high, a long row of fifteen-foot-high masts and several steel-lattice towers. The Muskeg stopped near the tallest of them, close to a ten-foot-square wooden cube made from marine ply. This box was raised a foot or so on skids and had a glass dome on top. It was dubbed the Auroral Hut; a photographic record of the sky was being taken automatically every fifteen minutes during the hours of darkness to capture an image of the aurora australis.

Getting down from the cab I could hear dogs barking nearby and was about to walk over for a closer look when Bloke suggested I help him feed them later. An exhaust pipe, some twelve feet high, throbbed away close to the largest of several box-like structures between five and eight feet high. These were access shafts into the base. Of the two largest, one was the front door into and out of the base, with steps up the outside and a series of ladders and landings on the inside descending twenty-six feet below the surface of the shelf ice. The other large shaft was covered in a tarpaulin with a substantial steel and wood gantry rising twelve feet above the surface and equipped with pulleys. This was the gash shaft, a sort of trades-man's entrance for getting stuff in or out of the base. The exhaust pipe disappeared down into a hole in the snow to the three diesel generators in the 'genny' shed. They were the same generators used by British Rail on their smaller trains. One would be continuously generating power; the second would be ready to start at a moment's notice. The third would be either stripped down for servicing, or ready to go.

Under our feet, buried in snow, were seven accommodation buildings laid out in an extended H-H-H: two dormitories, kitchen, dining room, lounge, offices and radio shack, garage, workshop and generator shed. On the corner where another building might have fitted was an ice cave in which lay a huge neoprene pillow tank holding two weeks' supply of Avtur. The smaller shafts on the perimeter of the base provided good ventilation for the base below, doubling as emergency shafts for a fast exit in the event of fire. Heating in the base came from electric fan heaters, which kept warm air circulating.

Imagine a giant had scraped away the snow around the base exposing enough of the structure to reveal the extent and relationship of build-ings to each other. My cutaway drawing (colour image 15) shows the base as it had been built five years earlier, on the flat surface of the site. The seven accommodation buildings had steel frames bolted on to a metal grid base. Each hut was seventy-two feet long, twenty feet wide and fourteen feet high. The huts had an inner and outer skin of one-inch marine ply. The gap between the inner and outer layer was twelve inches wide and filled with fibreglass insulation. There was a corrugated iron passageway connecting the buildings. The whole base was covered by drifting snow in the first few months of its completion and by the time I got there the floor of the base was twenty-six feet below the level of the surface snow. The temperature of the snow that had drifted around the base was a constant -24 °C, the average temperature of the air at that latitude, seventy-six degrees south.

Inevitably, people at home would ask about toilet facilities. When the base was built a deep pit had been dug in the ice where the toilet was going to be, at one end of the main tunnel. This pit was ten feet square and forty feet deep. A framework of joists was covered with marine ply at floor level and a cubicle built. Because the temperature was steady at -24 °C there was no smell. Mostly, everything was fine but human waste would build up below the cubicle to form what we called 'the turdicle', though strictly speaking it should have been called a 'turdigmite', since it grew up rather than down. When this happened someone had to go down with an axe to fell the turdicle. If you were the lucky man, there was just one thing to remember: keep your mouth shut.

It was our bad luck that the pit became full on our tour of service and we had to dig a new one. We started by 'burning' a hole, dropping aviation fuel on to old rags, which kept burning until it was so deep there wasn't enough oxygen. Then we started digging, filling oil drum after oil drum full of ice to be winched up to the surface. When we got to sixty-five feet we thought we had done enough. The pit was twelve feet square at the base but narrowed to six at the top. Before commissioning the new toilet, we realised we had created an excellent educational facility. Anyone who wanted could learn how to abseil and jumar or practise crevasse rescue techniques, literally at their own convenience.

With the resupply complete, the captain was keen to head north. The possibility of getting stuck in the ice for eight months was not one he relished. The noise and bustle of the last four days changed to a mood of contemplation and reflection. It is difficult to express the thoughts that went through my head as the *Perla Dan* headed out into the Weddell Sea. There was no regret, but it was a bittersweet moment, one tinged with apprehension. I thought of Jan who would soon be arriving at Port Stanley. The ship changed course and was soon hidden behind ice cliffs. We were alone in our cold world. Two years is a long time when you are a young man. I could not help making the analogy of starting a prison sentence. A few of us opted to walk back to the base and it was a some-what thoughtful group who climbed down the ladders into the base to find the beer flowing and a party in full swing in the 'Bondu Bar'.

Most fids spent two years at the same base though some were able to change bases halfway through. Senior scientists would only spend one winter, sometimes leaving a postgraduate to carry on the work. Today, with greater use of Twin Otter aircraft, a lot of scientists can avoid the winter and just spend the summer months there. The population of any base at any one time is made up of a mixture of first-year and second-year fids, the idea being that first-years can learn from second-years. During my second year there were twenty-three personnel made up of four geophysicists, two ionospherists and four meteorologists. In support were a doctor, a diesel mechanic, two tractor mechanics, a builder, two radio operators, a radar technician, an electrician, two cooks and two mountaineers. Of the twenty-three, eight were second-years and fifteen were first-years.

In early 1970, when I arrived, the original base, Halley I, was fifty-six feet below the surface having been covered by drifting snow year after year. We were occupying Halley II; researchers are now occupying Halley VI. Halley II, my home for the next two years, was built in 1967 about two miles east of the IGY hut, and it was already covered with twenty-six feet of snow. One of the rites of passage for new fids was a visit to the old base. This was more like a caving trip than anything else. The growing pressure of ice had squeezed rooms, passages and shafts so it was almost impossible to imagine what it had been like when in use.

Anything we found in the old base was bounty. On my first trip I recovered a case of maple syrup. A year later, two American Hercules aircraft flew in to bring two of our dog teams from the Shackleton Mountains where they were being used for geological survey work. The American flight crew asked us if there was anything we needed. As it happened, there was. We had run out of beer. Then they noticed that we had real, as opposed to synthetic, maple syrup. We had a few bottles left from my first visit to the old base, which we gave them. The Americans seemed overwhelmed by our generosity, though the beer was of far greater value to us. When I asked if they would like some more they were ecstatic. As the exchange rate between maple syrup and beer was so favourable, we dispatched a skidoo and sledge to the maple syrup mine. The Americans flew from McMurdo to Pole Station, where they won enough beer playing poker for us to celebrate Christmas and get through to the arrival of the next supply ship at the end of January.

Parties at Halley Bay were a regular event. Our employers had left us party boxes, one per month, with a variety of goodies including alcohol and chocolate. We also had a ration of a can of beer and a can of fruit juice per week. You could buy beer, but the limit was a case per week. When I became base commander, I asked the BAS shipping agent in Montevideo if they could supply a bulk purchase of wine. All those remaining for their second year said they would chip in. When the wine arrived we found fifteen of the ten-litre glass carboys had smashed on the journey, but we still had a lot – 350 litres. We drank wine with our evening meal on Tuesdays, Thursdays and Saturdays, when you could have as much as you liked, for the whole year. The bill came to four pounds fifty each.

In those far-off days, BAS also provided tobacco. As a very light smoker of four cigarettes a day, I gave them up in favour of a pipe, thinking this would embellish my explorer image. There was a good variety of tobacco and a surprisingly large stock. I started on Balkan Sobranie, which came in a sealed metal two-ounce tin. When the tobacco became dry, I would open a new tin and throw the old one away. There is a story about fids on one of the peninsula bases having so much tobacco that when the resupply ship departed they left cases of cigarettes on the sea ice to float away.

With the resupply completed and the ship on its journey north, there was much work to be done, and much to be learned by the new boys before winter set in. The ramp into the garage was the best way of getting large items in and out of the base but most of the time it was full of drifted snow. To minimise the hassle of digging it out, we had received corrugated steel – called Armco – to extend the existing arch out towards the surface. This should have been a relatively straightforward job but the bits of Armco we received didn't fit the Armco in the existing tunnel. This was the sort of self-reliance issue good fids relish; we couldn't phone up Armco and ask them to send the right stuff. The sheets of curved, corrugated steel, like crash barriers on motorways, were heavy, difficult to manoeuvre and unyielding. Even inexperienced fids could see that an Irish screw-driver – or sledgehammer – wouldn't solve the problem. The heavy-duty bolts fixing the pieces together had a tight tolerance. But we managed to screw up the last of them and seal the entrance with a heavy tarpaulin as a full-blown storm started to blow.

There were fifty Greenland huskies at Halley Bay, give or take a few pups. Greenland huskies are stronger and heavier than their Siberian cousins that are familiar from sled racing in northern Canada and Alaska. A team of nine Greenland huskies can pull half a ton all day. There were three mountain teams, the Mobsters, the Beatles and the Hobbits. There was another team not old enough to work yet; if they started too young they could develop arthritis, yet they needed to exercise and socialise, to get used to being around a sled and other working dogs.

Five weeks after arriving at Halley Bay, I had my first outing with a team of dogs, a training exercise for me rather than them. At least I could ski. Even so, the dogs spent most of the afternoon laughing at me. My sledging companion was Ian Leith, the doctor. Ian ran a physiological project looking at the relationship between thyroid and tolerance to cold. We had got on well on the ship on the way down and I was pleased to be working with him. On another sledge was the base's other mountaineer, Bloke Gyatt, like me a general assistant, and Dave Peel, who had a degree in glaciology and a doctorate in chemistry. Dave had his own experimental project, measuring the earth's pollution, which would involve a major tractor traverse the following spring.

A few days later, at the end of February, I took a couple of dogs, Canute and Pat, down to the first drum on the Great Antarctic Highway. This was the main route south, marked every two miles with an oil drum. The first twenty miles were straightforward but thereafter things became more difficult as I negotiated the Hinge Zone. A week later, Graham Wright took me out for a couple of nights. I had my own sled, learned how to put a tent up in a high wind, use the radio and navigate using sled wheel and compass. We went down the highway with the Mobsters as far as Drum H, a round trip of about nineteen miles.

Two years is not long enough to learn to drive a dog sled. It was really a case of the blind leading the sighted when it came to learning and teaching. I took over the Mobsters with their cute lead dog Shem. To start with it was hard work. The best plan was to let the dogs get on with it. They knew far more than we did, but as we became more experienced, so we learned to shout instructions at the right moment, or urge the dogs on when going uphill. By the time I left Antarctica I could do a sequence of figures of eights, which is not easy, nor, to be honest, very useful. On my last trip I covered the 130 miles back to base in four days, albeit with a light sled.

For now I was learning – not only interesting, but often very exciting. The dog sleds were built from hickory with laminated cross-bridges and a combination of stainless-steel fittings and leather thongs. The sliding surface was coated with 'Tufnol', a durable, low-friction resin. Each sled was designed to hold up to ten standard BAS sledging boxes. These slotted into the wooden stringers of the bed of the sled. As this was a short training trip we had light sledges, but on a big trip the boxes could be stacked two deep. Each box could hold twenty 'man days' of food, or else dog pemmican, a cooking set and whatever tools were required for the science project being done. Sleeping bags and all personal baggage went into 'P' bags. These were standard-issue Royal Mail bags. One would be placed at the front of the sled, just behind the cowcatcher – and the other at the back, in front of the handlebars. There were plenty of these bags; we had to process large quantities of mail, sticking the attractive BAS stamps on to specially printed first day cover envelopes for collectors. Finally, the tent, in its conical bag, would be placed lengthways on top of the load and the whole lot cinched down with six-millimetre nylon cord.

The dogs never stopped teaching me things. Towards the end of my second year at Halley, the glaciology department at Bristol University asked for temperature readings to be made at different depths beneath the ice shelf. This gave us carte blanche to go wherever we wanted to take readings. I decided to do the job myself, since my time on the ice was coming to an end, and take in some of the local sights, maybe even make the first as-cent of Christmas Box Hill, a dome of snow that rises 600 feet above the surrounding ice, and the highest place within sledging distance of Halley Bay.

To do the trip efficiently, I asked John Nockles and Tony Gannon to take a skidoo and Nansen sled, while I teamed up with Ian Bury, known as 'Guns'. We would take a dog sled and the Mobsters. John located a drum holding 2,000 feet of thin wire rope that was perfect for the job. John would also carry the winch and other equipment needed. We needed to travel 140 miles in two doglegs to where we thought we might find open water, and then find a depot of dog pemmican. On the final day, running low on pemmican, we had thirty miles to travel on a bearing in misty weather. We covered the distance and then stopped to put up the tent. As long as it was clear in the morning we should be within two miles of the depot and with binoculars we would probably see the depot's black flag on its aluminium pole. Shem was distracting me, making a fuss, pulling to one side and barking. All the others dogs were sitting or curled up in the snow but I wandered over to see what was bothering Shem. It was an aluminium pole, standing only eighteen inches clear of the ice and covered in rime. I checked the number cut into the metal: F17. This was our depot, almost hidden by drifting snow.

I prided myself on my excellent navigation, travelling 140 miles with no tolerance, until I heard about the camera. One of the meteorologists stopped to take photographs out sledging higher up on the ice shelf. When they started again he looped the camera over the handlebars but failed to notice the strap had broken. The camera was left behind on the snow. Ten days later, having weathered two storms, the dog team and their humans were returning to base. The outward tracks had long disappeared and the fids thought they were driving on a bearing. Then the lead dog, Frosty, stopped and started digging. There, at the bottom of the hole the dog had scraped, was the camera, none the worse for wear. Huskies can follow a scent under the snow. When we went on a routine trip, it was though we were on rails. The dogs were the true masters of route finding.

The other creatures that fascinated me were the emperor penguins. I got my opportunity to see them during my first winter, before they started breeding. We drove down towards the edge of the shelf in the Sno-Cat after Sunday brunch, stopping half a mile from a spot known as Mobster Creek. At two o'clock in the afternoon it was dark, with just the faintest glow in the northern sky. Leaving the comfort of the Sno-Cat's cab, we put on skis for the last stretch to the colony and as we got closer it got noisy. Very noisy. It was the sound of 8,000 penguins welcoming us with their call – *ka-kaar!* – a warm, raucous, welcome from a gregarious, sleekly plump and altogether magnificent bird.

There was no chance of missing them – all we had to do was head for the source of the noise. We could feel them before we saw them; or rather we could feel their heat, not exactly a wall of fire, but a definite increase in temperature. Then we could see them, unexpectedly, just yards away. My first impression was of their size; their heads came up to the level of my trouser pockets. I took off my skis and walked into the colony. The penguins did not seem to mind much. They did not have eggs yet and shuffled away if you reached out to them.

I didn't see them again until the sun came back. There was one trip in particular that stays in my mind. On a perfect day a couple of weeks before Christmas in my second year, we took a Muskeg down to the edge of the shelf ice and fixed an abseil rope to it. This was on a section of the coast where there had been a lot of calving that had left some very cleanly cut sections in the ice cliffs. It was a spectacular abseil but we had our eyes on an iceberg that had recently been frozen into the sea ice. From the top there was a fantastic view of the shelf and nestling under a section of cliffs we could see the colony about a mile away. On this occasion the birds were not pressed together to conserve their warmth, but spread out and sunning themselves in the mild weather and we were able to walk among them and take photographs.

It was on the way back to the abseil rope that we saw the crevasse. A section of ice cliffs had sheared so cleanly that it looked like a slab of marble. Running the full height of the cliff was a crevasse, curving upwards to a perfect blue sky. We stopped and I put on my crampons, stepped into the crevasse and started to climb. The width was perfect. I could back and foot quite easily, kicking my front points in and using my axe just to steady myself.

Like the huskies, penguins had senses we could barely guess at. In the September of my second year the geophysicists announced that the ice shelf we were sitting in had changed direction, albeit by less than one degree of arc. It also seemed to be speeding up. The Brunt had been measured moving in the same direction at the rate of a metre a day since 1956. How had it changed direction and what might have caused it to do so? I decided we should take a look at an area where some cracks had been developing over the previous year. It took us three days and a cold coming we had of it, Tony Gannon and I, at the worst time of the year. The temperature remained below minus forty most of the time, which made sledging difficult.

We had definitely come to the right place. Where once there had been mile after mile of shelf ice and old sea ice, there was now just ocean. A chunk of shelf ice the size of the Isle of Wight had detached and floated off into the Weddell Sea leaving behind clear water. Taking out a fag packet, I calculated the new iceberg must weigh in the order of seventeen trillion tons. We had a good look round and took photographs before finding a safe place to camp. It was so cold I couldn't sleep with my face outside the sleeping bag, which meant the moist air I exhaled started freezing inside the bag. After three days my bag was seamed with clusters of ice, like bunches of grapes. There was only one thing for it; I hung he bag in the top of the tent and cranked up the Primus stove. It took a whole day to thaw and dry it out. Tony, who used to walk about base with his sleeves rolled up, was able to sleep with his head outside his sleeping bag in any conditions. There was nothing we could do other than go back to base.

The iceberg had been driven by currents sweeping down the coast of the Brunt Ice Shelf, moving at a mile per day, heading for Halley Bay.

If it hit our bit of shelf we had no idea what would happen. In the event, we had a four-day blow during which the berg hit. We didn't feel anything but when the blow was over we went to assess the damage. A spot on the edge of the shelf known as Mobster Headland had gone: a quarter-mile square of ice 700 feet thick had simply disappeared. Mobster Headland was where the penguins were, or rather, had been. There was no ice left for them on which to congregate. We couldn't see any birds, even dead ones. Then there was a shout. Someone had seen a few penguins much further up the creek. We went to look and found the whole colony. By some premonition the penguins had known the danger they were in and carried their eggs half a mile up the creek to safety, balancing their precious cargo on their feet. We didn't find any sign of mortality.

Dave Peel's glaciological project measuring global pollution required us to make a 350-mile traverse from Halley Bay up on to the polar plateau. Once we reached the plateau, we would have to dig a pit every thirty-five miles to collect snow samples from different depths and consequently of different ages. That called for tractors rather than dogs. Having successfully navigated the Hinge Zone, we climbed the long slope up on to the polar plateau. The first part of this slope was slightly concave, indicating compression and therefore probably not subject to crevassing. Yet as we approached the top of the slope, it bulged slightly, becoming convex. I kept my eyes skinned. On ground like this you could find vast crevasses, the type that would eat both of our two-ton Muskeg tractors without blinking.

Nobody likes crevasses. I've never fallen into one but I've had my share of scary moments. Early one morning in the Bernina Alps, for example, I was confronted with a wide crevasse separating us from our climb. It was getting light; light enough to see the crevasse was nasty and deep. My partner took a good ice-axe belay and I set off, balancing across the uneven surface of the crevasse bridge with my heart firmly in my mouth. God knows how deep it was. Suddenly part of the bridge broke away and my right leg disappeared up to my hip. I froze. Time stood still. Then, as I started to withdraw my leg I heard the splash of a large lump of snow hitting water a long, long way beneath me. Very slowly I crawled across the remaining ten feet to safety. If you are in danger, you need to know what and where the danger is. When it comes to crevasses, whatever you know, you still stand a good chance of going down one.

I saw a crevasse the moment the Muskegs crested a slight rise. A dished line in the snow, about eight to ten feet wide, crossed our intended route, extending around 300 yards in both directions. We all got out of the tractors, reaching for our coffee flasks as we did so. I pointed out the crevasse to the others. It was about fifteen yards away. I tied the end of climbing rope round my waist using a bowline and tied a couple of loops with overhand knots to give myself enough slack to be able to take a good look while tying off the rope to a scaffold pole on the leading Muskeg. Taking a crevasse probe, I then walked gingerly towards the crevasse, stopping two yards from the edge.

I was about to start probing when movement to my left caught my attention. It was David Hoy, the tractor mechanic walking towards the crevasse. No problem. He was a second year and would know all about crevasses. The line of this one was quite obvious, but, to my horror, as he got to the spot where I would have stopped, David continued and walked out on to the sagging snow of the crevasse bridge. He had no idea of the danger he was in. I dared not shout to him in case he stopped and turned; that would stress the bridge more. He reached the far side of the crevasse, took one more step, and then, with a crack and a whoosh, the entire bridge, as far as I could see in either direction, fell into the crevasse. I crawled to the edge and looked down. The crevasse walls went straight down forever. David Hoy had been a very lucky man. If the bridge had gone two seconds earlier he would have been dead. It was the closest call I experienced in Antarctica.

Without ever discussing it, we fell into a pattern of working and sleeping that ran in thirty-five-hour cycles. It would take nine hours to travel the distance to the next dig spot. We would then have a meal, followed by a good sleep of fifteen hours or so. Then we would dig the snow pit, prepare the samples and finally load them into special zinc-coated, double-skinned boxes designed to take two 12-inch cubes. Back in the lab, they revealed a spike in radioactivity that coincided with atomic-weapon testing and the growth in our use of hydrocarbons, the story of the industrial revolution locked in the ice.

Despite our great care, the mission almost ended in disaster. On the last day, having descended 2,500 feet, we crossed the Hinge Zone but with only eighteen miles back to base our Muskeg blew a gasket. The temperature, unusually, was only a few degrees below while the 'black bulb' temperature was well above freezing. The other Muskeg went ahead with its precious cargo while Steve and I tried to fix the problem before the snow samples in the zinc boxes started to melt. Steve whipped the cylinder head off at double speed and we used a tin of emergency gunge to replace the gasket before the engine got too cold to work on. Then we drove like hell, if you consider four miles per hour to be fast. It's all a matter of perspective. We soon had the samples safely stored in the dog tunnel where it was a steady -24 °C.

Those who go to Antarctica are always quizzed about the temperature. It was a matter of pride that your base should be colder than someone else's base, and Halley Bay was the coldest. The worst wind-chill conditions I had to cope with were -40 °C with forty knots of wind, giving a wind chill of -66 °C. This will kill you very quickly. Fortunately, when there is a 'blow' the temperature rises.

Being the most remote and coldest British base allowed us to tease the other bases by mocking them as being in the 'Banana Belt'. Another joke that did the rounds was about an argument between the Americans and Russians. The Russians said it was so cold at their base that it took a week for them to dig a hole deep enough to bury their comrade. The Americans said their base was so cold that all they could do was sharpen their comrade's feet and hammer them in.

One day the temperature dropped to -53 °C, the lowest temperature ever recorded on a British base. It was my turn to check the dogs and turn the dog tunnel lights off. I put on my outdoor gear and called in at the kitchen to see if there were any scraps for the dogs. I took a bagful up to the surface, crossed the ice to the dog tunnel 200 yards away and removed the shaft cover. Then I set off down the ladder holding the bag of goodies in one hand and the top rung of the ladder with the other.

I took two steps down and removed my hand from the top rung to grab the next rung down, as I had done scores of times before. This time I missed. I felt myself fall backwards and kept falling for a long time. I expected to hear something break. I was expecting pain. When I hit the bottom I felt nothing. The ice I landed on was broken up, crunchy, like gravel. I stood up slowly, testing my limbs. Still nothing. The dogs were barking: 'What's your next trick?' I walked to the end of the tunnel distributing the kitchen scraps, climbed back up the ladder, replaced the shaft cover and went back to base. It was teatime and everyone was excited about the new record-low temperature. Someone said I looked pale and asked if I was okay. It could have been worse.

Cold affects us differently than heat. When the temperature rises from ten to twenty degrees the difference is very noticeable. At temperatures below zero the change in temperature feels much less. At temperatures of minus ten, it's only when you are exposed to wind that the cold really bites. It's the wind that kills you. Minus forty, on the other hand, really is cold. Minus forty will cause steel to become brittle, crack and break. I have watched the steel towing-bracket on a cargo sled crack like glass. It's at minus forty that Celsius meets the Fahrenheit scale. At minus forty, water cannot exist. It has to be ice. Without a film of water, ice stops being slippery, and snow becomes like sand. A cup of boiling water thrown into the air will explode into ice crystals that crackle and puff like a small firework.

The doctor during my first year at Halley Bay was Ian Leith, who was working on a project that linked thyroid activity to tolerance of cold and the ability to acclimatise to it. One of his experiments required six volunteers, including me, to spend ninety-six hours in a room where the temperature was a steady 5 °C. It was hell. We were allowed to wear a cotton T-shirt and a pair of jeans but that was it. The ordeal started at ten o'clock on a Monday morning. By one o'clock I wrote in my diary: 'I am already feeling very cold, shivering, teeth chattering intermittently.' The nights were, if anything, worse than the days. They were interminable. We were able to talk, and listen to music, and once a day someone would put a film on for us, but for all the distractions those four days were brutal. At least Ian taught me how to take a blood sample. I learned how to push the needle, feeling the tip go through the vein wall and not pushing so hard that the needle came out the other side. This was sometimes difficult: in cold conditions blood vessels shrink and tighten. I discovered I had a vein on the inside of my left elbow from which it was possible to extract blood however cold the conditions.

Ian also did research into the various natural rhythms of the body. The low level of stimulation of an Antarctic base in winter was an excellent environment to monitor these rhythms. In the hustle and bustle of modern life the stimuli one receives confuses the data. Ian's work included testing the natural cycles of human intelligence. Subjects would spend three minutes circling letters in a script as fast as possible. But there was another cycle I found even more interesting. Ian suggested we keep a record of how we felt emotionally during the course of our involvement in his project. I had a code for measuring my state of mind and noted the results in my diary, from one to five with one being most down and five being most up. Towards the end of winter I collated the information and drew a graph, using x and y coordinates where x was the time interval and the y axis recorded my mood. Drawing a graph, I discovered my moods ran in twenty-eight-day cycles. Every month I would have a brief downturn of two or three days.

I am still asked if there were any problems among the group as a result of the isolation, particularly during the hundred days without sun. By and large I think the base was a happy one. Unlike some bases, Halley was big enough for anyone wanting solitude to find it. There was, however, a division between those who liked to get out and do things like climbing and skiing, or just walking down to the coast, and those who hardly ever left the base. Those who stayed on base were sometimes critical of those who went out for putting their lives in jeopardy or immature behaviour. I never heard the more active group criticise those who stayed behind.

There was at least a custom at Halley Bay that everyone should have a summer holiday and see something of the ice shelf or go further afield. This might involve helping someone with a scientific project, but if someone had a project of his own that would be considered. Ian Bury, one of the cooks, organised the rescue of a seven-ton bulldozer that had fallen into a crevasse in the Hinge Zone three years before. This took three people, a lot of planning of the 'what if?' variety and several winches. But they got the bulldozer out and drove it back to base.

In August 1970, the base commander announced who would be his successor the following year, naming a member of the team who had been a warrant officer in the army and had also served a previous tour of duty, making him the most experienced as well as the oldest person at Halley. Then the message came from BAS headquarters in Cambridge: we want Vallance instead. Given that start, you'd be forgiven for thinking that when I took over in February 1971 I might have had more than my fair share of problems. In fact my period in charge was remarkably free of aggravation, despite all the pressures of isolation and the long dark winter. Then something totally unexpected – and unpleasant – happened.

In mid August, three days after the return of the sun, a group went down to Mobster Creek where someone who should have known better took it into his head to kill an emperor penguin. He did this by clubbing it unconscious, then cutting off its head. A first-year in the group tried unsuccessfully to restrain him. This wasn't just an act of mindless violence; it also contravened the Antarctic Treaty. His reason, he told me later, was to cook the bird on the next Saturday night and that anyone who wanted could try it. This struck me as a poor excuse. He also said he might do it again, so I made it clear that any further incident of that nature would be reported. As base commander, the sanctions I had at my disposal were limited; at worst I could recommend his fifteen per cent bonus should be withheld. I was willing to blame the last hundred days of darkness but I needed to rattle his cage a little. The whole base knew about it so ignoring what had happened wasn't an option.

I failed to anticipate what happened next. A senior second-year who had watched the penguin being killed posted a notice criticising my actions. I was making a fuss about nothing. When I tried to discuss it with him he refused to talk about it. I assumed that I would have the backing of the whole base, but instead found there was a small clique saying I had over-reacted. A few hours later I received a delegation of first-years supporting my action. They said I should throw the book at him. What surprised me was the speed with which this minor bit of foolishness escalated into a divisive incident with serious implications for morale. The atmosphere at base was distinctly unpleasant.

One penguin out of 8,000 wasn't such a big deal, but that wasn't the point. I suspected the incident had been contrived to cause trouble by people who were bored. They had succeeded. I called a meeting of the whole base including the duty meteorologists who would usually be in bed. There was real tension in the lounge with people in small groups whispering together. Calling the meeting to order I told them I was going to draw a line under the whole incident and wouldn't report it. There was total silence for a few seconds, then a buzz of conversation as people conferred. They had not anticipated that. I quickly moved on to remind them that we were subject to the Antarctic Treaty. I said that there would be no further contravention or I would throw the book at the perpetrators. Looking at those who had been involved, I asked if anyone had anything to say. Nobody seemed to want to say anything. I asked if everybody understood. There was a nodding of heads. I asked if there were any questions. There were no questions. I reminded them that we still had five months before the ship arrived and that we had to live and work together; it was my job to ensure the smooth running of the base and I expected their help and cooperation.

The incident was over and nothing more was said. The storm passed as quickly as it had arisen and the next few months passed in relative harmony. By late January, our resupply ship, the *Bransfield*, was on its way from South Georgia. It would not take long to get here and then we would face four days of hard work unloading. We were ready. The sea ice might be a problem, but nothing Captain Woodfield couldn't handle.

Two years before I had stood at the same spot on the edge of Antarctica, full of apprehension. I had been a different person then. Living in Antarctica had changed me. I had wondered at its beauty, at its power, at its indifference. It had changed my understanding of myself. It had changed my view of what I could achieve. I had revelled in the responsibility given to me. I had matured. There was now an important question that I had to ask the girl in Port Stanley. What, if anything, would Jan say when the mail arrived? What if she had not written? We had talked on the radio several times to the amusement of a considerable number of BAS employees who would listen in to our scheduled chats on Sunday mornings. But I wasn't sure.

A couple of years ago I had to buy Jan a new wedding ring to replace the one I bought her when I got to Stanley. Her first ring was no longer a ring, more a 'C'. While I was in the jeweller's I noticed a display of second-hand Rolexes. I was impressed by the prices. In 1969, on my way down to the Antarctic, I bought a Rolex Oyster Submariner watch in Stanley tax free for the princely sum of £47. A year after buying Jan's new ring my Rolex went on the blink. There's only one thing worse than an unreliable watch and that's an expensive unreliable watch. I asked the jeweller how much to get it serviced: several hundred pounds. No way was I paying that much to service a £47 watch. I asked the jeweller how much he would give me for it. He had a good look at it and said £2,500. The moral to the story is: don't ever buy a cheap Rolex – buy half a dozen.

My first 5.10 lead in America: *Twister* on The Twin Owls, Estes Park.

6 AMERICA

I arrived in Port Stanley on 7 February. Twelve days later Jan and I were married by special licence in the Stanley registry office. We lived in the Old Paint Store, a wooden house belonging to the Falkland Islands Government. I got a job teaching at the school in Port Stanley but not for long; I had a job waiting for me at Colorado Outward Bound School. Towards the end of April I boarded the *Bransfield* for its final sailing of the season and got off at Montevideo where I took a riverboat to Buenos Aires. From there I made my way northwards by bus, first to Jujuy on the Bolivian border, then on to La Paz. Unexpectedly, I met Neil Macpherson who had been base commander on Adelaide Island while I was at Halley. We had talked a few times on the radio. We climbed a peak together, Chacaltaya in the Cordillera Real, no more than a strenuous hike but at 17,785 feet (5,421 metres) my height record until the late 1980s. Then we caught a train to Machu Picchu, which we had almost to ourselves.

Not wanting to be late for my new job, I flew from Lima to Mexico City and took a bus to El Paso arriving at the border with Texas late in the evening. There were more than a dozen people on the bus, but I was the only one immigration stopped. My complexion might have had something to do with it. Someone had advised me to shave off my beard before crossing the border. I bought a razor in Mexico City and stood at the mirror in the Hotel Texas scraping away. The result was not good. The face in the mirror looked shifty. I'd acquired a deep suntan in South America. Anyone could see I had worn a beard and shaved it off very recently.

Immigration officials escorted me off the bus and into an air-conditioned shed. I was told to identify my luggage and then a uniformed officer who stank of stale sweat took everything out of my pack while another officer, this one in a dark suit, stared at me. A dog was brought in and failed to take any interest in me, my pack or its contents. The dark suit just carried on staring but the uniformed officer seemed disappointed, poking around a bit more and asking about my work permit. He waved me away with a parting shot: 'Why don't they hire our boys instead of foreigners?'

I thought it prudent not to answer back but I didn't like being called a foreigner – I was English, dammit! Nor did I tell him that my job offer had come from another Englishman, Gordon Mansell. I had applied for the job from Halley Bay and by sheer chance my letter was opened by Gordon, whom I knew quite well. He had worked at White Hall before moving to the States and was now in Boulder teaching graphic art at the University of Colorado. I boarded the next Greyhound to Denver. Passengers from the previous bus averted their gaze as I walked down the aisle or else looked at me as though I smelt bad. I felt like Arlo Guthrie in 'Alice's Restaurant'.

We crossed Texas, passed endless miles of dry prairie through Lubbock and Colorado Springs and on to Denver where I spent the first night in the YMCA near the bus station. Next day I checked in at the Outward Bound office in Denver. People were incredibly welcoming. Joe Logan arranged for me to spend a few days with a lovely couple, Bill and Kate Plitt, before I headed for Marble, high up in the Rockies near Aspen, and the Colorado Outward Bound School (COBS) training centre. Here I got a thorough briefing and some intensive training including the American Red Cross first-aid course.

After that I started work 9,000 feet up in the San Juan Mountains at the Red Cloud Ranch in Hinsdale County, the second least populated county in the United States. It had, in those days, just ninety-two inhabitants. Most of them lived in Lake City, which could have been the film set for a western with its wooden sidewalks and a saloon where almost everyone wore a gun-belt and sidearm.

The first three days of staff training involved a 'get-to-know-you' hike up a distinctive 14,000-foot mountain called Uncompahgre Peak, the highest in the range. My supervisor was Denny Hogan. Denny was very supportive and had a light touch; we soon became good friends. If there was a problem it would not be a problem for long. Another great thing about Red Cloud Ranch was Ann Hadlum, wife of the climber Des, a couple from Leicester who had worked for COBS for years. Ann's granola included a variety of grains, nuts and dried fruit mixed together and lightly roasted in oil and honey. I would take bags of it with me whenever I was away from base, which was most of the time. She gave me the recipe and I used it as mountain food thereafter.

I instructed on three courses, each lasting twenty-six days, all in the San Juans, but moving south down the Continental Divide each month. We would start with a few days of assessment and training, building teams that could operate in isolation as the course progressed. We taught the kids navigation, how to abseil, cross a river, make a shelter and camp cooking. Three days were spent in the wild without any human contact, the so-called 'solo'. I had instructed for Outward Bound in the Lake District but was impressed with the robust situations the American teenagers were expected to overcome. To finish, the students would plan a four- to six-day expedition designed to stretch them both physically and mentally.

There was a new dynamic, new to me anyway, created by the issue of race. I frequently found myself taking race into account when planning what I did with my group and when I did it. The white students were often motivated and fit, especially those from supportive families. They would probably enjoy the experience and become more self-confident as a consequence. Those students, often black, who came from poorer backgrounds, had the potential to derive far greater benefit. There was so much more for them to learn. About a third of the students were black, and most of them seemed to come from New Jersey. We would inevitably 'lose' one or two of them during the first or second day of each course. But it was these characters that would get the most out of it, as long as we could keep them long enough.

When possible, we would let the group find their own way to the next camp, first by leaving them alone for an afternoon, and then by letting them alone all day. Obviously we needed to know that they were safe, so we continued to observe them, hopefully without the group knowing we were there. One day I climbed 14,000ers to keep watch as my group negotiated the valleys between them. Perhaps the hardest part of each course was the three-day solo. The first I supervised was at a delightful spot called Balsam Lake at the head of Ten Mile Creek. The site was perfect, combining as it did, great natural beauty, remoteness, ease of hiding and interesting flora and fauna.

There was a black student who was quite a bit smaller than his peers. His friends called him Toff. When he was walking you could hardly see him under the large pack but he was cheerful and, despite the fact that he had developed some nasty blisters, kept up with the group. On one of the resupply days we walked down Ten Mile Creek to the infant Colorado River. This we had to cross to reach a good path that ran alongside the Denver and Rio Grande Railroad, which featured in *Butch Cassidy and the Sundance Kid*. We had to walk a couple of miles to a siding where the train company had left our provisions for the next week. To take the pressure off his blisters, Toff changed into a pair of trainers and put his boots in his pack.

When we got to the siding we had lunch before loading up our rucksacks ready for the hike back up Ten Mile Creek. No one noticed that Toff had taken his boots out of his rucksack when he was packing his share of supplies. It wasn't until we got back to the campsite that Toff remembered. He was very upset. His parents weren't wealthy and he was in Colorado on a scholarship. He felt he had not only let himself down, but his parents and his group. I told him I would go back and fetch them. I must be nuts, I thought, trying to think what I would need and grabbed a walking pole. I set off at a trot down the now-familiar track, realising too late that I should have eaten more and taken my headlamp.

When I got to the Colorado River, it looked fuller and faster than it had earlier. The day had been warm and snowmelt had been considerable. Fording the river, the water was halfway up my thighs where before it had only come up to my knees. Ideally, river crossings are best done in a group with everyone linking arms. I felt vulnerable. By the time I reached the siding, it was getting dark. I couldn't see well enough to find the boots. Damn. Increasingly frustrated, I was about to pack it in when I noticed a few inches of what looked like string. I pulled it and found a boot attached. I was saved.

I got back to the crossing point when it was almost dark and the river now looked really menacing. I was genuinely frightened as I waded into the water. I began muttering a sort of mantra: 'Don't fall. Do not fall. DO NOT FALL!' At least I had remembered my hiking pole. It took me a long time to get back to camp. I was tired and hungry and seriously scared of running into a bear. I whacked at stuff with the pole to make a noise as I walked up the trail ready to smite anything that emerged from the bush with it. By the time my head hit my neatly folded sweater I had covered forty-eight miles.

Jan's contract in the Falkland Islands ended on the last day of August. Mine ended, fortuitously, on the first day of September. We had not had

01 Hermann Woolley (1846–1922), my great great uncle and president
of the Alpine Club from 1908 to 1911.

02 My parents on holiday in 1940.

03 In my Sunday best, aged seven.

04

05

06

04 Nick Longland bouldering in the Churnet valley in 1960.
05 Climbing *Avalanche Wall* at Curbar in 1960. Note the gym shoes.
06 Climbing *Flying Buttress* at Stanage in 1959.
07 My Polanyi diagram.

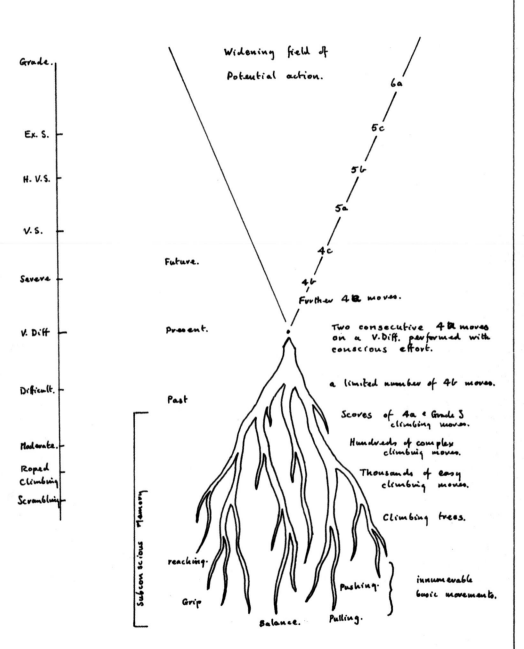

Diagram to illustrate how conscious thought and subconscious memory are focused into one single skilled action.

Widening field of Potential action.

Grade.

Ex. S.

H. V. S.

V. S.

Severe

V. Diff

Difficult.

Moderate.

Roped Climbing

Scrambling

6a

5c

5b

5a

4c

4b

Future.

Further 4b moves.

Present.

Two consecutive 4b moves on a V.Diff. performed with conscious effort.

a limited number of 4b moves.

Past

Scores of 4a & Grade 3 climbing moves.

Hundreds of complex climbing moves.

Thousands of easy climbing moves.

Climbing trees.

Subconscious Memory

reaching.

Grip

Balance.

Pushing.

Pulling.

innumerable basic movements.

07

MV.

08

09

10

11

12

08 Hjørundfjord, Norway.
09 La Meije in the Écrins.
10 Swami Lokeswarananda in the garden at Narendrapur.
11 The Swiss route on Les Courtes.
12 The north face of the Aiguille de Triolet.

13 An old iceberg in the Weddell Sea.
14 The *Perla Dan* in 'Third Chip'.
15 My cutaway drawing of the base at Halley Bay.

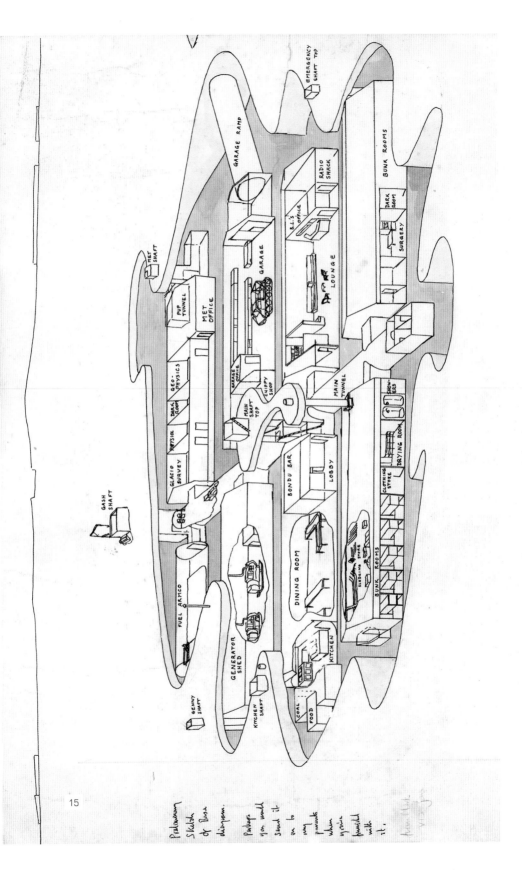

15

Preliminary
Sketch
of Base
diagram.

Perhaps
you would
send it
on to
any
persons
who are
familiar
with
it.

16

17

18

16 The surface above base at Halley Bay.
17 Filling the water tanks.
18 Throwing boiling water into the air in -40 °C temperatures – it instantly freezes!
19 Out with the 'Mobsters' on my birthday.
20 My lead dog, Shem.

19

20

21

22

21 Cutting up seal meat with a chainsaw. Note dog spans in the background.
22 The dog tunnel.
23 Mike Warden with the meat wagon.
24 Dave Hoy looking into the crevasse that he nearly fell down.
25 Me going for a swim on Christmas Eve, one of the two days
   when the temperature rose above freezing.

26 Rappelling down to the sea ice on the way to the emperor penguin colony.
27 Dr Dave Peel, doing what he does best: glaciology.
28 Me measuring ice core samples.

29

30

29 Me (left) and Ron Loan having a winter tea break.
30 Tony Gannon about to release a weather balloon.
31–33 Emperor penguins and their young.
34 Young Weddell seal.

35 Halley Bay (Base Z) at midday in early spring.
36 Me and Jan on the common behind Government House, Falkland Islands, in 1972.

time for a honeymoon after our wedding in Stanley so we planned to spend the next month in Colorado and then a month in California climbing in Yosemite. I had an open invitation to stay with the Plitts in Denver, so we were reunited there.

We wanted to do some climbing in Boulder and Estes Park but my main objective was one of the routes on the Diamond on Longs Peak. It was getting a little late in the season. Ice was falling from the summit rim in great sheets only to shatter into a thousand sparkling fragments as they fell. But I was fit and well acclimatised, having been at altitude for the past several months without ever dropping below 9,000 feet.

For this climb I teamed up with Dave Goth, a fellow instructor from COBS with whom I got on very well. We hiked up to Chasm View where we could take in the whole face. It was big and seemed incredibly steep. Doug Scott had likened it to climbing the Central Pillar of Frêney on Mont Blanc. A thousand feet of vertical granite began at a ledge system, known as Broadway, cutting across the face at 13,000 feet. Here we would spend the night. Once on the face, there were no ledges and no easy escape routes. We had chosen a route called D7, imaginatively named as the seventh route to be put up on the Diamond. D7 was also reckoned to be the easiest but it also went straight up the middle of the face, ending on the summit. With an early start, we hoped to climb the route next day.

From Chasm View, three long rappels took us to Broadway where we found a good bivouac spot. While we were slow getting off next morning, by midday we were halfway up the face and getting used to the requirements and discipline of big-wall climbing. Suddenly there was a yell, or rather a yelp. I looked up. Dave was about 130 feet above me on the belay ledge, if you can call a foothold a belay ledge. He had slipped, pivoting to one side, and in stopping himself had dislocated his shoulder. I jugged up to Dave's hanging stance and he told me what to do, since this had happened before. We got his shoulder back to where it should be and after a short discussion decided that with more than 400 feet of hard climbing still to go, it wasn't possible that we could top out that day. We would either have to bivouac on the face or abseil off. Neither option was appealing, but prudence won out and we were back at the campsite before nightfall.

It was now October. The weather would be cooler in Yosemite and I was desperate to get to grips with the Valley's legendary climbing. Jan and I had intended to hitch-hike from Boulder, but Dave Goth, still recovering from his injury on the Diamond, suggested we take a look at the rides advertised on the university noticeboard. In this way I met Larry, a college dropout in his mid twenties. Larry was pinning up a notice: 'Ride to California. Leaving Saturday morning. Share gas.' Perfect. I discovered Larry was pursuing the American dream, a latter-day prospector on his way west from New Jersey to seek his fortune. I asked if he had enough room for two plus two large packs. No problem. He drove a VW Microbus. Two days later we were driving down Interstate 70, passing signs to Vail, Eagle, Grand Junction, Cisco and Green River, where we turned north for Spanish Fork and Salt Lake City. As the sun dropped below he desert horizon, we pulled off the road to camp out for the night. We didn't bother with the tent but I suggested Jan check her trainers for scorpions in the morning, for which I got no thanks.

Crossing Bonneville Salt Flats next morning, the first twenty miles were dead straight and I wondered how far we would have to drive before finding breakfast. We'd driven 500 miles the day before and planned to do another 400 that day, but I discovered I was never bored. I could watch the high desert landscape unfold for hour after hour, staring at the distant mountains.

Returning from the bathroom in Reno, I walked back along a wide corridor lined with slot machines. Nearby a small group of tired-looking women dressed in fishnets and Playboy costumes were playing a desultory game of poker. They didn't look up. I paused to examine the change in my pocket, found a single quarter, stuck it in the nearest slot, and pulled the handle. Ker-boom. The slot machine started spewing quarters. I had hit the jackpot. I grabbed a plastic bucket and started scooping up the coins. As I headed for the cash desk, I could feel the bitterly resentful eyes of the bunnies on me.

Somewhere between Reno and Lake Tahoe, Larry announced he would like to see Yosemite. That suited us fine. We camped near Lake Tahoe and in the morning I used my winnings to buy one of those breakfasts America does best: freshly squeezed orange juice, a Denver omelette, blueberry muffins and coffee. We were getting close to Yosemite now and I could feel myself growing more and more excited, just as I had as a child going to the seaside for the first time. We drove past sequoias on Big Oak Flat, went through the Wawona Tunnel and suddenly – unexpectedly – it was there. El Capitan. I knew it was big and I thought I knew what 'big' meant, but I was not prepared for what I saw. We pulled over to take a longer look. I couldn't see anyone climbing, but further down the road a group of tourists were looking through binoculars and talking animatedly. I wandered down and asked them what they were looking at.

'Climbers! Here, try these.' One of the tourists passed me his binoculars. As the image came into focus I gasped. It seemed as though there were climbers everywhere, not just one or two, but dozens. They seemed to be concentrated on the right-hand side, where the classic *Nose* finds its way up 3,000 feet of mainly perfect granite. I started counting. There seemed to be several climbers on each belay, maybe fifty in total. What was going on? Then it struck me. It was a rescue. Someone was being lowered down on a stretcher. We had arrived in Yosemite on the day of the famous Olsen rescue. While quite high on the route, Neal Olsen had pulled a block off and broken his femur. It was one of the first really big technical rescues on El Capitan and the furthest anyone had been lowered down a rock face in history, taking thirty-one hours and spearheaded by the Yosemite pioneer Jim Bridwell.

The roads most people use to get about the Valley are mainly one-way loops. We drove round the big loop that filters tourists anticlockwise, and pitched our tent in Camp 4, not far from the Columbia Boulder, home to the famous boulder problem *Midnight Lightning*. Then we set out to find a much-needed shower. Camp 4 did not have any showers at that time but if you knew how to get inside you could get one in the washrooms of the more salubrious tourist trailer parks in Yosemite Village. I asked a man I thought looked like a climber wearing white painter's trousers and a T-shirt. He turned out to be Steve Wunsch, then one of the best in America. Not only did he escort us to the trailer park but told us how to get into the showers and where the fresh towels were kept.

Ken Wilson, editor of *Mountain* magazine, called Wunsch the 'prophet of purism' after his free ascents of several hard routes in North Wales. Wunsch had made the point that if you pulled or rested on a runner you weren't climbing free, which hurt the Brits, who always prided themselves on good climbing ethics. Even Joe Brown, who could do no wrong, had used the occasional peg to make his routes 'doable'. *Cenotaph Corner*, probably the most famous of Joe's climbs, had required two pegs for aid for several years after the first ascent.

Today Camp 4 is well groomed and tidy and Steve Wunsch works on Wall Street. But in the early seventies it was casual, scruffy and delightful. A few years ago the National Park Service wanted to bulldoze the place but there was a huge outcry, not only from American climbers but also from climbers all over the world. The powers that be were so impressedby the support that was given, Camp 4 was designated as a National Historic Site.

Our closest neighbours were three Scotsmen. That evening I wandered over to introduce myself and discovered I knew two of them. John Cunningham, my boss at Glenmore Lodge, had helped swing my appointment to BAS. John had himself spent six years in Antarctica, more than anyone else. His stories and anecdotes about his time down south had enlivened long evenings in snow caves on the Cairngorm plateau. I also recognised Fred Harper, chief instructor at Glenmore Lodge, and was introduced to Bob Smith. He was also an instructor at the Lodge. They had been planning to climb the *Nose*, but had been psyched out after their first attempt. Now they wanted to get as much climbing done as possible. This was fortunate for me; Jan did not want to climb all day, every day, and I was invited to join the Scots to make two ropes of two.

It was there, in Camp 4, that John Cunningham introduced me to the Yosemite climber Yvon Chouinard. I imagine it made no impression on Chouinard, but I remember it clearly. We were standing right next to the Columbia Boulder. Here was a man who understood climbing equipment. His company made the best in the world. And here I was talking to him in Camp 4 of all places. He had driven to Yosemite to meet with Cunningham who had been influential in developing modern ice climbing; John had helped Yvon with his seminal book on the subject. I did not know it then, but our paths would cross again – and again.

Like everyone else I knew, the first climb Jan and I did in the Valley was Royal Robbins's iconic *Nutcracker*. Graded 5.8 and five pitches long, it was one of the very first routes to be climbed in America using the 'new' clean ethic: no pegs and no hammers, just nuts for protection. Robbins discovered using nuts as protection in Colorado, from the British climber Tony Greenbank, who had brought some over from England. Within a couple of years Robbins was a devotee and *Nutcracker* was part of his mission. It's now one of the most popular routes in the Valley. Not everyone was convinced that the peg hammer would soon be redundant. Yosemite cracks are often parallel and nut placements didn't look convincing compared to a well-driven piton. But by the early seventies the revolution transforming Yosemite climbing was well underway. The stage was set for a rapid evolution in rock-climbing gear.

We didn't have a car and were trying to work out how to get to Manure Pile Buttress, as the home of *Nutcracker* is known, a name that doesn't do the cliff justice but might keep the numbers down. Robin Barley, an anaesthetist and well-known climber from Yorkshire now living in Canada, was camping quite close to us. He heard our conversation, told us he knew how to find it and asked if he could join us. It was an excellent climb. I loved the granite, its solidness, the friction and the uncompromising economy of holds, the warmth, the feel of smooth rock against my hands, the feel of rough rock against my hands. I knew I could never grow tired of this place. Indeed what I liked most about Yosemite was the rock, the endlessly varied granite – the complexity of its colour. The big draw in the Valley is its famous big walls: the *Nose*, *Salathé* and so on. But the sheer perfection of some of the single-pitch climbs, whatever the grade, blew my mind.

The first route I did with John Cunningham was at the base of El Capitan, a strenuous line called *Moby Dick*. Like many of the short routes on El Cap, it was made by a huge flake of granite lying against the main cliff itself. After we had rappelled down we were walking back to our packs when I noticed an almost brand-new three-inch chromoly Lost Arrow piton. I scooped it up and after ten paces found another peg, this time a knife-blade, not quite pristine but good enough. John was not to be outdone, and we spent the next half hour grovelling in the dirt looking for more loot. I found two more pegs but John came away empty-handed and, forgive the pun, spitting nails.

Next day John told me he had seen a bear trying, and almost succeeding, in reaching my bag of food suspended on a rope between two trees. We were both using the same rope and as a consequence the two trees were bending towards each other, making the bags an easier target. John helped me rehang the two bags and as we went back to our tents, I told him that any bear that got my bag now would deserve it. In the morning, the base of my bag had been torn out. I don't know how, but my theory was it must have stood on another bear's shoulders.

With the Scots, I climbed *Lost Arrow Spire*, a classic route combining a fabulous walk up a switchback trail looking across to Yosemite Falls, a long rappel, then four pitches of quite awkward and very exposed pegging. Sadly we didn't have enough time or the right equipment to rig the classic Tyrolean traverse from the summit of the spire to the rim. Anyway, it was crowded enough with four of us crammed on its tip. There are few easy long routes in Yosemite but the best of them is *Royal Arches*, starting close to the Ahwahnee Hotel on the north side of the Valley. It's not hard, about 5.6, but in seventeen pitches takes you from the floor of the Valley to the rim, near North Dome. Jan and I got up early to give ourselves plenty of time, but as we walked through the grounds of the hotel we exchanged greetings with a distinguished looking man who, on hearing our accents, asked us if we were from England. He wanted to know what we were doing and seemed intrigued by our climbing gear. It turned out he was a US senator.

Now running late, we quickly found the start of the route and made good time up the clean granite until we reached the notorious Rotten Log pitch. Here we had to cross a wide defile by scrambling up an old rotting pine that had been there long before the route was established. (It finally broke up and was washed away in 1982.) We negotiated the log easily enough but the final few pitches were made harder by granite gravel, like little ball bearings, washed down the slabs from the top.

We had been warned about the descent, but that didn't stop us having an epic in the gully to the east of Washington Column. It took us ages. Three years later I combined *Royal Arches* with an ascent of North Dome – a really great day out giving 3,000 feet of climbing on near-perfect granite. Much later our daughter Jody and I slept out on the top of North Dome and after stashing our packs on the summit climbed *Crest Jewel*, an elegant route with ten pitches of quite hard slab climbing.

Jan and I had a similar experience on a notorious route called *Selaginella*, five pitches long and in the opinion of many undergraded at 5.8. It was our second route of the day, and we'd been rather slow, not getting to the last and hardest pitch until after sundown. I found it difficult in the gloom, and Jan found it very difficult in the dark, especially so because I had to pull her through a large manzanita bush which bars the exit to the climb. Manzanita is the only member of the plant kingdom I know that is made from cast iron. It is also deeply malevolent. Having escaped the bush, we still had to get down the Yosemite Falls trail in the dark with its zigzags and drop-offs. I had twelve matches and with frugal use we managed to get so far but when they ran out we were stuck. I had just started looking for a bivouac when the moon rose over the Valley's rim bathing us – and the trail – in its silvery light, enough for us to stroll to Camp 4.

At the end of our month in Yosemite we flew home, stopping over in Montreal for a couple of days to visit Len Mason, the friend of my father who had first taken me climbing in 1955. Three years after leaving Britain, we arrived back on a bright and frosty autumn day, with smoke from burning leaves rising straight up into a cloudless blue sky. It felt like the perfect day to return to England, the end of an era, a day to celebrate the end of youth. It felt like the start of something entirely new.

The summit plateau of Kinder Scout in the Peak District, photographed on the August
bank holiday 1973, while making a photographic survey of car parking in the national park.

7 A PROPER JOB

After a few days with Jan's parents in Hastings we drove north to stay with mine in the Peak District village of Great Hucklow. I needed a job, and hoped to find one as an instructor in a mountain centre somewhere. John Evans, a director at Colorado Outward Bound, had offered me a full-time appointment in Colorado, but Jan and I needed to spend time at home and renew old friendships. It was good to know John would hold the job open for a few months.

In a stroke of good luck, I saw an advertisement for a new post based at the Peak District National Park headquarters in Bakewell. It was an educational job and although not what I'd had in mind, it paid well, more than I could expect working as an outdoor instructor. The successful candidate needed 'a degree in environmental studies or other relevant discipline'. My CV fell some way short; I had a teaching certificate from Goldsmiths and mountain leader qualifications. But I applied anyway and found myself on a shortlist of six out of almost 200 applicants.

The interview process involved a full day of activity with a class of schoolchildren bussed in to Monsal Head, a local beauty spot in the Wye Valley. We would be evaluated on our teaching skills and knowledge of the national park. It was November. The sky was a dirty grey. It was not really cold, but a misty drizzle dampened spirits. An officer from the national park, Theo Burrell, asked for a volunteer to open the batting. It struck me that the first candidate would have the advantage of novelty before the kids got really wet and cold – and bored. I didn't hesitate. I stuck my hand up.

As the children gathered round, I was in the process of putting a quick lesson plan together in my head when I noticed an empty litterbin lying on its side near the car park entrance. It was surrounded by rubbish – drinks cans, polythene bags and so forth. I set the bin upright and asked the students to collect ten bits of litter each and put them in the bin. While they did, I gave them a short sermon on the evils of litter. Soon the bin was full and the area was clean. The other candidates would not have the opportunity to score litter points. Later that afternoon, shortly after getting home, I received a phone call from Burrell offering me the job and asking how soon I could start. I suggested the beginning of the following week. After I had started, Ivor Morton, the vice chairman of the board, took me on one side and told me that they had been impressed by my 'bravery' in volunteering to go first. I thanked him but didn't reveal my secret.

My five years working for the national park – my first proper job, perhaps my only one – were productive and much of the time great fun. Working in local government didn't particularly suit me, but it was a pleasant enough place to work, there was no unreasonable pressure, and hell, I liked living and working in the Peak District. I made good friends who I still keep in touch with. We're part of a walking group called The Escape Committee. To be a member you must have worked for the national park and be retired. It meets once a month to cover six to eight miles before a pub lunch where we toast our good fortune.

I worked within the information service although I might more appropriately have been based at the park's study centre at Losehill Hall near Castleton. Within the service were five full-time staff and twenty part-time staff who ran the information centres across the Peak District. A senior colleague, Peter Freeman, was a tireless promoter of park issues and landscape interpretation and put the 'national' into national park, having worked in parks around the country including Dartmoor and Northumberland and would later work in the Lake District. Pete was also a climber and mixed work and pleasure in an imaginative way. He decided to make an audio-visual about the recreational value of the national park. What better way than to make a presentation about climbing? He didn't have to twist my arm very hard to get my help. The programme was shown at Edale information centre and featured five famous Peak District climbs: *The Sloth, Peapod, Left Unconquerable* and *Surplomb*, and *The Prow* on Raven Tor, then still an aid route. Pete was the first to admit he was not in the top rank of rock climbers but he was one of the best aid climbers that I've known. On a trip to the Cheddar Gorge we climbed *Bird of Paradise*, a technical, steep and very exposed aid route, which, on the final pitch, made me wish

I was elsewhere. This was shortly before Ron Fawcett came along and climbed it free, just as he did *The Prow*. We also climbed *Coronation Street* together, probably the finest non-mountain rock climb in Britain.

At work, Pete took me under his wing. He taught me the importance of giving a name to any scheme or project that you initiated. By giving it a name, you established your ownership of the project and denied the opportunity for someone else to take the credit. As the first 'youth and schools liaison assistant' I was able to define the job myself. Its scope was quite broad and at times I struggled to stop myself being spread too thinly. My first big project was to create what would today be called a database, providing information for teachers and group leaders that could be sent out on request. I called this the 'The Schools Service', starting with a set of free information sheets on a variety of national park subjects for use by teachers and group leaders. Subjects included the history and philosophy of national parks, their geography, geology, geomorphology and biology, and topics like industrial heritage. Each information sheet could be cut down into manageable blocks and added to, corrected or revised whenever the need arose or time permitted.

From time to time teachers would enquire about doing voluntary work and I did my best to accommodate them though it wasn't part of my remit. During my third year, a new job of volunteer organiser was created in the national park ranger service. The post was for a senior officer with a correspondingly higher salary than mine. This rankled with me and I said so to the director for park management. He suggested that I should apply for it. That hadn't occurred to me but I did as he suggested and got the job. There was no limit to what I could do in my new post.

One request was to cut hawthorn in the national nature reserve at Miller's Dale. I was asked for help with drystone walling and footpath repair work. Some of these projects required higher levels of skill than the volunteers had. How could I get them trained up? The answer came from the British Trust for Conservation Volunteers (BTCV). I established a small group of regular volunteers, whom I called the Peak Park Conservation Volunteers (PPCV) and affiliated them to the BTCV who helped with training. Within six months I had a dedicated, skilled, self-motivated team who could tackle most of the work volunteers could be expected to tackle.

In the spring of 1978 the Labour government announced a new training scheme, the Youth Opportunities Programme, an important job creation scheme. The national park had just committed to a major improvement of the Pennine Way, with a particular emphasis on the very difficult and boggy section from Snake Pass to Bleaklow. I got an application in very early and as a result of this serendipity ours was the first YOP scheme in Derbyshire and one of the first in the country. We called the project 'Task Force North'. Much of the work was experimental, trying to use local materials to make a dry path through or over the peat bogs that form ninety per cent of the moorland plateau. Terram, a kind of unwoven matting, was used to form some kind of base, disastrously as it turned out. It all had to be removed over the course of time. The National Trust pioneered the solution but it proved expensive. They helicoptered gritstone slabs from the back of a low-loader on the Strines Road up on to Derwent Edge. Some of the slabs were so big that they had to be lifted singly, though most of the seven-minute trips delivered three slabs. These have now become strong, effective pathways that are a pleasure to walk on and may last a thousand years.

I had some luck getting Task Force North off the ground. My opposite number at the Manpower Services Commission, the government agency responsible for employing new YOPs, was a climber called Henry Folkard. It was good to be working with someone who I could relate to, and it was Henry who came up with the name Task Force North. It was important that we should keep the youngsters motivated and we did this quite easily by rotating groups between the various work sites. Although the work was often similar from site to site, the location changed on a regular basis.

There was an unexpected bonus. Most of our new recruits were city kids. Working outdoors in the Derbyshire countryside was something they appreciated and we could turn to our advantage. We soon had three teams of between eight and ten youths. The week after we launched we got a visit from a government minister eager to tell the press a 'good-news' story. Many years later I found myself working with Henry again on a number of projects for the British Mountaineering Council, most importantly the purchase of Horseshoe Quarry in Stoney Middleton.

Most of the jobs were, of necessity, unskilled. Footpath work was ideal, but I also had a contact in the Nature Conservancy Council who authorised a scrub clearance project in the reserve in Monks Dale. Once we were up and running we could think about broadening our range of activity, training those who wanted to learn more specialist skills such as building and repairing drystone walls. Within three months we had a specialised unit tackling basic drystone wall projects led by a young man called George Sampson who lived in Grindleford. George was a fast learner and became a successful landscape gardener in the Peak District.

Working for the national park, first as schools officer and then as volunteers organiser, I found I could make a difference and I enjoyed the work. It wasn't the ideal introduction to the unforgiving world of commerce, where mistakes could end in bankruptcy, but I had considerable autonomy. I was used to planning, managing and implementing projects and the success I had with the volunteers had boosted my self-confidence. But five years had taken its toll. Working in local government can be soul-destroying; some people, like Henry Folkard, are committed and hardworking. Others are time-servers. I was ready to move on.

In November 1977, towards the end of the first phase of the YOP scheme, something happened that triggered my resignation. Each team of lads had an adult assigned to them, also drawn from the ranks of the unemployed, as a supervisor. The supervisors drove the vehicles needed in the course of the team's work. I discovered that one of the supervisors was using his group vehicle and fuel credit card at weekends without permission. When challenged the supervisor admitted this. I should have suspended him on the spot, but because the first six-month period was about to come to an end and we were expecting a new set of unemployed kids and supervisors, I told him to work the last week of his six months rather than have to lay off his whole team. That was my mistake. I knew next to nothing about employment law and because I didn't handle the sacking correctly I found myself involved in an industrial tribunal.

I wrote a report and was told my attendance was optional. The day of the tribunal was also the day our daughter Jody was born, a week overdue and after Jan had been in hospital for thirty-six hours with me alongside her. Unfortunately the chairman of the tribunal wasn't impressed by modern fatherhood. He took the view that I should have been attending the tribunal rather than the hospital.

'Babies are born every day. Why is this one so special?'

The tribunal found in favour of the supervisor and gave him a substantial cash award at the expense of the taxpayer for wrongful dismissal. The decision was not only difficult to comprehend, it soured my view of my job and I made up my mind to go. And by then, a whole new adventure was coming to fruition.

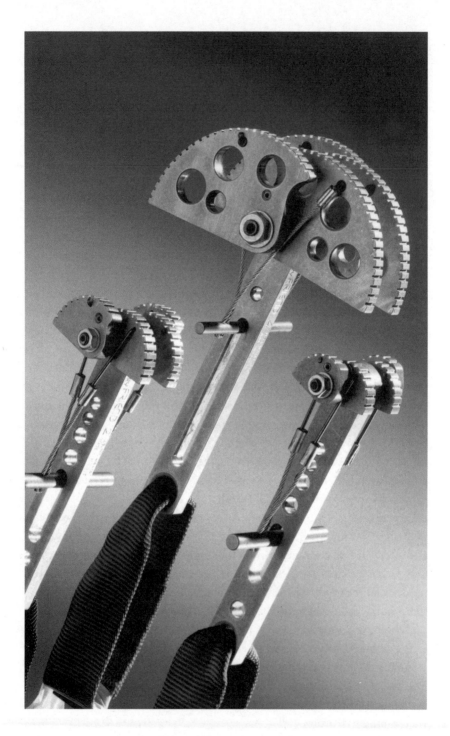

Advertising photograph made for the first generation of Friends. *Photo: Angus Stokes.*

8 MAKING FRIENDS

Ray Jardine's letter in early 1977 came out of the blue. I had to read it several times before I realised I was being offered the chance of a lifetime. I knew Ray from climbing in Yosemite. I had done some of my hardest climbs with him. We'd even done two quite hard first ascents on Washington Column together. A few months younger than me, Ray was from Colorado and had grown up in the outdoors. He was also a computer engineer who had worked in the aerospace industry. By the mid seventies, he was among the best rock climbers in the world, and in 1977 would be the first man to break the 5.13 barrier with his route *Phoenix*. As far as Ray was concerned, Friends were simply part of his ambition to climb harder and faster.

Ray had been developing a camming device since 1971. Aware of how nuts could swivel in the parallel cracks of Yosemite, he'd developed a sliding nut that would jam in place. He was also aware that the Lowe brothers Mike and Greg were working on a design, called the Cam Nut, which Ray acquired. These worked on the mathematical principle of the constant angle spiral, and were spring loaded. The same principle had already been used in climbing for clamps that slid up a rope and then locked on a spring-loaded cam, the work of Swiss guide Adolf Jüsy and engineer Walter Marti – the 'Ju-Mar'. Jumars went on sale in 1958. Greg Lowe, who was an imaginative gear innovator, had produced an earlier camming device in 1967 actually called a Crack Jumar.

Lowe's Cam Nuts, which looked a little like half a Friend, went on sale in 1973, advertised through the pages of *Climbing* magazine. Yet when Ray used them for the first time they fell out and he gave up using them. They were fiddly to place and clearly unreliable. Even so, the idea had piqued his interest. Drawing on his aerospace experience he spent months in the Colorado workshop of friend and gear inventor Bill Forrest, developing prototype camming devices. Finally he had the idea of placing two pairs of cams either side of a stem that were not only spring loaded but cammed independently of each other – like the suspension on the wheels of a car that shared an axle. These would become Friends.

I had done a lot of climbing with Ray. We first met when I was working for Colorado Outward Bound and between courses he took me to classic climbing areas like Eldorado Canyon, Estes Park and Boulder Canyon. Yet I didn't feel I really knew the man. Although we had great fun climbing together, we weren't close. His Hyperlon plastic rucksack had biblical texts written in waterproof ink and when asked to find something in his glove compartment I was surprised to find a Colt .45. I was more at home with Ray on a crag than in a social environment.

My first experience of Friends was much later, in 1975. Ray was very secretive, carrying a blue nylon bag around which clinked and rattled. The first time I used them was climbing with Ray on Washington Column. I had to swear an oath of secrecy before the blue bag was opened. This secrecy led to their name. Kris Walker, one of the trusted few, was about to ask Ray if he had brought along his bag of prototypes, and then had to do a swerve to avoid spilling the beans to some uninitiated climbers. He referred to them as his 'friends'. Up until then, Ray had referred to them as 'grabbers' – not so catchy. It speaks highly of Ray's companions that his device remained such a well-kept secret for five years, although there was one attempt to steal the design. Ray climbed *Hot Line*, listed in the *Guinness Book of Records* as the hardest route in the world, but his second left a Friend behind in one of the upper pitches. When Ray discovered he was one Friend short, he suspected skulduggery. Next morning he got up early, rappelled the route and retrieved the Friend.

His prototypes were an odd selection: some beautifully made with polished aluminium and carefully filed edges. Others he just slung together to test out a new idea but retained in the armoury because they worked. I picked up a number three and automatically used its trigger to open and close the cams, then walked over to a nearby crack and placed it. Ray was stunned.

'Who told you about Friends?'

'Nobody.'

'So how did you know what to do?'

The truth was that I didn't. I'd simply done what felt natural. It was a clue that Friends were well designed.

That day climbing on the Washington Column we made the first ascent of a route called *Power Failure* and I learned a great deal about Friends. One of the belays was from two number 4s placed in a vertical crack. As I hung there in slings I thought I saw the Friends move. I moved position slightly and realised I'd been right. They really did move. My God! I kept absolutely still and started sweating but then I got cramp and had to shift position. The Friends moved again. Growing used to this, I became fascinated with how they seemed to follow me about, always turning to absorb a load. A couple of days later we climbed another new route we'd spotted from *Power Failure*, a mind-blowing crack a hundred feet high that would have been unprotectable without Friends. It wasn't hard to see their potential.

As Jim Bridwell put it, responding in *Climbing* magazine to early criticism that Friends were unethical:

> When I did the first ascent of many routes in Yosemite, pitons were
> the only means of protection. A placement involved hanging in while
> one selected the correct piton from the heavy rack, sticking it into
> the crack being careful not to drop it while you extracted the hammer
> from the holster, pounding it well into place … Then came nuts, crude
> at first but improving in design. At first it seemed like cheating because
> they were too easy to use, but soon they won acceptance and created
> an explosion of a sustained free climbing activity … Friends are
> possibly the biggest technical breakthrough since the nylon rope.

I encouraged Ray to develop the Friends project, mainly because I wanted a set for myself to use in Britain. I even gave him fifty dollars to send a set to England when they eventually went into production. Now he was writing to ask if I would consider making them in Britain. I was being given the opportunity to manufacture a product that would, if my judgement were correct, influence the course of climbing worldwide.

Ray's offer still causes me to do a double take. Not only was the letter a surprise, it seemed illogical. I was not an engineer, or a designer, or an accountant. They certainly didn't teach me much about business at school. What on earth was Ray thinking about? Success is a mixture of vision, confidence, single-mindedness, trust, communication and – most important of all – luck. Add to this an in-depth knowledge of the product, a genuine belief in it and an understanding of the market. I met a few of those criteria, but I was untested.

When climbers ask why Ray chose me, I tell them how I was the first person who saw Friends to understand them fully and see their potential. Ray never told me that in so many words, although later on that's how he described it. I remember saying it might be possible to manufacture Friends in England, but that wasn't a suggestion, more of a passing comment. When it comes down to it, I think Ray was getting desperate. The Lowe brothers had ditched the idea and for various reasons he didn't want to deal with Yvon Chouinard.

In his letter Ray was specific that the manufacturing rights would be personal to me. If I agreed to make Friends, Ray promised me exclusive rights worldwide. In return, I would pay him a royalty. We never got down to even discussing this principle let alone the detail. Ray should have taken out the patents to protect his interest. In the end I took out the patents in his name but at my expense. Later I realised that this was all highly unusual.

When dealing with Ray, I was very much the junior partner. Friends were his baby and though he consulted me on design it was usually about cosmetic details such as size and position of the lightening holes on the cams, for which I did a lot of testing. He wasn't interested in my business, only in his innovation. When I came up with the curved-wedge design for what would become Rocks, Ray was quiet and non-committal. At this point I didn't know what we would call them, but when they went into production, he told me he did not like the name and didn't want to distribute them in America. He was just as adamant that we shouldn't manufacture Friends with a flexible stem, even though we had done a lot of testing and were very confident in the product's viability. In the end we started manufacturing them without Ray's approval. We did however continue to pay him his royalty on both his design and the flexible Wild Country design. We also had no choice but to make a different arrangement for distribution in North America.

I soon learned that business is mostly common sense but there are techniques and rules of thumb that can be immensely helpful. I was living in Great Hucklow at the time, and used to help a man called Angus Stokes run the village youth group. He was the only businessman I knew. An ex-teacher who had graduated in biochemistry, he was a little older than me and had found a niche market for a product that killed the green gunge in fish tanks and garden ponds without killing the fish. His wife, Margaret, was a friend of Jan's, and our kids got on well together.

Angus was doing well, and he drove an Aston Martin. On the mile of straight road near the village he would reach 130 miles an hour and still have time to brake before the corner. Angus would prove an invaluable sounding board. When I needed advice he was usually able to give it, and if I just needed to talk, he was a good listener too. Angus and I had a mutual friend called Jack Badger living in Bradwell, the next village. Jack taught at a technical college in Sheffield and had access to a tensile-testing machine that was underemployed. This was also very useful for me and Jack got a kick out of seeing my aluminium stems shatter or one-inch nylon slings behaving like overgrown elastic bands.

Jack introduced me to a metallurgist friend called John Ridgeway who was a senior manager in the Sheffield tool industry. When two different metals are in close proximity, there is an electrolytic reaction similar to that in a battery. I went to see him to get some advice about the problems of dissimilar metals and electrolytic corrosion. John was fascinated by the Friend samples I had taken along. He quizzed me at length about various aspects of my business plan and asked me if I had worked out the pricing structure. I had to admit that I hadn't, but that things were tight. He gave me a lecture on pricing manufactured products, which I never forgot. From the wholesale cost of a product, materials and labour should take a third. Overheads – rent, electricity, advertising and promotion – should take another. This left a final third as gross profit. From the gross profit I had to take Ray's royalty, the cost of bank borrowing, corporate tax and my salary. A healthy business, John told me, should make a net profit of ten per cent of turnover.

As I was leaving, John asked me what percentage Ray would get. I told him I hadn't agreed a figure with Ray, but we were looking at about ten per cent. John's eyebrows shot up.

'Ten per cent is too much. Six per cent is the usual maximum.'

In fact, Ray and I had already discussed it and Ray had told me: 'Fifty per cent each, half for you, half for me.' This seemed a little optimistic on Ray's part and I found myself giving him a brief tutorial on the difference between gross profit and net profit. As it turned out, Ray made a lot of money from Friends, enough to fund his continuing adventures.

I had an informal chat with Mr Rigby, my bank manager, who told me to make a business plan and suggested a number of bullet points. What I came up with was a map. I used a large sheet of drawing paper to write down in detail everything that had to be done before Friends could be put to the market and the order I should do them in. This, I later discovered, is called a 'critical path analysis'. Some of the items could be produced in series, some in parallel. My map impressed the hell out of Mr Rigby. He wanted to know where I had learned how to do this sort of thing. It seemed like common sense to me. As someone who finds maps useful and easy to understand, the graphics helped me not only in getting the bank to give me a loan but also in serving as my constant planning aid. Years later, I gave the original document to the Mountain Heritage Trust along with one of Ray's original prototypes.

The new company was started with £5,000 of capital in the form of a bank overdraft facility. This was an era when bank managers still had a degree of autonomy and were expected to use their discretion. Mr Rigby, at the Bakewell branch of Midland Bank, had handled my personal account for six years. He explained why it was necessary for me to give the bank a financial guarantee, and how I could do this by taking a second mortgage on my house in favour of the bank. That way, if the company went belly up, the bank wouldn't lose out. Then, of course, there was an arrangement fee, and, unavoidably, an insurance fee in case a bus ran me over. It was at about this stage I realised I might have chosen the wrong occupation.

Looking back, I don't think I had any idea how lucky I was in the people I met and the help and advice I received. My guardian angel was working overtime the day I went down to Birmingham to meet with Graham Turner of Dependable Springs. His Birmingham accent seemed much stronger than it had on the phone as we spent a few minutes in small talk. The arrival of coffee seemed the cue for business. The easiest way to explain what I needed was to show Graham a Friend. I showed him how the trigger worked and passed it over. While he played, I explained some fundamentals about climbing in general and Friends in particular: the need to hold a falling climber, the requirement to have strong springs. After a few minutes Graham placed the Friend on his desk and said there was no problem in providing me with what I wanted. He would make a selection of samples for me to experiment with. Picking up the phone, he asked for Joe to come to his office. When Joe arrived, Graham waxed quite lyrical as he explained to Joe how Friends worked. I found another Friend for Joe to play with as we sat round drinking coffee.

I asked Graham how much the springs would cost. He smiled. 'Just a few pence.' Then he continued. 'But the price is not important. The difficulty will be paying for them.' I asked what he meant. 'Most of the companies you will be dealing with will give you thirty days credit but they will all want, and probably expect, to be paid promptly when the thirty days are up. Paying one invoice won't be a problem, but paying all the invoices will be a problem, especially if they all have to be paid at the same time. Have you done a cash-flow forecast?'

I had to admit that I had not. In fact, I only had a vague understanding of what a cash-flow forecast was. Graham explained how business was a balancing act between money that you owed and money that was owed to you. Because time was involved, how much money you had was fluid. Because business transactions usually had a time element, you could work out how much money you would have to pay out at some future date, and how much money you would have available to pay the bill.

At this point Graham's wife Brenda arrived. She picked up the Friend, just like Joe had, and started to play with it while Graham explained how it worked. His spiel was getting quite good. Brenda asked if we were having lunch. We could go to a local pub, or send out for sandwiches. We settled on sandwiches. When the sandwiches arrived we chatted about families and they asked me about climbing. It turned out that they were both very keen swimmers and ran the local swimming club. It was nice to hear them talking about something they felt passionate about. I was discovering that business people were just people, and these people were very genuine.

After lunch Graham produced a piece of graph paper and proceeded to write down a list of Friend components in a column, springs at the top, then stem, axle, cams, trigger bar, wire rope, swages and scroll pins. He paused.

'What do you call these things?'

'L wires.'

He wrote that down too.

'We could make those for you. I'll give you a price. What about packaging?'

Then he asked how much different components would cost, how many Friends I could make each month and how many I could sell. In the next column Graham started writing figures using a pencil. At the top of the next column he wrote January, in the next, February, and so on. For the rest of the afternoon I got what amounted to an accelerated tutorial in business studies. At one point the sample springs were brought into the office, each with a price attached. The most expensive was 2.7 pence, the smallest 1.9 pence. At the end Graham wrote in the 'springs' row, 250 x 2 x 2.7 x 6. Then he wrote in the May column £82.50.

'Why in the May column? I asked.

'I'm going to give you four months' credit. That means you will be able to make and sell your first two months' production and get your money into the bank before you have to pay me. If you can get extended credit from any other suppliers, do so.'

At this point, my problem was not so much the cost of each component, but the quantity. Most of the components could only be manufactured in relatively big batches of thousands rather than hundreds. Fortunately, batch size was not a problem for Dependable Springs.

I gave up my day job at the end of October 1977, following my frustration with the industrial tribunal, and for the next twenty years Jan and I lived with a financial sword of Damocles hanging over our heads. As time passed, and the business grew, so did the size of the overdraft, and of course, the guarantee. To give him his due, Mr Rigby took a keen interest in my venture. On one occasion, when the company had been trading for about two and a half years, I was invited to lunch at the north-east head office of the bank. The other guests were all wearing suits and I remember feeling somewhat underdressed in slacks and a sports jacket, but that I was also at least fifteen years younger than any of the others. Towards the end of the meal the bank employee who had been waiting on us came into the room with a silver platter on which there was a sealed envelope. Our host opened the envelope and read the note inside.

'The arrival of an envelope like this,' he announced, 'usually heralds a change in the bank lending rate. However, I am delighted to tell you that Ian Botham was 149 not out at Headingley and that England has won the test match.' The odds that morning had been 500/1 against. I still see Mr Rigby from time to time when I go to Bakewell; he was one of the last old-style bank managers.

There was another decision I had to grapple with: patents. I had been led to understand that patenting is very expensive. Normally the inventor takes out the patents but Ray thought I would be able to handle it even though I had no knowledge of patent law whatsoever. The Yellow Pages offered up a company in Sheffield that did patent work and I found myself in a

Mr Haughton's office surrounded by dusty files and overflowing ashtrays, anticipating a large invoice. Here I learned about 'prior art', 'obviousness' and 'novelty'. I also discovered taking out a patent need not be expensive. Mr Haughton told me there was something called a provisional patent, which cost about £200. It gave you a year in which to decide if you wanted to go for a full patent. I could afford to take out patents in Britain, the USA, Germany and France. I was not certain if the last two were necessary but in retrospect it was a good decision. It would have been comforting to have wider patent protection but I didn't have the leeway.

The perceived mechanism of the Friend itself was not patentable. A device had been patented in 1901 for use in mills to hold a portable weighing scale, which used cams in the same way as Friends. The cams were used to fit the sixteen-inch gap between joists in the ceiling and only required about an inch of expansion. The protection our provisional patent afforded us was all to do with the trigger. The way the four cams could be controlled with one hand passed the novelty test and could be patented. Mr Haughton gave me some homework. I had to try and define all the ways a Friend could be triggered and to write down any other devices that used expansion to form an anchor. Various attempts had been made to design expanding protection for cracks. Slide-nuts had been used in parallel-sided cracks, but there was a problem with friction. Even with a modest wedge angle of 12 degrees, one of the wedges had to move with respect to the other in order to get any expansion. This in turn required movement with respect to the rock. Ray's prototype camming device had a constant angle of 15 degrees. After testing on other rock types, in particular limestone, we reduced the angle by 1.25 degrees to 13.75 degrees. This very specific angle would prove crucial and has defined the optimum shape of cams for the last thirty-six years. Ray had met with the Lowe brothers and used their devices, but the Lowes had made the camming angle too big, or 'greedy'. That made their device unreliable. When Ray suggested they reduce the angle they correctly pointed out that this would reduce the expansion ratio, thus decreasing the range of crack size the unit could fit. They said they had tried cams and they didn't work and that was the end of it. I still find it astonishing that Ray failed to get Friends manufactured in America. I would have assumed that American business culture would have made manufacture in the States easier, but here I was, a beneficiary of Ray's obsessive climbing agenda. He simply did not want to commit himself to a life dominated by business.

At long last, Wild Country was ready to begin production. With funding secured, I wrote to Ray inviting him come over to Britain to help me get started and, as bait, to do some climbing. I needed his input as an engineer. The summer of 1977 was not easy. I still had a full-time job, a six-month-old daughter and a very limited budget to launch a complex new business. I used up my holiday allowance by taking a couple of days off every week. Ray, his partner Suzie and I spent a lot of time trying to find companies who could provide components. We had to meet close tolerances on the mechanical side and the aerospace alloys were harder to find and more expensive than they were in America. Even so, I was learning a great deal about accounts and metallurgy while picking Ray's brain for any engineering crumbs I could.

When he arrived in England, Ray was climbing superbly. He'd recently made first ascents of landmark 5.12s in Yosemite like the roof on *Rostrum Roof*, *Owl Roof* and *Phoenix*, the first 5.13. On *Owl Roof* Ray couldn't figure out how to climb its off-width overhang. His belayer John Lackey was watching carefully and figured out a possible but radical solution. John climbed out to the lip and managed to get a firm hand-stack jam. Then to Ray's surprise, he cut loose and inverted, pulling his legs round and up above the rest of his body. Jamming his feet he was able to move his hands up again and struggle to an upright position to finish the pitch.

Ray was happy to do classic British rock climbs and I lined up various friends to climb with him on days I was at work. This was when Ray made the first ascent of *Ray's Roof* at Baldstones, a route Ray graded 5.11c and which still retains a reputation for power and technicality. The afternoon we discovered *Ray's Roof*, we had just climbed *Ramshaw Crack* with its cruel hand jams, debilitating arm-bars, relaxing arm-locks and crafty foot-nests. I spent the next several hours holding Ray's rope. It eventually took Ray four visits before he worked out the upside-down moves on the over-hanging, bulging, rounded off-width. As Ray said at the time, it was like trying to layback up a basketball. Kurt Albert is credited with the intro-duction of redpointing, but Ray was using the same tactics as early as 1975.

The first route in Britain to be protected by Friends was a classic layback crack first climbed by Hugh Banner – *Insanity* on Curbar Edge. I had tried it a couple of times but had not had the bottle because of the difficulty in protecting it. The first Welsh route on which Friends were used was *Cenotaph Corner*. We had driven over to stay at Ynys Ettws, the Climbers' Club hut in the Llanberis Pass. It was a bright summer evening and even at nine o'clock there was still plenty of light. There was just enough time to climb Joe Brown's classic route. We hiked up to Dinas Cromlech and Ray climbed the route in seven minutes flat. In the Lakes, the first Friends were placed on *Fallen Angel*, the classic E4 on Pavey Ark in Langdale.

One particular memory stands out. Ray and Suzie were off to climb *Kipling Groove* at Gimmer Crag above Langdale. Colin Foord and I were planning to climb *Gimmer String*. Ray had brought some Californian sunshine with him; the sky was blue and there was not a breath of wind. There was however another party on *KG* and from their accents we knew they were from Birmingham. Ray caught up with them on the stance at the start of the last pitch. Colin and I could hear every word. The conversation went something like this.

'You must be from America.' A monosyllabic grunt confirmed that this was indeed the case. 'I have a friend climbing in Yosemite at the moment. Do you know Yosemite?' Another affirmative grunt. 'He sent me a postcard of Ray Jardine climbing this massive roof called *Separate Reality*. Do you know it?'

There was a pause before Ray spoke: 'I'm in it.'

The silence that followed was profound.

I told Ray he should send the photo, taken by John Lackey, to Ken Wilson, who was still editing *Mountain* magazine. Ray said something about the photos being the wrong format but didn't let on he'd already done so. Soon after *Mountain* dropped through the letterbox with the image of *Separate Reality* on the cover. Ken had simply run the cover as a landscape to produce one of the best climbing magazine covers ever published.

On a visit to Scafell with Martin Wragg, a member of the Mynydd Climbing Club and Wild Country's lawyer, Ray climbed *Phoenix* and *Ichabod*. Lyn Noble took him to Gogarth where he did several routes, and I had a great day with him on Cloggy doing *Scorpio*, *Vember* and *November*. But if the climbing was going well, our work together was frustrating.

We were trying to introduce an unknown, complex piece of safety equipment to the small market of a minority sport. A simple aluminium wedge would sell in the shops for about £1.20. We had to drill four or more holes through five aluminium components, mill a slot in one of them, turn a chromium-nickel-molybdenum steel axle with two threaded ends and two nuts then add a trigger unit with two bits of wire rope, four drilled holes, four copper swages, four L wires, four scroll pins and two cam springs. And after all that we had to get it on the market for £7.

We were miles away. There simply wasn't enough of a margin to do what had to be done. We would drive to a possible supplier, tell them what we wanted and discover it was too expensive, or the minimum quantity was huge, or the quantity one had to purchase before the price was reasonable was far greater than we could manage. It was a case of two steps forward and one back.

We had planned to use Nicopress-coated copper swages from America to bond the wire rope and the L wire together. These little swages were easy to use but they cost 3p each and we needed four per Friend. What, I wondered if we were to make our own swages? I sent off for some samples of copper tubing and purchased a fine-bladed high-speed hand-operated saw. This worked like a treat. Using the saw I could make about one per second. Having cut off enough for a few days production I would flatten the round section into an ellipse. After a bit of testing I got a success rate of 100 per cent and the finished swages looked attractive. Most people wouldn't be able to tell the difference between the Nicopress swages and mine. And the price? Copper tubing: 2p. Cutting: 1p. Shaping: 1p. Total: 4p x 4 = 16p. Cash saved: 12p per Friend.

I couldn't use a DIY approach on everything but remembering Graham Turner's suggestion I went on a charm offensive. I would try to get an appointment with the highest-ranked executive I could in the company I had targeted. I would put one of the prototype Friends on their desk, usually the number 3 because it was easy to see the cams working and the unit felt good when triggered. I would start to trigger the cams on the number 2 Friend I would be holding. Soon they would pick up the Friend on their desk and start playing with it like an executive toy. Next they would start asking questions about how Friends worked before moving on to ask about my sales forecasts. At this point I would mention the difficulty over cash flow. Human nature exists even in business. Once they had the Friend in their hands, they wanted to be involved and would ask how they could help. In the end I managed to get four of the targeted companies to give me three months' credit. This was unprecedented, but even companies that had only given me two months indicated that because Wild Country was so small their finance departments would probably be relaxed about late payment. Just don't mess them about. Tell them you will be late paying them. Tell them when you intend to pay them and stick to it. In this way I was able to use the income from the sale of Friends to fund materials invoices three or four months after

I received the materials. The face-to-face approach worked well with the smaller supplier companies and because Wild Country was a very small company, it was no skin off the noses of bigger companies to give us more latitude than they would allow their big customers. Not only did the charm offensive help me tremendously, by making it possible for Wild Country to start trading, it was the start of some special relationships. Wild Country kept those suppliers for many years and in most instances the special payment terms too.

The major stumbling block was a supplier of aluminium. World War Two saw a rapid development of aluminium alloys for aircraft production. Metallurgists found that adding zinc, among other alloys, to aluminium produced a big increase in its tensile strength. Pure aluminium has a tensile strength of two tons per square inch. Compare this with the alloy 7075 T6, developed by the Japanese and used by their air force. This has a tensile strength of over forty tons per square inch – twenty times as strong. The 6000 series of alloys, using silicon and magnesium, aren't quite as strong but have different advantages; they're easier to weld, cheaper and less prone to corrosion. We used 7075 for the stem and a 6000-series alloy for the cams.

We had great difficulty with the aluminium alloys, especially finding a supplier of 7075, but there was one major breakthrough. Ray had rejected casting as a method for producing the cams because the process would leave them with half the strength of 6000 series. He assumed we would have to cut the cams out of quarter-inch sheet aluminium. Then, during a trip to the British Aluminium Company in the West Cumbrian town of Workington, an engineer asked me if I had considered using extrusions. I replied I hadn't. What did it entail? He took me 300 yards through the factory and showed me a huge machine that was spitting out sixteen-metre lengths of window frame every thirty seconds. Like toothpaste from a tube, extrusion involves pushing a plastic material through a hole. The shape of the hole that you push the material through dictates the shape of the extrusion. In the case of toothpaste the hole is circular. Aluminium is extruded at 400 °C at a pressure of 50,000 pounds per square inch. By cutting the shape of the Friends' teeth into the cam die, all the cross-sectional detail was in place when the semi-plastic aluminium emerged. I could see immediately that this was the solution. Not only would this make it easy to manufacture the cam shape within tolerance, it also had the advantage that the cams could be extruded with teeth rather than having to machine them later. The problem remained of finding an aluminium extruder who would do small orders.

When Ray and Suzie went back to California at the end of August, I could tell Ray was thinking he had wasted his time and had little faith I would be able to produce the goods. There were a number of irons still in the fire but no reason to suppose that these enquiries would yield anything new or different. Then I found a supplier who would extrude a quarter-ton of 7075 stem alloy and not long after another extruder who would make small quantities of the 6064 cam alloy. More importantly, the supplier agreed to amortise the cost of the dies, meaning they would allow me to pay for the extrusion dies over a period of time.

Finally I found Garry.

Garry was a long-haired hippy with a cowshed in Leicestershire. What was unusual about Garry's cowshed was its three-phase electricity, a bank of drills and milling machines, various circular and band saws and, in pride of place, a 1200cc straight-four-cylinder Honda motorbike. Garry could do the job. In fact, Gary could do anything. Not only could he make Friends, he liked doing it and would do so for a price that was a third of the next best quote in quantities I could live with. There was a hiatus while the lead times unwound but in less than eight weeks I had sent a set of pre-production Friends to Ray. Shortly afterwards Ray called me, amazed at how I had produced a rabbit out of the hat. More importantly he gave me the go-ahead to start production. Garry would help with production of early batches until we were up and running in Derbyshire.

Testing the finished product proved straightforward. I had access to the tensile testing machine in Sheffield, courtesy of Jack Badger, but I needed dynamic testing too. I found a quiet place in woods near Hathersage where I could lob a big rock wrapped in nylon webbing into space to simulate a fall. The test site was a flat clifftop split by a long crack. I could reach down from the top and place a number three Friend. Clive Jones, a climber and physics graduate with big shoulders, stood on one side of the crack and I on the other. We then tossed the rock, which weighed almost 200 pounds, over the edge. The stone smacked into the ground. At first I thought the Friend had come out or broken, but it was still in place. I had simply underestimated how much the rope would stretch. The next time we got a result. We saw the rope tighten and the Friend pivot and align itself. As the full load hit, we felt the earth move as the crack widened and closed but the Friend was still in place. With a little more testing we soon got to the stage when we were confident to fall off ourselves, which made the rock redundant.

There was one final bridge to cross. I still needed a name for the company. I had been using the working title Wild Mountain Workshop but it was too contrived. I wanted a name that reflected the adventure of mountaineering while not being out of place with the technical nature of climbing equipment. I needed a name that would be acceptable in America while also working worldwide. It wasn't until the end of October that I found it. I was reading the new climbs section of *Mountain* and came across a route on a crag in Eldorado Canyon climbed by Duncan Ferguson, who I had met while climbing with Ray. He had given it the name *Wide Country*. Being dyslexic I misread 'Wide Country' for 'Wild Country'. 'What a pity,' I thought, 'that would have been a great name.' I turned the page, and then quickly turned back again. I reread the item and realised my mistake. I *could* use the name Wild Country. Thirty-six years later I still like it and have never thought of another name I preferred. So thank you Duncan Ferguson. Dyslexia rules KO.

I made up an advertisement myself, sketching a version of the photograph John Lackey had taken of Ray and doing the text with Letraset. I chose a font called 'Cut-in Bold'; it was the closest I could find to the style the National Park Service used for signs and trail markers. It looked as though they had been branded into wood. Then I sent the artwork to *Mountain* magazine. We were ready to go.

Steve Bean, my business partner for eight years, testing fresh sea ice at Halley Bay.

9 TOMORROW'S WORLD

Hanging off my arms, fifty feet above the ground, my last piece of protection some distance below my feet, I prepared to jump. Nobody, I reflected, gets a chance like this. It was late January 1978, the weather was perfect, a clear blue sky, and with a hard frost and a thin covering of snow the looming gritstone quarry of Millstone Edge looked its best. The presenter and producer of the BBC technology show *Tomorrow's World* were busy doing last-minute checks. One of their crew fiddled with a remote-controlled camera pointing straight up directly below the crack I was climbing. Very shortly, I would be accelerating towards it. Should anything go wrong, I would destroy both it and me. The main camera was some fifty feet out from the crack's base where it could zoom in on me or pan out to frame the whole crag. I was most of the way up a route called *Dexterity*, a straight in, two-inch-wide crack devoid of handholds or footholds: a clean and simple line that would show off Friends to the best advantage. I could climb it quickly without messing about and because it was slightly overhanging when I jumped off I would fall into thin air and not bump into anything hard on the way down. What could possibly go wrong?

I had written to the BBC the previous September telling them that I had a product that ticked all their boxes and could make exciting television. I didn't really expect to hear back and for a few months I didn't. This was, after all, the biggest technology show on British television. Then, in mid December, *Tomorrow's World* producer Andrew Wiseman phoned to say they were interested. Could I get a letter from 'a suitable person' to vouch for the product? This was a problem. Only fourteen people in the world knew about Friends and thirteen of them were in America – and the producer was in a hurry. I phoned Peter Boardman, a friend who was then the national officer of the British Mountaineering Council. I had climbed some of my best routes with Pete. I arranged to meet him that evening at New Mills Torrs, near to where he lived. I could tell Pete wasn't particularly impressed, but I was used to experienced climbers failing to understand the potential of Friends. The important thing was that he agreed he would write the letter.

Andrew Wiseman and presenter William Woollard arrived the afternoon before shooting. They were both professional and relaxed; William took a shine to Jody, my one-year-old daughter. It turned out he had a son the same age. Over tea Andrew filled me in: we needed to write a brief script to include a bit of climbing history and some background to climbing protection. I suggested we go up to Millstone Edge to familiarise them with the site before it got dark and to see if there were any snags with the locations I'd chosen. Then we went home to draw up a plan.

The item would open with William halfway up *Embankment Route 2*, standing in slings, protected with a top rope held by Clive Jones, the young physics graduate who had been helping me test the pre-production Friends. Woollard would talk about the history of climbing protection starting with pitons, then nuts, and finally he would introduce the next great development: Friends. He would unclip a Friend from his harness, trigger it, place it in the crack, pull on it, then clip a sling into the webbing loop and stand in it.

I had already told Andrew Wiseman I would be willing to take a big fall in the interests of great television, although my interest was more in great advertising. At the crag next day, Andrew asked me what I had meant by 'taking a fall.' I explained I would climb up the cliff using only Friends to protect myself and jump off above my last piece of gear.

'How far will you go?'

'Thirty feet, maybe? Would you like to see the climb I was thinking of using?'

As we picked our way over the quarry floor Andrew explained they weren't supposed to let anyone with a commercial interest appear on the programme. But with a chuckle he answered his own question. 'I don't expect that we'll find anyone else to jump. Are you sure you can do it safely?' I showed him where I would place the Friends, where I would climb to before I jumped off and where I would end up, assuming everything went well. Then I showed him where I would end up if it all went wrong. He seemed impressed.

William Woollard had never been rock climbing, but his micro-lecture and demonstration on the history of climbing protection, the development of pitons, nuts and Friends, delivered twenty feet up *Embankment Route 2* was impressive. He seemed completely relaxed, chatting to the camera about the history of climbing gear as though he'd been doing it forever.

Then it was my turn. Andrew asked me if I was ready, fixed a tiny radio microphone to the inside of my collar and told me to take care of it. I had asked Lyn Noble, principal of White Hall Outdoor Centre and a very experienced climber, to hold the rope. I was in good hands. I checked my knot for the umpteenth time just to make sure I had tied it on to my harness correctly. The cameras started and someone did that thing with the clapperboard. Then I began jamming my way up the crack of *Dexterity* until I was thirty feet off the ground and placed a number 3 Friend. This was my back up. I moved up again and placed another number 3 a few feet above the first and clipped that one too. This was the unit that would hold my fall when I jumped off. I was almost ready.

I climbed up until my feet were just above the top Friend. This is where I had intended to jump, but I would only have one opportunity to get this sort of publicity. So I climbed a little higher, glanced down at Lyn, composed myself and let go. The ground rushed up to meet me, the rope tightened, the air was knocked out of my lungs and I came to a halt about eight feet above the camera. If I had climbed any higher I really would have hit the ground. I started to sell Friends in early February 1978. On 16 February *Tomorrow's World*, with the segment on Friends, was broadcast, four minutes and forty seconds of prime-time television exposure. Good timing or what?

Not all my attempts at generating publicity were so successful. The famous climber Pete Livesey wrote a column for one of the climbing magazines and asked me for a sample set of Friends so he could review them. I gave him a set asking him to let me have them back if he didn't like them. The review was printed and Pete didn't like them: too mechanical, too difficult to place, too difficult to get out. The next time I saw him he grinned his famous toothy grin at me. 'When are you going to send them back?' I asked knowing I wouldn't see the Friends again.

'Trouble is,' he replied, 'a lot more people can climb my routes now.' At least when Rocks came out he gave them a glowing testimonial.

At first I sold Friends by mail order, which meant I got the cash up front, but climbing shops weren't happy. If there was a new miraculous product available then retailers wanted some of the action too. I sometimes wonder what would have happened if I had continued as the only source. But it was a fact I couldn't supply the entire world market from my tiny workshop in Derbyshire, and that persuaded me that distribution was the way to go. That posed a problem. I had to give retailers credit, which put a strain on my dodgy cash flow, so my credit terms were 'two weeks net cash'. By April 1978, shops were ordering Friends at the rate of one or two sets per order but then a breakthrough came: a buyer at Alpine Sports in London called Dick Turnbull ordered ten. Ten sets!

It wasn't time for the champagne yet, but ten sets, thirty Friends, was a significant order. Two weeks later there was another order from Alpine Sports. I explained I couldn't let them have any more Friends until they had paid for the first lot. Martin Green, the owner of Alpine Sports, hit the roof. He told me nobody imposed two weeks trading terms on his company. I really needed the money and kept my nerve. No more Friends till our trading terms were met. We were soon sending them consignments on a weekly basis and getting paid on the nail.

In May disaster struck. John Kirk, a Sheffield climber, was using a Friend when it fell to pieces in his hand. The cams were retained at each end of the axle with a small clip spring-loaded on to a small groove. The clip had come off and the cams had followed. The climber was left holding a bunch of spare parts. I had tested this component thoroughly, whacking a cam with a peg hammer on an axle clamped in a vice. It was a severe test and I must have done this 200 times. I set about trying to repeat the problem but to no avail. I was never able to repeat the failure. The groove for the clip was less than a millimetre. I think that wear on the narrow cutting tool caused the tolerance problem and quality control – that being me – failed to notice. The truth was I didn't have the facilities for sophisticated inspection. I needed a design that was more straightforward and easier to inspect.

I redesigned the axle so that it terminated at both ends with a conventional nut and published a recall notice. I couldn't afford this and was resigned to the probability that it would force the company into receivership. The alternative was to sit and wait for news of the first fatality. As it turned out, doing the right thing enhanced the reputation of the fledgling company, but I don't recommend it as a way to get publicity. Of the relatively small number of Friends returned, only a few were faulty, but I didn't know that at the time. There may still be climbers out there who have first generation Friends with clips and who never bothered to send them back for replacement. If sales had not been growing at an exponential rate I think the recall would have been the end. Dealing with the recall in America, my biggest market, was particularly difficult and produced logistical problems for several months. I lost a good deal of sleep and learned a potent lesson.

The following year, there was a fatality involving a Friend on the Diamond on Longs Peak in Colorado. It was several months before I was able to get a copy of the accident report, written by Mike Covington, and found out that Wild Country was not at fault. The leader had completed a pitch on one of the harder climbs that involved a long traverse to the left to reach a corner, where he placed a Friend. He then climbed up the corner and belayed at the top. The second climber fell at the start of the traverse and slammed into the left wall of the dihedral. If the Friend had come out or broken as a result of the fall, the second might have swung more gently into the wall and survived. But the Friend did what it was designed to do and stayed in the crack.

Some people get a kick out of doing deals but I am not one of them. I don't think of myself as a businessman. I'm a climber who got lucky and was able to make a living out of my pastime. If I had to have a label I think 'entrepreneur' would hit the spot. When my shiny new company was up and running and my confidence in my new product began to seem justified, I had time to consider what I wanted to achieve at a personal level. What sort of lifestyle did I aspire to? I was working hard, as hard as I had ever worked, and there was very little in the way of spare time, money or holidays – and not much prospect of such things.

The idea crossed my mind that I should find a business partner, but I had no idea how I could do that. I doubted a classified in *The Times* would work: 'Small business in hazardous, undeveloped market requires worker and investor. Long hours, low remuneration.'

As it turned out, I didn't have to look far. During my stint as base commander in Antarctica, I had chosen as my deputy Steve Bean. Unlike most of those on the base, Steve had left school at fifteen and done an apprenticeship in diesel engines, his expertise in diesels being the reason he was on the base. Despite his lack of higher education, Steve was highly intelligent and after Antarctica had done very well for himself. When he came back to England, he had got a job as a salesman in a North London company that leased heavy construction machinery. It was a small business in a much larger group of companies. Within a year Steve had been promoted to sales manager, and to managing director within three years. Under his management the business he ran became the most profitable in the group. At just twenty-eight, Steve was made a director, the youngest by fifteen years. Steve was the business partner that I needed, and he would be the businessman that Wild Country needed as an under capitalised, but dynamic young company.

Steve had heard that I had given up my day job and was setting up my own business. He invited himself to spend a weekend at Great Hucklow to see what I was doing. I think Steve expected to find some half-baked plans with me on the verge of financial disaster. At that stage, May 1978, I was selling Friends by mail order and having no difficulty shipping everything I made. Steve was impressed and suggested a separate marketing company. He would buy every Friend I made and market them. This was not what I had in mind. What I wanted was a business partner to shoulder some of the work and responsibility, so that I could continue climbing and not become a slave to my own company. By the end of the weekend, Steve had agreed to give notice to his employers. He would take a fifty per cent cut in his current salary and match my capital investment of £5,000. In retrospect, this perfectly equal division of the company was a mistake. Steve began commuting from Gillingham to Derbyshire during the week, working for Wild Country by day, and house hunting in the evenings.

In September, eight months after the launch of Wild Country, we hit our first year's sales target of 3,000 Friends with a turnover of £18,000. Thus began a fairy-tale partnership that would last for seven years without an argument or harsh word. In that period our turnover doubled each year.

Wild Country had started by renting space on the first floor of an old stone-built factory called Townhead Works but known locally as the Old Boot Factory, eight miles from Sheffield in the village of Eyam. We rented 200 square feet of space. All we needed at that stage was a table, a few tools and a sewing machine. We soon needed more space. Our landlord, who had a printing business on the ground floor, asked if we would like to buy the building and lease the ground floor back to him. A few calculations on the back of an envelope suggested his asking price of £25,000 was too much. Our landlord then suggested £20,000.

Steve kicked me under the table before I could agree and said we couldn't afford more than £15,000. I bit my lip and within five minutes we had an agreement to purchase the whole factory for £17,000, including a separate two-storey outbuilding where we set up our manufacturing workshop. When we moved to Tideswell two years later we sold Townhead Works and the workshop building separately for a total of £130,000.

We rented a factory unit on Alma Road in Tideswell and instead of automatically buying second-hand equipment and adapting it, we got the best and most suitable available. Instead of sawing each cam by hand with a rotary saw, we bought a specialist saw that kept a very tight tolerance which would saw a four-metre length of cam extrusion by itself with minimal oversight. Not only did the new saw do this by itself but it did the job quicker while giving the cams a better finish. The bigger cams took longer to cut than the smaller cams but now we could load up lengths of number-4 cam and leave the machine to do the job after we'd gone home for the day.

We had some good fortune during this reassessment. The axles on which the cams rotated were made from a tough steel alloy called EN24, made to our specification by a subcontractor called Frank Harlow Engineering in Sheffield. We had used Frank Harlow right from the start and hesitated about taking on the manufacture of this component ourselves. The toolmaker in charge of the shop floor at Frank Harlow was Raymond Brocklehurst. Raymond was a big man, sixty-three years old with hands like bunches of bananas. If Raymond ever tightened anything by hand you would need a wrench to loosen it. Raymond had been around metalworking since leaving school at fifteen and could find an answer to any engineering problem.

I had just picked up a consignment of axles from Frank Harlow, when Raymond came out to help put them in my car. He seemed a little embarrassed and asked if he could talk to me – in private. He asked if I had heard that their managing director had announced his retirement. I hadn't, but I knew Raymond spoke highly of him. He told me he had met the new man and hadn't taken to him. I could see where the conversation was heading and I could see Raymond didn't know how to ask.

'If you want a job, Raymond, I'll give you one.' It was one of the best decisions I ever made. Raymond was well known in the metal-bashing world of Sheffield. He took advice on what machinery we should buy and recommended we buy some of it second-hand. He would vouch for it. We bought a bank of drills, which was old, cost peanuts and would carry on working forever. Transporting the drills to Tideswell cost more than the drills themselves.

A lot of our efforts went into making our in-house assembly jobs more efficient. Raymond had an innate skill for designing and making jigs, fixtures and fittings to do just that. Not only that, he won the respect of the shop floor where his authority was biblical. Some of our employees were very young and would go to Raymond for advice about anything and everything. Then again, so did I. Raymond was old school: a conservative working man who always wore a tie. Soon after he started at Wild Country he tackled me about the staff calling me Mark rather than Mr Vallance. I smiled, thinking he was taking the mickey, but he was serious. I shrugged my shoulders and said that my name was Mark and that's how I wanted to be addressed.

When Raymond reached the age of sixty-five I asked him what he wanted to do about retirement. A shadow flickered across his face. 'I haven't given it a thought,' he said, but his slight hesitation was a giveaway. Ten years later, when he was seventy-five, we talked about it again and he asked if he could work four days a week. When he turned eighty, he reduced his work down to three days a week. One evening I had a phone call from the shop-floor manager. Raymond had been taken into hospital, just a precaution, nothing to worry about. He died two days later before I had a chance to go and see him. I think those were the only days in his whole life that Raymond had not turned up for work.

I also hired a young man called Mike Townsend who worked in the workshop. He had come to us straight from school and had been with us for about two years when Raymond arrived. He arrived at his interview with his mother and though he was a big lad, standing six foot two, he seemed to be petrified. I got in touch with his tutor at Hope Valley College who gave Mike the worst reference I have ever seen but I hired him anyway. Mike was very shy and kept himself to himself but surprisingly he settled in well even though it was a few months before I was able to have a proper conversation with him. I was surprised to discover that his ambition was to become a self-employed lorry driver. He was saving up to buy a lorry and to get his HGV licence. Mike lived close to our factory and his mother Jean asked me one day if we had any part-time work. The short answer was 'no', but on a whim I suggested she had a week's trial. She started on Rocks assembly, moved on to Friends and later moved to sewing. I can't remember when she moved to quality control. It was always difficult to find good quality controllers but she was the best. I forgot about Mike. He worked hard, was never late, would always do overtime if offered the opportunity, and just got on with the job. One Friday he came to my office before leaving work. I asked him what I could do for him.

'I've come to give my notice,' he said.

'What's the problem?' I asked.

'No problem,' he said. 'But I got my HGV licence last week. Would you like to see the lorry?'

We walked down to the Royal Oak where his wagon was parked. It was old, but it seemed to be in good condition and was polished like a sports car.

I like to think that Wild Country was a good employer and a happy place to work. When I sold the company in 1998 there were two employees of twenty-five years' standing, two of over twenty years and three of over fifteen years.

Wild Country needed to have a sewing capacity so we could sell Friends with a sewn nylon loop. So I did some research into heavy-duty bar-tacking machines. In the case of Wild Country, heavy duty meant exactly that. People's lives depended on it. I discovered I wanted something that wasn't on the market. The Singer 269 was strong and reliable but could only handle metric 40 nylon thread. I needed one that could use metric 20, which had the necessary strength without the bulk of a thicker thread. Anything that stood proud of the webbing would be abraded. Forty-two stitches in metric 20 would give each loop the strength of 1 kN – and it would look good too. I bought a second-hand machine from a dealer in Leeds and took it to Mr Smith at a company in Stevenage called Mechatron. Mr Smith reckoned Mechatron could do anything when it came to heavy-duty sewing. He showed me a machine developed to sew canvas to plywood. The needle reminded me of my spinal tap.

Mechatron put a forty-two-stitch cam on the driveshaft timed to deliver thirty stitches per second. This worked well apart from one small problem. At such a high rate of stitching, friction melted the nylon thread. This was not so good for high-strength stitching. Mr Smith suggested we use silicone spray to solve the problem. He also recommended directing a cooling jet of compressed air directly on to the needle. We started with huge aerosols, spraying it on to the nylon webbing and the bobbins of thread. This worked well, but was messy – and expensive. A better method was to place the whole bobbin in a deep tray of silicone. After an hour the thread would be saturated. We would stand the bobbins on a grill and let them drain for twenty-four hours. This was more controllable, less messy and much cheaper. I was now able to make sewn-sling loops for Friends, and in due course made them colour coded. The product was complete.

After I launched Friends in early 1978, a string of camming devices hit the market. Some of them worked, some didn't. The best ones, and the only ones that worked, were TCUs – three-cam units. They worked in a similar way to Friends but, like a three-wheeled car, were not as stable. TCUs did have an advantage over Friends: they could be made narrower. But they couldn't be made any bigger than a number 1.5 Friend.

When one of these new devices appeared I would look at it and wonder why whoever had made it had bothered. It reminded me of the kettle I was forced to use in a holiday house I'd rented. However carefully I tried, I'd leave pools of water behind. How could a well-known company put something on the market that couldn't do something fundamental to its purpose? It was the same with these new camming devices. Sometimes it was obvious the designer had little or no understanding of the geometry and physics involved. Most of them had 'greedy' cams, where the camming angle was too big, meaning the unit would slide out of a parallel-sided crack. At least these devices were expensive, which made them even more uncompetitive.

One well-respected German company produced a device with two cams. We had tried a similar design that we called the Cosmic Cam and made a few prototypes. It worked up to a point but while one side of the device worked, the other side didn't. One day, the late, great German climber Wolfgang Güllich came into the factory saying he wanted to climb *Master's Edge* at Millstone Edge. This famous challenge has three drilled blasting holes about twenty-five feet off the ground. Wolfgang wanted a cam to place in one of these holes that didn't compromise it as a foothold. I told him I could make a unit with four cams to fit the holes that still allowed the climber to use it for his feet, but it would take a day or two.

Wolfgang, alas, was impatient. He tried the route using the German cams, fell from above the holes and landed flat on his back on the quarry floor. He arrived at my house, driven there by his friend Norbert Bätz, in considerable pain but not badly injured. He had been lucky. Norbert had driven him to hospital in Chesterfield but had not been impressed with Wolfgang's medical care and so brought him to my house for lack of anywhere better. They were both keen to get home. A friend of mine, a professor of paediatrics at Sheffield University, was coming to dinner. I asked him to assess Wolfgang and make a recommendation regarding travel. Three days later Norbert drove Wolfgang home where the diagnosis was a broken spur off two vertebrae and severe bruising. A month later Wolfgang made the first ascent of the 8b *Kamasutra 218* in the Frankenjura.

When Friends first appeared, the word 'magic' was frequently used to explain how they worked. The concept had been around for years but it required good three-dimensional thinking to understand how the cams rotate and interact with the walls of a crack. When a number of companies around the world, including several that were well respected, failed to make a competitive product, Wild Country's dominance was emphasised. Our rapid early growth in sixteen countries inside six months established Wild Country as a global brand very quickly and led to the Queen's Award for Export less than ten years after the company was launched.

We were given strict instructions about who should attend the Queen: someone from the shop floor, a representative from middle management and a senior manager. I took Pat Hammond who assembled Friends and Rocks in Tideswell, and Fred Johnson, shop-floor manager at the tent factory we'd opened at Alfreton. The Audi got quite a shock when I polished the paintwork and we had the surreal experience of trying – and failing – to find the entrance to Buckingham Palace. We went round the Victoria Memorial twice before a policeman, seeing the special identification ticket in the windscreen, beckoned us down a lane of cones. We found ourselves in a surprisingly large car park and were told to stay in the car. Four soldiers searched the boot and used long-handled mirrors to check under the car and that was it – no more security.

We were directed up a broad staircase carpeted in pile deep enough to get lost in. Anything that could be covered in gold leaf had been. From a large landing we entered a vast room, equally ornate, and for the next forty minutes the room filled up, Pat and Fred chatting away to the people near them and having a good time. When the room was uncomfortably full, a door opened and several uniformed men started to organise us into groups. We were quite high up the order, but still had a fifteen-minute shuffle before we got to the front of the queue.

Entering an even larger room, with a more relaxed ambience, one of the uniformed men announced: 'Mr Vallance, Wild Country.' I found myself shaking the Queen's hand. I have no memory of what she said but as he took my hand the Duke of Edinburgh said: 'Camping equipment isn't it?' I was not about to argue. I was simply impressed the Duke of Edinburgh had remembered any of his briefing. There were 200 other companies for him to remember. A tray of drinks floated past and I took a glass of claret, which turned out to be Château Talbot. Perfect. I wandered round, talking to people who looked as though they wanted to talk. Everyone was in the same situation; they hadn't done this before either. The whole of the Cabinet was also present and Margaret Thatcher was very busy, with a constant double ring of people round her, answering questions and arguing. I noticed Michael Heseltine, who had left the Cabinet the year before, was almost as busy as Thatcher.

Of all our export countries, I thought hardest about Japan. It was a big market and clearly Wild Country needed to be there, but how does a company with a workforce of five make an impact on a country 10,000 miles away with more climbers than Britain? It was not the sort of place you could tackle on a small budget. Then Dennis Gray, general secretary of the BMC, called me. 'How would you like to go to Japan for a couple of weeks?'

The Japanese Alpine Club had invited the BMC to send six climbers to Japan for two weeks in May. The team had been finalised several weeks before but one of the team had dropped out and they needed to find a replacement quickly. I snapped up the offer, but with the proviso that I could have a day to myself in Tokyo. Then I phoned my contact at the Department of Trade and Industry's export office. This was a contact that had doubted the veracity of our camping trip to Germany to develop our export strategy. This time I was asking if he would pay for a trip to Japan. He laughed and told me he might be able to do something the following year. I told him I needed a list of recommended sporting goods importers to Japan and some official letters of introduction. I got three, the best being a chap called Jiri Endo who looked like the good guy from *You Only Live Twice*. He had led the Japanese team that made the second ascent of the Harlin Direct on the north face of the Eiger in 1970. Endo-san worked for a Swiss company in Tokyo called Liebermann, which imported a diverse range of upmarket sporting goods: Fischer skis, Salomon ski boots, Edelrid ropes, Lafuma rucksacks – nothing but the best. They also imported Rolex watches, Cartier perfume and Chivas whisky. After my visit they were able to add Wild Country climbing gear to their list. Their first order was for a thousand Friends plus 200 of the soon to be available number 4.

We were not the strongest climbing team Britain has fielded but what we lacked in skill, we made up for in enthusiasm. We flew Cathay Pacific and had managed to get drunk and then sober up by the time we reached Hong Kong. By the time we'd changed aircraft and reached Tokyo we were drunk again. The minibus from Narita airport to our destination, on the far side of Tokyo, took four hours. By then we were ready for bed but our hosts wanted to party. We had a formal welcome dinner sitting cross-legged round a long low table with an unopened bottle of Suntory whisky at each place setting, the same stuff Bill Murray was advertising in *Lost in Translation*.

Our hosts were kind, leaving us in bed until six in the morning before rousing us. We sprung into action and were only an hour and a half late for our visit to the Japanese Alpine Club, where everyone reached for the fresh orange juice rather than the sake, beer or whisky on offer. That evening we were driven to a youth hostel near a granite crag about fifty miles from Tokyo. I woke early to a flawless blue sky above and a temperature inversion below. There was an astonishing view of Mount Fuji rising out of a sea of cloud. When I got back to the hostel the others were stirring. We were about to be sandbagged.

The previous night we had eaten late and sat up drinking with our hosts afterwards, but there was no sign of them now. We had instead a fresh group that looked alert, keen, fit and ready for action. I was introduced to Naoe Sakashita, small and strong, with a big smile and excellent English – he had translated Yvon Chouinard's book *Climbing Ice* into Japanese. It also turned out he had a very good sense of humour, which was just as well. Naoe had made the first ascent of the north ridge of K2, surviving a bivouac above 8,000 metres on the way down, and attempted Annapurna in winter.[1]

Our hosts showed us a great time and we climbed at a different crag every day. It was May, when the cherry blossom is at its best. The problem

---

1. The following February the BMC hosted a return visit. At the request of the Japanese this was held in Scotland, a hazardous plan as they might have spent a fortnight watching rain fall. Happily, the sun shines on the righteous. The delegation had cold, clear weather and the best snow conditions for years. Naoe Sakashita was one of the guests and though I was busy, I managed to squeeze in two great routes with him, *The Chancer* on Hell's Lum in the Cairngorms and *Smith's Gully* on Creag Meagaidh.

was the party each evening, thrown in our honour by that day's hosts. The most memorable climbing venue was Mount Tanigawa, a thousand-foot cliff that was shockingly loose. There were three of us on the climb: Naoe, a former army cook turned adventurer called Nigel Gifford and myself. We were three pitches up, dodging rockfall, wanting to be else-where, when Gifford said to me, 'If there was a way out of this with honour, I'd take it like a shot.'

Just at that moment there was a loud cry and a body came whizzing past our stance and then slammed into the cliff face. 'Bit of a nip in the air,' Gifford said, somewhat tastelessly. The body in question belonged to one of our hosts. I was surprised to see the body start to move, but after a sixty-foot fall the only damage done was a broken arm.

'The honourable thing to do would be to rescue him,' I said.

Naoe sorted out the rope and rigged an abseil around a big spike of rock. He was about to set off down the cliff when I thought I saw the spike of rock move. I grabbed him by the hand and pulled him back up on to our stance. Then I pulled the rope out of the way, and gently kicked the spike with my foot. Without much force, it tumbled down the face, shattering into small splinters of rock. After we got our injured host down, an ambulance whisked him off to have his arm set. We were then shown the nets they put across the river to catch dead bodies released from melting avalanche debris. After that we were shown the memorial to those killed on Tanigawa. I remember the total was getting on for 900, and that was in 1980. God knows what the score is today.

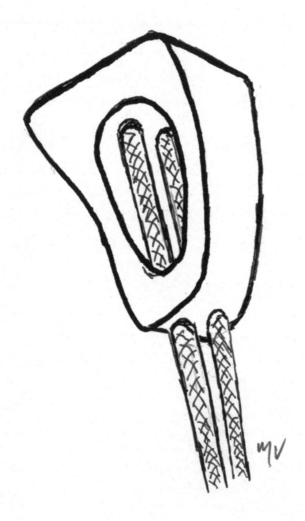

Rocks, the most copied design and biggest selling rock-climbing anchor ever made.

10 YOU DON'T NEED A HAMMER TO CRACK A NUT

The development of kernmantle ropes in the 1960s made falling off a rock face a lot safer than it had been in the days of hawser-laid ropes. It wasn't just because of their strength and elasticity. When I started climbing in the fifties, I was taught to tie on to the end of the hawser rope and use a waist or shoulder belay. The waist belay was considered to be better than the shoulder belay but no formal tests were ever carried out. The kernmantle's superior handling led to the development of devices that greatly improved the ability of a belayer to hold a fall. Salewa brought out the Sticht plate, named for its designer Fritz Sticht, a simple slotted disc that today looks crude but was once ubiquitous. (I would spend many hours playing about with different geometry for one-rope and two-rope devices, not without success. Wild Country's shaped Variable Controller was simple and effective, while the Single Rope Controller was great for climbing walls and clip-ups without resorting to the complexity of some competing devices.)

Another major development was nylon webbing. The first time I saw nylon webbing was when John Harlin and Chris Bonington walked into the Bar National in Chamonix after their first ascent of the Right-hand Pillar of Brouillard. Harlin was wearing a swami belt made of one-inch tubular webbing. Nylon webbing was originally manufactured for the US Air Force, in which Harlin had served. Webbing took over from nylon rope for slings and has become thinner, lighter and stronger. Padded canvas climbing belts had become available in the late sixties but it was the availability of webbing that made the development of the modern harness possible.

Pitons were not acceptable in Britain unless placed by top climbers. Even then they were kept to a minimum. When Joe Brown first climbed *Cenotaph Corner* in 1952 he used two pitons for aid, one below and one at the top of the niche high on the route. Because British climbers were historically reluctant to use pitons, there was consequently a more pressing need to improve alternatives. There was no point in having a rope that didn't break if the anchors that were used to secure it failed to hold. In the same way that new belaying techniques and devices became possible, the full potential of the kernmantle rope was more fully realised with the development of new rock anchors like the MOAC and then the Friend. These developments resulted in greater safety and gave rise to harder climbing.

Everyone knows how engineering nuts were used to protect cracks; any climber who wanted could make them at home. In 1961, climber John Brailsford, father of the famous cycling coach Dave and an engineering technology teacher, created one of the first purpose-designed nuts, the Acorn, turned on a lathe from extruded aluminium. There were other innovations like the Peck Cracker and the Rockcentric, developed from the basic geometry of a hexagonal engineering nut. Most important of all was the development of the wedge. The first wedge-shaped nut I saw was at a party to celebrate the first ascent of the Troll Wall in 1965. It was handmade from aluminium, the work of Alan Waterhouse from the company Troll. But the hole for the rope thread was drilled horizontally meaning there was only one way to place it. Then John Brailsford drilled two holes lengthways through the wedge offering two placement options. This opened the door for the first commercially successful nut, the MOAC, named for the import company Mountain Activities. Chouinard Equipment gets the credit for the first set of nuts, called Stoppers, that gave climbers a range of sizes from a quarter of an inch upwards. Why it never occurred to British climbers to make a range of different sizes of nut seems very strange.

After starting to manufacture Friends I was repeatedly approached by shop managers asking if Wild Country would manufacture a range of nuts. Chouinard Equipment was very erratic in its delivery of Stoppers and there was an obvious opportunity. But I didn't just want to copy the Chouinard product as shop owners urged. My ethical scruples would turn out to have a more concrete reward.

I had experimented with various modifications of the wedge shape in the warm summer of 1975, two years before founding Wild Country. At that time I was involved with whittling down the aid used on the piton-scarred cracks at Millstone Edge, routes like *Time for Tea* and *Regent Street*, often in the company of Jim Reading, a tough ex-army boxer and very good climber. These routes required nuts smaller than the ubiquitous MOAC and I made some prototypes that worked quite well.

These prototypes weren't any better than Stoppers but they were by necessity of a different design. Millstone Edge was an old quarry that had been used by climbers to hone their pegging skills. The repeated use of pitons over the years had created scars you could get your fingers into: holes, finger pockets and other features. These made it possible to climb the old pegging-cracks free while also offering placements for differently shaped nuts. Two of my prototype designs in particular worked well where others didn't. They weren't better for every placement, but I kept them on my rack and used them quite frequently when the placement called for them. One was like a vase and the other was barrel-shaped.

Over the next couple of years the remaining cracks at Millstone Edge went free, the biggest prize of all being *London Wall*. Jim Reading and I did *White Wall* with one point of aid, watched closely by Steve Bancroft and John Allen, who climbed it free half an hour later. (I placed a peg above a small overlap to protect the top part of the route and was by chance at Millstone when Ron Fawcett climbed it without the peg.) Jim climbed *High Plains Drifter* across the road at Lawrencefield Quarry towards the end of this spree, and now that all the cracks had been climbed free, there wasn't much call for my barrel- and vase-shaped nuts. I kept one of each on my rack for a while before relegating them to my box of good ideas that weren't all that good.

Looking back at the time I spent trying to create a better nut, it seems ridiculous that it took so long to put the two curves together, the vase shape with the barrel shape. I remember the moment when the logic of the design hit me. *Eureka!* It was so elegant, so simple. I had been working on the sizing of a range of nuts where each nut would be 1.175 times wider than the next size down. The smallest nut I felt confident about manufacturing was 7 millimetres wide. It would have 2.5-millimetre drill holes and 2.5-millimetre wire rope, giving it a breaking load of 700 N. My maths indicated a range of nine nuts from 7-millimetre to 25.4-millimetre – one inch. When plotted on graph paper it produced an attractive, gentle curve.

My desk was untidy with sketches and sheets of graph paper with various logarithmic curves. There was something about the 1.175 multiplier I really liked so I drew this one with more care than the others. When I finished, I went to put the kettle on for a cup of coffee and while the water was boiling I made a half-hearted effort to tidy my worktop. I gathered papers into piles: one for barrel shapes, another for vase shapes and a third for nut sizing. When I came back with my coffee, I set it down clumsily on a pencil, the mug tilted sideways and some coffee splashed out, threatening to ruin my drawings. I hurriedly pushed the papers out of the way, mixing them up so that they overlapped. Then I looked around for a tissue.

When I turned back to the desk, there it was: the convex curve of the barrel overlapping the concave curve of the vase, winking at me. I will always remember that moment. I looked at those curves and I knew I was looking at the future. I took a pencil and sketched the whole nut: my vase shape and barrel shape incorporated into one unit. I sketched it out again and could see the advantages.

Most nut placements are not perfect. The contact area may be small, or the taper angle too acute, or not acute enough. An experienced climber will be able to make a considered judgement about the safety of the placement but with conventional nuts they just had to accept placements were poor. With my new design, the climber didn't need to try and fill the crack. All they needed were three points of contact, two on one side of the crack, and one on the other. Whatever the taper of the crack the nut would be stable, like a tripod. Until that moment good nut placements were dependent on the similarity between the shape of the nut and the shape of the placement. With this new geometry, good placements could be found wherever three points of contact could be found.

I quickly found the box of old Forrest Foxheads, given to me by Bill Forrest himself the evening he met Ray back in 1972. I took them to the workshop. No one was using the high-speed belt sander, which just tore its way through aluminium, and within ten minutes I had half a dozen usable prototypes. I was impatient to try out my new design so phoned Nick Longland to see if he was free that evening. We agreed to meet at Higgar Tor, where I discovered my optimism was justified. Every time I tried a new placement the nut settled naturally into a solid placement.

Then I discovered something I hadn't anticipated. The nut was chiral – meaning 'handed'; it could be flipped around to offer the opposite shape to a crack. Not only did the new nut have the stability of a near-perfect wedge placement in many more situations than conventional nuts, but, by being chiral, placement opportunities were doubled. Nick, who had been the first of my climbing partners to use Friends, was now the first to see what was to become the biggest-selling piece of climbing protection of all time. Nick doesn't get excited without good cause, but I think he came close that evening.

I wanted to show the new nuts at the autumn trade shows. During September I refined the design. It took seven stages to get there. The curves on my first prototypes were too extreme. By reducing the convex curve the new nut was not only easier to place, but it seated better too. I also reduced the curve on the shallower concave surface. Another important change was to introduce a flat area at the top of the concave side. This was an important modification, which made the nuts much easier to clean. By the time we placed the order for the first set of extrusions in September 1980, I was confident that we had got the best design possible. After thirty-five years the geometry of the extrusions hasn't changed. It's good to get it right first time.

I applied for a patent in the USA but not Europe. My greatest concern was that Chouinard Equipment, now called Black Diamond, would copy my design, which indeed it did. I remember the first time I saw the Chouinard copies. Their production model was very similar to my first prototype, before I had really got to work on it. I felt oddly disappointed, saddened even, that the man I respected most in the climbing business had made such a poor contribution. But I didn't let it upset me for long.

In that era, the biggest trade show in the UK calendar was held in late autumn in Harrogate. Business was brisk. Shops that only ordered Friends in dribs and drabs were placing substantial orders. Sporthaus Schuster, a major retailer from Munich, placed the biggest order I had ever seen. The buyer wrote out the order on his triplicate ledger then guided me to the bar where he bought me a beer and handed me my copy: a thousand of each size, 9,000 altogether, half for delivery in January. I was glad I had a drink in my hand.

When I was proved right about the threat from Chouinard, I stood my ground. Taking out a patent is not particularly expensive but defending a patent is very expensive indeed. Patent lawyers are the most expensive of a very expensive breed. Because it was an American patent, and I was the one bringing the case to court, I had to do so in California. I had been advised to use a particular firm of lawyers, but when I got in touch with them I found Chouinard had already retained them. Their defence was 'prior art', claiming a group of climbers called the Stonemasters, including climbers I knew like Mike Graham and John Bachar in California, Rick Accomazzo in Boulder and Fred East from Las Vegas, had used a nut with a convex curved side. My case rested on the absence of a concave surface on this prior art, which meant they lacked the three-point stability Rocks had. It was like my vase-shaped nut, but without the barrel-shaped one. They had got close but failed to see the total picture.

I spent a miserable couple of weeks before Christmas flying round the western USA deposing members of the Stonemasters at colossal expense until I ran out of money and had to instruct my lawyers to settle out of court. Every time I deposed one climber, Chouinard's lawyers would find another. A little salt was rubbed into the wound when I heard that while I was sweating in California, Chouinard was on holiday in Antarctica. Halfway through this saline experience I drove up to Joshua Tree for the weekend and ran into Rusty Baillie and his daughter Rowan. The place was almost deserted. After a good day's climbing we visited one of the hot springs a few miles down the road from the park entrance and as the sun went down we soaked in our choice of hot pools. I felt much better during my last week in Los Angeles. Years later, I sat near Chouinard at a dinner somewhere, and we talked about it. He couldn't understand why I had kept fighting a losing battle. I told him that simply by taking on Chouinard, I had served notice to everyone else that I wouldn't be bullied.

So many aspects of my life came together in California. A good example was my ambition to climb the *Nose* on El Capitan, that elegant buttress of rock sculpted by glaciers a million years ago into the finest climbing challenge on earth. I first read about the *Nose* in 1968 in an early edition of *Mountain* magazine. In his article 'The Sorcerer's Apprentice', Robin Wood described a route way beyond my experience and almost beyond my imagination. It was not only difficult, it was intimidating in a way that not even the biggest Alpine routes can be. Its first ascent, sieged by Warren Harding and friends over an eighteen-month period and finally completed in 1958 after forty-seven days on the face, was an epic story. They'd fixed fragile manila ropes all the way up it that frayed and broke in the cold of winter and storms.

By the early 1970s, when I was working for the Peak District National Park, an ascent of the *Nose* was still an outlandish prospect. It still hadn't been climbed in a day. I was doing a lot of climbing with Peter Freeman, my colleague in the information office. Pete really wanted to climb the *Nose* as well, to the point of obsession. A project that big would be a huge commitment for both of us; just getting enough time off work to make the trip worthwhile was difficult enough.

Then we had some luck. Pete had been responsible for looking after a visiting American park ranger, John Kinney, who was doing a lecture tour in Britain. Kinney arranged a letter of introduction to the Yosemite park superintendent. Pete and I were invited to give two evening lectures each at the Yosemite Visitor Centre. Pete would talk about national parks in Britain and I would give my Antarctica lecture, which I titled 'A World Park' for the occasion. The Peak Park's senior management saw this invitation as 'enterprising', a coup that reflected well on the Peak Park and its management. As a consequence, Pete and I ended up spending five weeks in California and were well rewarded for our lectures with free accommodation in a tent-cabin for the duration of our stay. The cabin was made from heavy canvas stretched over a wooden framework on a concrete base about ten feet by twelve. There were two beds, a wood stove and as much wood as we wanted. There was even electric lighting and a fridge. Luxury.

It was usual when climbing the *Nose* to fix ropes up to Sickle Ledge and stash your haul bag there to get a good start the next day, or the day after – or maybe the day after that. For some, this was as far as they got. Because of weight limitations on the flight, we were operating on the bare minimum of equipment. We were able to borrow three somewhat-tatty ropes from John Dill, the ranger responsible for rescue and one of Ray Jardine's sworn brethren who kept the secret of Friends. Thanks to John, we could also drag the haul bag up to Sickle, fix rappels down to the foot of El Cap and have a good night's sleep in our cabin with an early start the next day. Hopefully we'd make it to Dolt Tower before dark.

Sickle Ledge, 600 feet above the valley floor, is quite a friendly place and a great launch pad for the serious climbing above. There's a rope swing and some hard free climbing before you get a chance to relax on the lie-down ledge of Dolt Tower. Maybe the grand designer took pity on ordinary climbers; there are three flat ledges on El Capitan – Dolt Tower, Camp 4 and Camp 6 – at helpfully regular intervals.

The first three pitches above Sickle are not hard and should have broken us in gently but the heat was already building. By the time we got to the security of Dolt Hole sweat was running into my eyes. At least at Dolt I was in the shade belaying while Pete got to grips with a bolt ladder and pendulum. This swing has an overlap that you have to hurdle, while running, to have enough momentum to reach the first of the Stoveleg cracks. Pete got it in one and was soon clipped into a hanging belay, pulling the bag across. Once in the Stovelegs the character of the route changes. The route finding is obvious but the climbing is harder and more exposed. Up to this point I had been tense and cautious, but on such wonderful cracks I began to enjoy myself. Annoyingly, sack hauling was a new skill I was yet to master. The bag was a struggle to control, weighed down with four 1-gallon polythene water bottles wrapped in duct tape, then wrapped in our two sleeping bags to protect them. We had granola for breakfast, salami and cheese for calories, crackers to put underneath the salami and cheese, and coffee for morning and evening.

Normally I cope with heat quite well, but that day El Cap was a furnace. I remember resting my forehead against the rock while hauling and watching sweat trickle down the hot granite to evaporate after only a few inches. The temperature was 96 °F in the shade, but there is no shade on the Stovelegs. Though we had practised, our lack of familiarity with big-wall techniques slowed us down. We had to get to Dolt Tower before dark. My memory of climbing the third pitch of the Stovelegs is one of determined bloody mindedness, a combination of strength, fear and not wanting to spend the night sitting in slings knowing there was a flat ledge less than a rope's length away. I've climbed harder and more strenuous pitches of climbing, but this is the one in which I take the most pride.

It starts as a finger crack and over the next 130 feet gradually widens to about six inches. There was a new angle peg at about fifteen feet and a two-inch bong ten feet above that. Then there was a gap of about twenty-five feet before I was able to place a large Hexentric nut that looked solid, and then – nothing. The crack reared up above the Hex for a full eighty feet and with every move it would get harder and more strenuous. Eighty feet of unprotected off-width climbing above the last Hex placement ended at a tiny triangular recess with a very short but strenuous pitch to the safety and comfort of Dolt Tower.

I thrust my right arm and shoulder into the crack using an arm bar to keep me in balance. To begin with I could get quite good foot jams, but as I got higher the crack became too wide for foot jams and I had to rely on heel and toe placements. Climbing as fast as I could, I could feel myself tiring fast as well. There was no way back now. I was not capable of climbing back down what I had just come up. I was totally committed. I tried not to think about the fall I would take if I failed to get to the ledge. Slowly, eighty feet became fifty, fifty feet became twenty and then five and I was on the ledge, gasping, feeling sick, with sweat pouring down my face, stinging my eyes.

Safe.

I disposed of the last little pitch quickly and soon we were on the bivouac ledge. I was exhausted, dehydrated and suffering from cramps that attacked me at random. The rock was radiating heat. I didn't need the warmth of my sleeping bag until three o'clock in the morning.

Next day I had no appetite for the route. I was scared, not terrified-scared, but a long, long way from my comfort zone. We had barely done a third of the route but already I felt spent. We found the top of the rappel route and, rather dejected, started to descend. Just abseiling off proved hard enough. There were three rappel routes from Dolt Tower, but two of them required ropes of fifty-five or sixty metres. Ours were not long enough. On the second abseil I was short of the next station. Bouncing on the rope and reaching down I could just touch the top bolt. I attached a nylon sling to my harness but it took three tries to clip it. Then I carefully untied the overhand knot in the abseil ropes and let them go, swinging down to hang from the sling. It didn't take an overactive imagination to see what would happen if the bolt was bad – and a lot of them were in those days. As quickly as possible I clipped into the other anchors, now adrift in a vertical ocean of granite 300 feet above the ground.

Having explained the problem to Pete, the haul bag appeared and then the abseil ropes with the overhand knot reinstated. Pete had clipped one end into a long sling that attached to his harness. But as he came closer, he ground to a halt. I'd forgotten Pete was lighter than me. The ropes wouldn't stretch as much. Using nylon slings, I made a daisy chain eight feet long and threw him the end. Pete clipped it securely to his harness and then we checked the whole system: Pete would undo the overhand knot, slide off the end of the thinner of the two ropes and his weight would pull the ropes through the top anchor. Hopefully there would be enough friction in the system for him to fall on to me slowly. It worked as planned and I fielded my man. The last two abseils were shorter and we were soon safely on the ground.

So El Capitan and the *Nose* remained unfinished business, and when Hugh Banner asked me if I would like to team up with him I jumped at the chance. Hugh had been among the very first climbers outside the Rock and Ice Club to repeat the routes of Joe Brown and Don Whillans. He made the third ascent of *Cenotaph Corner*. He also did the first ascent of *Insanity* at Curbar, the first route I had done when Friends arrived in Britain, and a route the Rock and Ice had failed on.

It had been raining and the Valley felt fresh. To warm up, on our first morning we went over to Glacier Point Apron, 1,200 feet high, and climbed *Coonyard Pinnacle*, a 5.9 slab – named for a distortion of Yvon Chouinard's name – that had beaten me on two previous visits. The difference was on my feet. Gone were the once-ubiquitous EB rock shoes. I now had a pair of Asolo Canyons, the best rock-climbing footwear I'd ever experienced. They were comfortable too.

As we climbed up to Sickle Ledge to fix our ropes, we watched two Swiss climbers we had met in Camp 4 climbing quickly ahead of us towards Dolt Tower. They would not be holding us up. Both were big lads and I took some comfort from knowing they would have weighted the bolts before Hugh got to them – Hugh weighed next to nothing. Next day we jugged up to Sickle, collected the haul bag and headed for Dolt Hole and the bolt ladder pitch, which Hugh dispatched quickly.

We had discussed ad nauseam what gear to take. Pete and I had only nuts. Hugh and I had two complete sets of Friends from number 1 to 4, including half sizes, and two complete sets of Rocks, 1 to 9. I ended up leading the same big off-width crack that had cost me so much on my first attempt seven years earlier. This time it was much easier. The temperature was cooler and I did most of the climb in my old Helly Hansen pile jacket. I climbed up using Friends as and when needed, then pushed a number 4 Friend ahead of me for fifty feet. Leaving it there, I used the other number 4 Friend to protect the rest of the pitch. We were soon sitting on Dolt Ledge eating dinner. I savoured a large tin of peaches in heavy syrup thinking of the dehydration and cramp I had suffered first time around. After sorting out the sleeping arrangements, Hugh passed me a small white pill that he insisted I take, swallowing one himself. He wouldn't say what it was, just that it wasn't illegal. It turned out to be Valium, enough to see me off to sleep without causing problems in the morning.

Next morning we had a couple of straightforward 5.9 pitches that took us to where Ray Jardine's variation branched out leftwards to Eagle Ledge and Eagle Corner. A short and strenuous traverse to the left took us to Eagle Ledge followed by a long, straightforward groove to join the original route at the Grey Bands. One of the great things about the *Nose* is its near-perfect rock. If you were to take the individual pitches and rebuild them elsewhere, most would be two- or three- star climbs. Here, on the Grey Bands, was the only bad rock on the whole route on a mainly horizontal traverse. I attached the haul bag to my harness and manoeuvred it as I climbed the pitch belayed by Hugh. Another easy pitch took us up to Camp 4 where we spent the second night.

I was now enjoying myself and early next morning tackled what I think is the most beautiful aid pitch in the world – the Great Roof. Ray spent fifty days or so over several months trying to free it but was thwarted by water oozing from the crack and the size of his fingers. He left it for posterity, which arrived, sooner than many expected, in 1993, in the form of Lynn Hill, a former gymnast, five-foot-one tall and with slimmer fingers than Ray. Lynn not only made the first free ascent of the *Nose*, one of the greatest ascents in climbing history, but she went on to climb it free in under twenty-four hours. The Great Roof pitch went at 5.13, but the technical crux turned out to be a few pitches higher in a section called Changing Corners, graded 5.14.

The Great Roof is long and its architecture magnificent, but on aid it is straightforward. Starting as a friendly dihedral, it rises vertically for the first seventy feet then starts to curve over to the right until you are traversing horizontally, aiming for a tiny stance a few feet beyond the end of the roof. This ledge is about eighteen inches long and four inches wide, right on the apex of the buttress and happily protected by four very substantial bolts. Here grey and yellow granite gives way to the most perfect white El Cap granite. I found myself standing on a tiny ledge on the edge of space, the most exposed place I have ever been. And I absolutely loved it.

It was here, at this significant, intense, almost religious place, that I allowed myself to think that perhaps we were going to succeed. The top was getting closer but there were still ten pitches to go. I didn't think we'd top out that day but the cracks in this section of perfect rock seemed as though they were made by craftsmen and we floated up, past Pancake Flake and Super Crack, past the Glowering Spot and then two short pitches to Camp 6. Perhaps the top was within reach but the weather was settled, we had lots of water and saw little point in risking an uncomfortable night in slings if we misjudged it. That evening we sat on the big triangular ledge with 3,000 feet of fresh air below us, watching the stream of traffic pouring into the Valley for the Columbus Day weekend. We talked about the routes we had done, the routes we wanted to do. I was on an endorphin high.

Next morning we took our time climbing the last five pitches that led to the final overhangs. The weather continued to be perfect, the rock, perfect, the views, perfect. Hugh got the final pitch up the overhanging headwall, following the line of twenty-six bolts Warren Harding had drilled through the night on the first ascent. He disappeared above the overhangs but in clipping so many of the bolts to the rope he left himself with appalling rope drag, poised on the abyss, and had to belay early. I unclipped the haul bag from the belay and watched it swing into space, out and out. My stomach tightened. Eventually the bag swung back towards me, coming to a stop forty feet in space. Then it started to rise and I knew that Hugh was hauling. Then it was my turn.

I became ultra-cautious, remembering how a climber had fallen 3,000 feet here when his jumars became detached from the rope. Every thirty feet I would tie the main rope into my harness just in case. At the top, with a lot of food left and even some water, we sat around snacking and enjoying the horizontal, brewing coffee and then falling asleep. We woke as the sun went down and then, as we walked down Yosemite Falls Trail, Hugh's brand-new Chinese headlamp failed. Pulling out our sleeping bags, we laid them out next to the path and were soon asleep. Next day I phoned Jan from a public phone in Yosemite Village to let her know I was fine. She told me the latest edition of *Mountain* had arrived. The cover photo was of me inside the crevasse in Antarctica on the last occasion I visited the emperor penguins.

———————

While we were climbing the *Nose*, every morning and early evening we would hear a very loud whistle that seemed at the time a complete mystery. When I went to collect the ropes we had used to get to Sickle, I discovered its source – an attractive blond woman with a walkie-talkie and a whistle, which she blew very hard. Mystery solved. I said hello but it turned out she was Spanish and didn't speak much English. Shortly before we finished our ascent of the *Nose* we had climbed past a team of three Spaniards who were putting up a big new route that finished a few hundred feet to the left of the*Nose*. It involved a lot of bolting. I took a couple of photographs from our last belay and forgot all about it. The Spanish woman was their ground crew.

At the time a rumour was doing the rounds about new rock boots from Spain with incredibly sticky soles. Nobody seemed to know exactly where the boots were made, or who made them. Jerry Moffatt, then arguably the best rock climber in the world, had managed to get hold of a pair of Firés, as they were known, in America and used them to make the first ascents of *Ulysses* on Stanage Edge and *Master's Wall* on Cloggy. But Firés weren't available to ordinary mortals and we had few clues to go on: no advertising, no sightings and no shoes. We had only one piece of information, and that was probably unreliable: the boots were manufactured within fifty kilometres of Alicante – maybe.

We came up with a cunning plan. My business partner's wife, Hillary, spoke fluent Spanish so we bought a cheap off-season package deal in Benidorm and then hired a taxi driver with a bit of nous. They found the Boreal factory in the afternoon of the second day, in a small village called Villena. The owner, Jesús García López, wasn't going to give Wild Country the distribution rights for Britain without making us jump through a few hoops. He wanted to visit our headquarters. At the time all we had was our little workshop in Eyam, not quite the corporate castle that might impress. So we booked Jesús into the best country hotel we could find in the Hope Valley. He arrived with a marketing consultant, a mountaineer called Miguel Ángel Gallego. Somewhere in the murky labyrinths of my brain, a little bell started to ring.

It was clear to both Steve and myself that Jesús was not impressed by our little fourteen-by-eleven-foot manufacturing base. Over dinner that evening, from under this cloud, I tried to engage Miguel in conversation, with Hillary kept busy doing the translation. As we talked, the little bell in my memory grew more insistent. He told me he had recently been in California and suddenly I knew who Miguel Ángel was, one of the Spanish climbers who we had overtaken on that last morning on El Capitan.

'And you made the first ascent of the Mediterranean Route?'

Miguel sat up straight. By chance I had the prints of our El Capitan climb in the car, including ones of the Spanish. Miguel could not believe they were genuine. He hadn't seen us go past them, a few hundred feet to his right, being busy placing a bolt with a star drill. While the photos didn't prove I was a good businessman, they did prove I was a climber, and that seemed to do the trick.

I had one more ace up my sleeve. I'd already asked Jerry Moffatt if he would represent Boreal in Britain for a percentage of sales. We would import and distribute the boots; Jerry would use his considerable profile to market them. Ordinarily, I didn't like sponsoring climbers on principle. Most sponsored climbers I knew were paid to use gear and say nice things about it. My name for them was 'hired guns'.

I preferred a very different approach to raising the company's profile: the Wild Country Foundation. Its explicit aims were the promotion of adventure in climbing and the preservation of the climbing environment. I wanted to make a forceful statement to the climbing world that a company was willing to take a stand in favour of certain values to do with sustainability and strong ethics, much as Patagonia does now in the United States. We gave tens of thousands of pounds over the years to various projects and organisations, not least the BMC's access and conservation committee but also to environmental projects in Nepal, Poland and elsewhere, and in supporting Terry Gifford's international mountain literature festival. It seemed better to support the community and its environment as a whole than simply hire good climbers.

Yet I had no problems paying Jerry. He was already committed to the product and became involved with design and development. We made several trips together to the factory in Spain. I used to enjoy these trips, but there was one big problem. The famous American soloist John Bachar, who was the distributor in the USA, was Boreal's biggest customer. He also had large carbuncles on his feet. John thought Firés were comfortable, but although they were incredible sticky, they were not a good fit for most climbers. They looked like boats, and it hardly mattered which shoe you wore on which foot. We had to do something about the fit if we were to keep our dominant position. I did a few sketches but Bachar vetoed my designs. So next time I went to Spain I took with me a pair of lasts, made from blocks of wood, that would fit Jerry and myself. These rock shoes came out very well, far better than I had hoped for. We made a stiffish shoe version, which became the Quartz. Then we made a softer one that really hit the spot. This became the Boreal Ace, one of the best-selling rock shoes of all time. Ultimately, our distributors across Europe became Boreal's distributors too.

Friends had made a huge impact on the climbing world and put Wild Country on the map. Within a year, we produced Rocks, which, though less exciting than Friends, became the market leader overnight, grabbing eighty per cent of the market, a level almost unprecedented in business. Less than a year after our meeting with Boreal, Wild Country had produced another rabbit out of its corporate hat. Firé shoes, with their new rubber, allowed everyone to move up a grade overnight. It became noticeable in pictures of hard climbs in magazines and guidebooks that all the climbers were wearing the characteristic light-grey shoes.

Finally, another great product fell into our lap. When we appointed Simond to become our distributors in France we discovered they were about to launch their Chacal ice tools. This was a radical design, the greatest single advance in ice-climbing equipment ever, and we were distributing those too. It seemed we could do no wrong.

Out running on Eyam Moor. *Photo: Mike Browell.*

11 SUPER NOVA

When I was fifteen I started making my own outdoor clothing. My mother had a 1925 Singer electric sewing machine and I wanted an anorak. I found a lightweight, gabardine raincoat that had seen better days and set to work. From a sartorial standpoint, my efforts left something to be desired. But I did manufacture a reasonably waterproof and more or less windproof garment in which I could walk and climb.

Encouraged, my next project was a duvet jacket. I got the cambric material and the goose down from a new shop on Deansgate in Manchester called The Mountaineer run by the famous rock climber Peter Crew and the founder of Mountain Equipment Peter Hutchinson. The Mountaineer was the first of a new breed of climbing shops and the first to import Pierre Allain's specialist rock climbing boots from France – the forerunner of the EB. A down jacket was an ambitious project, involving quilted wall compartments, but by the time I was finished my jacket looked pretty good. Alas, it had a fatal flaw: it was ridiculously warm. I sold it to my gliding school friend Tony Maufe, the proud owner of the oldest airworthy glider in the country. Apparently it can get damn cold in a glider and Tony appreciated my jacket's qualities. It served him well for over thirty years.

By the time I was eighteen I had made three anoraks, a wind-shirt and a tent, and gained experience sewing a variety of fabrics including Ventile and proofed nylon. Some of these items were more successful than others, but each success gave me more confidence and I learned from my mistakes, which were many and varied. My experience with my mother's old sewing machine did not make me into a skilled machinist but it did show me how fabrics are joined together. I never shied away from design problems or from tackling items that might seem difficult.

Two years after the launch of Wild Country I was at a party in Llanberis and found myself talking to Ben Wintringham. Ben's dad Tom Wintringham had been an experienced military man, an influential communist and a founding journalist on the *Daily Worker*. He had commanded the British Brigade in the Spanish Civil War, got to know Ernest Hemingway and fallen in love with a beautiful American heiress and volunteer nurse who treated his wounds. Ben had been very young when his father died but he was no less adventurous. He had a passion for fast cars and a flair for design, as well as being a talented rock climber. He was also great company.

It didn't take long for me to detect that Ben was not his usual cheerful self. I asked him what the matter was; he told me his company Wintergear was filing for receivership on the Monday morning. Despite having some great designs, Ben's tent-making business, which he ran with his wife Marion, was on the brink of collapse. Steve and I were looking for opportunities to grow our business, so I asked Ben if he thought we would be able to work together. I suggested Steve and I meet with him and Marion. If that went well we should meet their bank manager. By Wednesday we had an agreement cobbled together and within a week Wild Country was in the tent business. Ben and Marion owned fifty per cent of the refinanced business and Wild Country owned the other half.

There was nothing fundamentally wrong with Wintergear. The designs were good and the tents were strong. What it needed was more targeted management. The order book was overflowing but production was not. Not only were we failing to catch up, we were falling further behind. The first thing we did was put the prices up. This did several things. It made the company profitable and it slowed down sales of tents, not a lot, but enough to calm things down. The business was no longer in a state of panic. At first we continued manufacturing in a small unit between Llanberis and Caernarfon we shared with Laura Ashley. But whatever we did, the market for quality mountain tents seemed to be growing and we still struggled to keep pace with the order book.

What we did not anticipate was the Falklands War. Ben and Marion had developed a Gore-Tex bivvy bag especially for military use. It was used throughout, unlike many competitors who skimped with nylon on the groundsheet, and had two zips, rather than the standard bag's main zip and Velcro opening. Velcro makes a lot of noise when you open it, not so good if the enemy is close or you're on a long stake-out. At the time

37 The Diamond, Longs Peak, Colorado. The main face
   can be seen rising dramatically from Chasm View.
38 A really comfortable bivvy on Broadway.

39 Jan at the top of Washington Column after climbing seventeen pitches of *Royal Arches*.
40 Jan climbing *Nutcracker* (5.8), with Robin Barley watching below.
41 John Cunningham at the top of Lost Arrow Spire.
42 Me on the crux of *Left Unconquerable* (E1), Stanage. *Photo: Peter Freeman.*

61

62

63

61　Himalchuli West (7,540 metres). The three-kilometre rock ridge leads
　　to sunny snow slopes and the summit.
62　Paddy fields bursting into life on the lower slopes of Himalchuli.
63　Shishapangma (8,027 metres) from Base Camp, thirty kilometres away.
64　Everest (8,848 metres) on the left, Cho Oyu (8,201 metres) and other
　　peaks seen from the Pang La.
65　Graham Hoyland filming for the BBC on the north side of Everest in 2000.

57 Bill Supple guarding the entrance to our New England office and warehouse.
58 Inside Outside in Hathersage.
59 Broad Peak (8,047 metres) from near Concordia. Our route is hidden by the
    rock ridge on the left skyline.
60 On Himalchuli West (7,540 metres) having negotiated the steep rock ridge
    visible in the background.

55

56

53 *Supercrack of the Desert*, one of the finest hand cracks I have ever climbed.
54 ... so good I climbed it twice.
55 Discussing the finer points of rock-shoe design with Jerry Moffatt (*centre*) and Wolfgang Güllich (*right*).
56 Andy Elliott with a Wild Country tent at Camp 2 (6,000 metres) on Broad Peak. K2 in the background.

51

52

49 Riccardo Cassin and Jody wondering where to go climbing.
50 Jody climbing *Orange Plasma* (5.11b) in Tuolomne Meadows.
51 The Great Roof on the *Nose* of El Capitan, one of the finest pitches anywhere.
52 Working man's hands on top of the *Nose*.

47 The Wild Country workforce on the day that the Duke of Devonshire opened our new factory. *1* Mark Vallance. *2* Mike Longden. *3* Raymond. *4* Garry Walker. *5* Dave Shaw. *6* Steve Foster. *7* Fred. *8* Andy Bowman. *9* Ted Howard. *10* Pat Lewis. *11* Dick Turnbull. *12* Sally Turnbull. *13* Jerry Moffatt.

48 Mount Fuji.

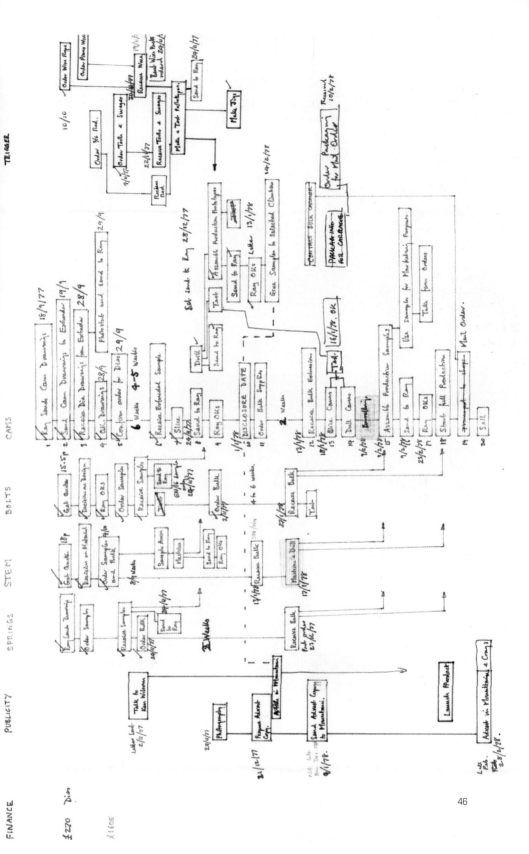

43 Ray Jardine climbing *Phoenix*, the first 5.13.
44 Ray Jardine climbing *Crimson Cringe* (5.12a), Yosemite Valley.
45 The remaining prototype 'Jardine' Friend, now in the Mountain Heritage Trust's collection.
    Photo: John Coefield.
46 The critical-path analysis for the Wild Country start-up.

64

65

66

67

68

66 The Old Man of Hoy.
67 Nick Longland on the crux moves of the Old Man.
68 Training in Lanzarote using £4,000 worth of carbon fibre
    loaned to me by Mike Browell, who took the photograph.

the Ministry of Defence had not given approval for Gore-Tex. So Winter-gear sold these bags direct to soldiers by mail order. They were hugely popular. When you are out fighting in the wilds of the South Atlantic and it's cold and wet, a waterproof, breathable bivvy bag is worth its weight in gold. Because we sold them direct, we could give soldiers a good discount and still make a decent return on the product. Everyone was happy.

The Wintringhams had started their company to make dome tents. Their first had three poles crossed at the apex. This design was easy to make, but because there is only one crossover point for the poles the tent was floppy in windy conditions. It was nicknamed the Jelly. Dick Turn-bull, then at Alpine Sports in London, suggested a design improvement. North Face made a geodesic tent called the VE24 based on a design by the American architect Buckminster Fuller. This had four poles with five crossover points, which made the tent more rigid. Dick suggested they take this design and add an extra pole to create an entrance vestibule for wet gear and cooking, something Americans didn't need in their warmer, drier summers. The Super Diamond was an instant success, so much so that North Face copied the idea for their VE25.

The credit for the next tent also goes to Dick. The Super Diamond was quite a big tent and heavier than it needed to be when used by two people, which was most of the time. It would sleep three people, but what was needed was a strong, two-person mountain tent. The result was the Quasar, the most successful mountain tent ever made because of its compact design, high strength and aerodynamic, wind-shedding shape. We made two special single-skin Gore-Tex Quasars for the Polish expe-dition leader Andrzej Zawada, leader of the first winter attempt on K2. These tents used half-inch 7075 T6 aluminium alloy poles.

We pitched one in Outside and while we were admiring it somebody asked how strong it was. I said I thought it would take the weight of an adult. There was a short argument about this so we had to try, although I had my fingers crossed. We lifted a volunteer so he could lie across the centre crossover. No problem. The tents were used on an exposed shoulder on K2 at about 25,000 feet, performed well and were then aban-doned. Two years later an American expedition discovered they were trying to pitch their tents on top of the old Polish camp. They dug down and found the Quasars were in perfect condition and provided excellent accommodation for the Americans and various other expeditions in subsequent years.

After Wild Country had been manufacturing and selling tents for two and a half years Ben and Marion announced at a board meeting they wanted to have a tent catalogue. Steve and I resisted. We didn't want to create more demand with a six-month back-order book. They remained adamant. The reality was Ben and Marion wanted their old company back. Our bank managers were brought in to come up with a fair valuation and we negotiated an amicable separation. Wild Country would continue making the existing line of tents but we would change the names of any that still had their original Wintergear names: thus the Super Diamond became the Super Nova, the Emerald became the Trisar and the Quasar remained the Quasar as it was a Wild Country design.

Later, when I wanted a big geodesic tent for a Himalayan trip, I designed the Terra Nova, a four-person tent. As a result of its success we made a smaller version which used the same pole set as the Super Nova but gave the tent a rectangular shape more suitable for three people than Buckminster Fuller's hexagonal design. The new design also had two new pole crossing-points, which added strength and rigidity.

Many climbers had tent stories, which I would inevitably get to hear. Usually they were about the storm that wrecked all the other tents on the campsite except for the Wild Country Quasar or Super Nova. We did various tests to try and create a standard for mountain tents and discovered ours seemed to be stronger at high altitudes than low altitudes. This got me wondering. We knew from wind tunnel tests that the Super Nova would start to break up and disintegrate in winds of more than eighty knots at sea level, but we had lots of information about the same tents withstanding winds of 120 knots on the South Col of Everest. It took me some time to figure out that it wasn't the wind's speed causing damage but the density of air. The higher you go, the thinner the air gets. Or to put it another way, there are fewer molecules in the atmosphere. At 18,000 feet the air pressure is half that at sea level. At 25,000 feet it's a quarter. So a hundred-knot wind will snap the poles like matchsticks just off the beach in South Georgia, whereas on Everest the pressure of the wind is only a quarter of that at sea level.

My favourite tent story was about the camper who arrived on a beach on the Greek island of Corfu, pitched his Trisar on the sand, zipped his rucksack inside the tent and, having developed a thirst, wandered down to the bar at the end of the beach. Halfway through his beer the wind got up and, looking down the beach to check on his tent, he was horrified to see it rolling like tumbleweed towards the sea. By the time he reached the water's edge the tent was twenty yards offshore, upside down and heading for Italy. His pack was keeping it stable with the tips of the poles pointing upwards. He threw himself into the water and pulled the Trisar back to shore with the guy lines in his teeth. But when he opened it to sort through his gear, there was only the smallest quantity of water in the tent and his camera and passport were dry.

Having made a firm commitment to the mountain tent market, we needed some consolidation. I thought that with our factory space in Tideswell we would have plenty of room, but I was wrong. Twenty-five minutes away, in Alfreton, there was a trading estate with a choice of factory units and, more importantly, a skilled local workforce. Coats Viyella had just laid off almost 300 machinists. We rented a factory on the industrial park and over the next five months took on thirty of them. We were beginning to anticipate the sewn goods market. The tents were not cheap but they were gaining a reputation for performance.

When we started making harnesses I found only one manufacturer who made webbing I thought suitable. I could only buy end of run or end of reel lengths; it would be some time before I could order enough to have it made to my specification. The company was Swiss owned but based in Croydon. I made an appointment to see the sales manager but when I got there he escorted me directly to the managing director's office. He seemed a little uncertain about how to begin. Over coffee, which I needed having just driven 200 miles, he told me they had been asked by another company not to do business with me. I have to admit I was more than a little surprised. There was only one company in Britain that made climbing harnesses at that time.

'If you don't sell me the webbings I need,' I told him, 'do you think I will go away and forget about making harnesses?'

The sales manager smiled and exchanged a look with his boss.

'We thought that if they were so worried as to ask us not to supply you, that you must be a big threat.'

I told them I wasn't, but that I intended to be. Sometime later I met the production manager of our competitor who said disparagingly that Wild Country only knew how to do bar tacks.

I could never understand how the Whillans harness had such a following. Everything about it seemed counterintuitive. I had bought a Forrest swami belt and leg loops in America and much preferred it. I wrote to

Bill Forrest to ask if I could manufacture his harness under licence. I never got a reply. Then I noticed that Troll, the company that made the Whillans, were advertising the Forrest harness. I decided to design my own version of the swami and leg-loop combination and called it the Black Belt. I was quite pleased with the way sales went.

When the Australian climber Kim Carrigan became sales manager at Mammut in Switzerland, we suddenly had access to webbings that were not only more attractive and colourful than our existing supply, but were technically superior too. There was a one-inch tubular webbing using all the colours of the rainbow. The slings we made with it were instant bestsellers. Later I specified a webbing based on the colours in the Wild Country logo – black, yellow, black, orange, black, red, black. This looked classy and also sold like hot cakes.

In the early years of Wild Country, establishing the business was more than a full-time job. It took over my life. I worked long hours and found my opportunities for recreation were limited. To keep in shape I started running. I started with a three-mile circuit from my house in Great Hucklow, up the long hill to Bretton where, at 1,200 feet, the Barrel Inn looks out over the plateau of the White Peak, then down the hill to Foolow and back across the fields through Grindlow to my house. Doing this reawakened something that stretched back to my childhood.

After seeing the 1953 Everest film I wanted to take our summer holiday in the mountains. My father was a keen hillwalker and knew the Lake District well so we spent the next six summer holidays based in Langdale. A flame was lit that has burned all my life. We walked every day, rain or shine. If the weather was good we walked in the hills. If it rained, we would do a low-level walk. In the course of those six years I got to know the Lake District fells pretty well.

The first hill I climbed was Lingmoor Fell, an undistinguished feature on the south side of Langdale. That first year, 1954, we climbed Helvellyn by the light of a bright full moon, and Scafell Pike, the highest mountain in England, for which I made my little Union Jack. The following year we repeated the exercise adding Scafell, the second-highest mountain. The year after, we added Great Gable to the pot. All these mountain days concluded with a ham and egg tea and ginger beer supplied by Sid Cross at the Old Dungeon Ghyll Hotel.

During our third holiday, on a dull, wet day, my father suggested a circuit of the passes of the central Lake District. We had been hoping the weather would improve but had got fed up waiting. Our route took us along the now-familiar path up Mickleden to Rossett Gill, down to Angle Tarn, over Esk Hause, past Sprinkling Tarn and on to Wasdale. As we walked over Black Sail Pass, and passed the youth hostel, the rain eased off and finally stopped. By the time we got to Buttermere we were drying out and ready for tea. Thus fortified, we followed the road over Honister and Seatoller to Stonethwaite and up Langstrath. It was getting dark as we descended the Stake Pass, reaching our campsite just before eleven o'clock. We had covered a distance of thirty miles, not bad for an eleven year old, but even more impressive for my nine-year-old brother Stephen.

At our campsite in 1960, my father, who was reading the *Manchester Guardian* after breakfast, told us that Alan Heaton had become only the second person to complete the Bob Graham Round. Then my father explained the Bob Graham Round was a sixty-six-mile route around the fells of the Lake District, with 27,000 feet of ascent to be completed within twenty-four hours. I was impressed, and tucked this snippet of information away for future reference. It would be a few years before this challenge got on to my agenda but the seed was sown.

When my colleague Peter Freeman and I were planning our trip to Yosemite, Pete thought we needed to get fitter and suggested we go running in our lunch breaks. My first serious outing was the Marsden to Edale fell race, organised by Tanky Stokes who owned a popular climbing shop in Sheffield. This twenty-four-mile course over Black Hill, Bleaklow and Kinder Scout is a Peak District classic. After that, the business took over.

By then, running was becoming a part of my life. I can't remember when I stopped disliking it, or when I found that I liked it, but I extended my regular route up past the Barrel Inn, along the Roman road and ridge, over the stile and down across Eyam Moor and back again, a distance of eight miles that included a height gain and loss of 950 feet. Within a few months I was able to do this run in under an hour. Gradually I whittled that down to fifty minutes and eventually – and significantly – on my fortieth birthday I did it in forty-four minutes and fifteen seconds, a personal best never to be repeated. Six days later I ran the Leicester marathon in three hours and fifteen minutes, another personal best.

Some of my best days running in the mountains were spent with my climbing partner Mike Browell, a landscape architect from Sheffield and visiting professor at the China University of Mining and Technology in Xuzhou – and an enthusiastic member of the Dark Peak fell running club. Mike was also my conscience. He is eight years younger than I am and every now and then he phones me up and suggests a trip. I've done a variety of walks and events with him including a number of trips to Scotland, usually to knock off more Munros in a day than is usually considered respectful. My usual response to any suggestion from Mike was to say 'No.' But Mike always had a way of making what, at face value, appeared to be a debilitating, muscle-cramping, knee-grinding epic into a light-hearted day trip that any middle-aged man ought to be able to manage without complaint.

One early morning in late June, his wife Lynda dropped us in Marsden and we set off up the familiar track that starts the classic Marsden to Edale. He wanted to trot. I didn't. Things had got seriously out of hand. We wouldn't be stopping at Edale; we were planning to keep going the whole length of the Peak District, over the middle limestone plateau with its deep dales before a long cruise down Dovedale to finish.

It had started a few weeks previously when Mike ever so casually asked if I had ever done the Derwent Watershed. My mind raced. The Watershed. The great epic of Peak District bog trotting. 'No,' I said, not thinking fast enough. He knew perfectly well I hadn't done it. He also knew I wanted to do it and most importantly knew I felt deeply guilty I had not even attempted it. This was a set-up.

The result was that on a less than perfect day in early June with thunderstorms as well as sunshine, we had a great day out, completing the forty-two miles in a comfortable eleven hours, setting out from Hope car park as the church clock struck five and arriving back as it struck four. In fact it was so comfortable that we now found ourselves committed to this traverse of the whole Peak, moving at a fast pace into ever-thickening mist past Wessenden Reservoir on the well-used Pennine Way.

The first hour or two of a long walk always seems to pass most slowly. Today the combination of poor weather and the early hour demanded an effort of will to keep going. Like all really big tasks, the trick was to concentrate on the job in hand and not think of the final objective. Thus, in the course of a mere hundred minutes, we arrived at the top of Black Hill. At this point the change of gradient – from gently up, to gently down – and the change of terrain – from boggy tussocks to smoother grassy moorland – persuaded me, along with the nagging of my companion, that a bit of trotting might not be such a bad idea. The mist started to clear, our route finding, or rather Mike's route finding, was tediously perfect, and within another half hour Black Hill was history. The clouds were thinning and Bleaklow lay ahead. So far, so good.

Bleaklow, as aficionados of the Dark Peak will know, is a big place, and not to be taken lightly, but as the first slow hours were behind us, within another fifty minutes we were at Bleaklow Head and soon after nine o'clock had found the two litres of lemonade hidden by Mike the previous day at Snake Summit. The sun started to make an appearance and life seemed good.

It is my opinion, not shared by everyone, that the National Trust has done a superb job laying a sinuous line of paving stones over Featherbed Moss to Mill Hill. These heavy millstone slabs are wonderfully varied, both in colour and texture and while they may be visible by those flying over the moors before final approach to Manchester Airport, this magnificent footpath is not visible from the higher ground of Kinder or elsewhere until you're almost on it. More importantly, it has changed what in most conditions is one of the most dreary and soul-destroying sections of moorland into an easily negotiated and pleasurable hike. The only problem is that it does form a slight dogleg.

'How about making a beeline for Kinder Downfall over the North Edge?' said Mike.

'No way,' said I.

By midday the White Peak, now under a clear blue sky, and the prospect of food drew us on. The day before I had left a big plastic bag hidden behind a drystone wall by the road near Perry Dale. It contained two 1-litre-bottles of lemonade and Coke, a large pack of cheese and onion sandwiches and a half-pound of marzipan. It also contained a fresh T-shirt, a clean pair of socks and a fresh pair of very comfortable Nike trainers. I dumped my sweaty T-shirt, peat-stained socks and muddy fell shoes to be collected later.

Mike mocked my fresh attire and insisted we set off after a seven-minute lunch break with me tying my shoelaces and stuffing sandwiches into my mouth. First, a mile of road to Peak Forest, then the gloriously easy grass valleys of Dam Dale, Hay Dale and Peter Dale to Monks Dale with its ten-minute section of difficult, bouldery stream bed – and so to Miller's Dale.

Getting to upper Dovedale was, from an aesthetic point of view, somewhat contrived. We linked tracks and country roads for seven miles keeping to the west of Taddington, Flagg and Monyash to reach the Dove near Pilsbury Castle.[1]

My taskmaster was urging me to break into a trot at this stage but I managed to resist the temptation until we reached the fine, valley-side footpath that leads into Hartington village. Here we enjoyed huge ice creams – Mike tut-tutted but agreed to have one too – and drank cans of cold Lucozade bought at the only shop we passed all day. It was four o'clock, we were feeling good and we knew that nothing could stop us. Beresford Dale, Wolfscote Dale and Dovedale offer ten miles of the finest valley scenery in Britain and on that wonderful, midweek summer evening they sped past in a haze of euphoria and exhilaration. At Thorpe Cloud we were met by Jan, who had hiked up from the car park with our dogs, but we still had business to attend to. After thirteen hours and almost fifty magnificent miles of Dark Peak moorland and White Peak dales, the national park boundary was a mile ahead at Coldwall Bridge. I got there at six o'clock, a few minutes after Mike.

'What kept you?'

When Bob Berzins asked me in the spring of 1983 if I had ever heard of the Bob Graham Round he seemed quite surprised when I said I knew quite a lot about it. Bob had been talking to Don Barr with whom I had climbed *Smith's Gully* on Creag Meagaidh the previous winter. If we were to stand any chance we needed to take advantage of the long days and short nights of June. Our plan was to do it alpine style, carrying our own food and drinks and doing all our own route finding. With no training, no research and the wrong sort of food – Mars Bars and Kendal Mint Cake – we set off from Moot Hall in Keswick at midnight on 26 June in the anti-clockwise direction.

We gradually dropped further and further behind schedule so when I said I had had enough and told the lads to go on without me, their reaction was one of relief. Neither of them had wanted to be the first to admit defeat. As the oldest, they expected me to be the first to drop out and they were more than ready for me to do so. That we managed to cover forty miles to Harrison Stickle by six o'clock was not a bad effort considering that it is usual to have pacers, route-finders and helpers to ease the burden. I think that had I taken more suitable food, we might have succeeded first time. Chocolate and mint cake was difficult to eat on the hoof.

---

1. If you find yourself wanting to do this route, I suggest turning left at Miller's Dale and following the River Wye to White Lodge on the A6. Then head south up Deep Dale to get to Monyash and so to the Dove. This is a better route and will give you a full fifty-mile day out.

That summer, Don asked me to climb the north face of the Eiger with him; I jumped at the opportunity. During his first Alpine season, at the age of seventeen, Don had climbed both the Walker Spur and Croz Spur on the Grandes Jorasses, the Cecchinel-Nominè on the Grand Pilier d'Angle and the Central Pillar of Frêney on Mont Blanc. How could I pass up a chance of climbing with someone like that? Don would go to Chamonix before me, and when he thought the weather was settled he would phone. I got a phone call, but it was the BMC with bad news. Don was dead. Two days later I got a postcard that read: 'Conditions too dangerous at present. Going to the Verdon.' In the Verdon he climbed with Pete Harrop and Paul Dawson, friends we had in common. Don had just led the top pitch of a route called *Le Petit Coin de Paradis*, and was belaying on the edge of the gorge when he was struck by a single bolt of lightning.

Death in the mountains is an all too common event, but nobody close to me had ever died before. I had felt bad when Pete Boardman died on Everest, but the sort of Himalayan climbing he was doing carried a high degree of risk. I mourned his death but it seemed at the time it was somehow inevitable. Don's death really hit me hard. I had not known him long, but I knew him well. I found some relief in the thought that another person's death could diminish me that much.

Bob and I now wanted to do the Bob Graham Round as a tribute to Don. We discovered that rather than eating chocolate and glucose we should be using food with more fibre, fat and oil, like the recipe Ann Hadlum had given me in Colorado. I also carried peaches in heavy syrup. On the hill, I carried marzipan and XL, an isotonic drink from Norway.

Late in the evening on 2 June 1984, Bob and I set off up Skiddaw in the opposite direction to the year before. The previous weekend I had been in Scotland and climbed the classic *Shibboleth* on Slime Wall in Glencoe. I was as fit as I had ever been, both climbing and fell running. It was overcast but dry when we started, with very little wind and we moved well and had no difficulty with the route finding. We got to the top of Blencathra a little ahead of schedule and made excellent time down the steep ridge to Threlkeld where we had hidden a plastic bag with lemonade, cheese sandwiches and fruit cake.

The route up to Clough Head was easy enough but it started to rain and I felt a bit low until I remembered that three in the morning is when the body is at its nadir, the time when the KGB knocked at your door. When it started to get light, the rain stopped and we got on to an easy rounded ridge on short springy turf over the Dodds, running effortlessly from summit to summit, past Raise and White Side until we reached Helvellyn. Still on the ridge, we crossed Nethermost Pike, Dollywaggon Pike and the steep zigzags down to Grisedale Tarn. Now came one of the more annoying outliers, Fairfield, returning the same way for another steep but easy descent from Seat Sandal to Dunmail Raise, where Bob's fiancée Barbara waited with breakfast. Bob had Ambrosia rice pudding; I had my granola baked in honey washed down with lots of full cream milk and a tin of peaches in heavy syrup.

After fifteen minutes we were on our way again up steeply to Steel Fell and running most of the plateau of High Raise to the Langdale Pikes. This was home ground for me. There is a long, rather boring section before you cross the Stake path but we were both feeling good, managing to run the flat sections and comfortably ahead of schedule. We crossed the top of Rossett Gill and found the little spring above the col without difficulty. After summiting Bowfell we were able to stay high over Esk Pike and Esk Hause, zigzagging between the various summits of Scafell Pike.

I was getting worried about my feet and made an unscheduled stop on Ill Crag to cover the soles of my feet with white zinc oxide tape. If I had gone much further, I think I would have caught it too late. Thanks to my efforts, it was only when I got to the final section of road that I suffered. We passed the summit of Scafell Pike at a trot and on to Mickledore. We had opted for the Broad Stand route up Scafell but when we got to the awkward slot of Fat Man's Agony we found we had no power in our arms. Neither of us could do the steep pull-up and we had to rest for a couple of minutes to get the blood to our arms rather than our legs. Soon we were on top of Scafell and heading down to Brackenclose, the Fell and Rock hut at Wasdale. This would be our last rest, a final chance to get the 10,000 calories I calculated I needed to complete the round.

Yewbarrow is a bit of a slog and the circuit of Red Pike, Pillar, Steeple, Kirk Fell and Great Gable is a good day out on its own, but heading north to Honister the running became easier. We only had three more summits, Dale Head, Hindscarth, and when we got to the third, Robinson, it was all downhill. At the road I suggested to Bob he go ahead as my feet were hurting. We still had the best part of two hours to complete the last four miles to Keswick. I alternated between running and walking and reached Moot Hall twenty-seven minutes inside the twenty-four hours.

Bob managed to get to the pub before closing time and I slept well in the back of the car. I have a list of about five days of which I am most proud. Saturday 2 June 1984 is one of them. What we didn't know is that to become a member of the Bob Graham Club we should have registered with the secretary before setting off, rather than retrospectively, as we assumed we could. Just doing it was reward enough.

Inside Outside: Jan and our pointer Harry inspecting the building work at the shop in Hathersage.

12 MOVING THE CENTRE

Wild Country's export success led us to set up our own sales office and warehouse in North Conway, an attractive town in the Mount Washington Valley in New Hampshire's White Mountains. Our landlord was the distributor of Ben & Jerry's ice cream, and every so often they would bung us a box of twenty-four or forty-eight which were judged unfit for human consumption, usually because someone had dropped the box and it had landed on a corner. We kept a deep freeze in the office to cope with such tragic events. My favourite was – still is – cookie dough.

Mount Washington to the north dominates the head of the valley, notorious for the highest wind speed ever recorded – 231 miles per hour – at which point the anemometer broke. The main street is lined with outlet stores where you can get Levi 501s for $20 and Ralph Lauren shirts and Rockport deck shoes for knockdown prices. Cars with licence plates that say 'Live Free or Die' give way without a trace of aggression to pedestrians. I used to go there two or three times a year on Wild Country business. It was great to take a day off to go climbing with our sales rep, Doug Madara. When John Bouchard, one of America's finest alpinists, was in town I would try to get myself invited to have a lobster dinner. The deal was that I got the lobsters and Sauvignon Blanc while John's wife did the cooking. I think John got the best of the deal. I would usually stay with Rick Wilcox who instead of a guest bedroom had built a guesthouse next to the one he lived in, surrounded by several acres of woods and his very own lake complete with beaver dam. Once, going back to England, Rick flew me down to Logan Airport at Boston in his Cessna. I felt like a big shot walking across the tarmac and into the first class lounge and perhaps I even looked the part because I was bumped up to business class for the flight home.

On one of these trips, Jan and I arranged to spend a few days driving up to Maine to see the natural fireworks of New England's forests in the autumn, visit Bar Harbor and go mountain biking in Acadia National Park. Bill Supple, CEO of Wild Country USA, had booked us into The Inn at Canoe Point and told us we'd like it. We did. We almost missed the narrow driveway that led down through pine trees to a house built of pine on the granite rocks that fringed the beautiful inlet with the Atlantic Ocean beyond. It was almost too perfect, like a stage set. Step down from the front door and you could walk around the decking just inches above the high-tide mark. Bill said it was difficult to get a booking. The names of more than one former vice president were in the visitor book.

Bill also suggested we stop at Freeport, fifty miles east of North Conway on the way up to Bar Harbor, to take a look at the outdoor retailer L.L. Bean, which was, and still is, an outdoor store without equal. I was impressed. The main retail facility was a modern multi-level emporium – 20,000 square feet of retail space. The interior was light, spacious and beautifully finished in rough-cut timber with oiled hardwood detailing. Good use had been made of reinforced glass. The ambience was uncluttered, spacious and relaxed.

In the middle of the ground floor was L.L. Bean's famous duck pond complete with fish. A broad spiral staircase curved up through a wide opening in the ceiling to give access to a restaurant and a large area dedicated to women's outdoor and sports clothing. This was one of the busiest parts of the shop though it was laid out in such a way not to seem crowded. Apart from a very extensive outdoor and casual clothing department, footwear, camping, small boats and kayaks, packs, road bikes and mountain bikes, there was a large display of hunting, fishing and shooting equipment which reflected the store's origins, and a well-stocked book store, travel and map section. When L.L. Bean founded the company in the early twentieth century, hunters and fishermen would call in to purchase bait and a cup of coffee in the early hours. It was easier to keep the shop open twenty-four hours a day, all year round, to cope with the unorthodox hours hunters and fishermen kept. The store is still constantly open and the mail-order business is still expanding after a hundred years.

L.L. Bean wasn't a specialised mountaineering store – far from it. It only stocked basic climbing gear, but for the average outdoorsy American family it was a treasure chest. I spent half an hour looking at the display of outdoor tools: Leathermen, folding tools, Swiss army knives, and so forth.

At the time of my first visit, in 1986, the business had a turnover of just over a $100 million, of which twenty per cent was retail and the rest mail order. On a visit three years later, the turnover was £500 million and by 2012 it was $1.5 billion. They must be doing something right. When I decided to open Outside, my own outdoor shop in the Peak District village of Hathersage, the success of L.L. Bean, located 200 miles north of Boston, was instrumental. If L.L. Bean could have a thriving shop out in the sticks, then why shouldn't I?

———————

In September 1985, when we were at ISPO, the main European trade show held each year in Munich, my partner Steve Bean told me he wanted to sell his shares in Wild Country and end our partnership. Although this was a bit of a shock, it did not come as a total surprise. We had had our first significant disagreement a couple of months earlier about the manufacture and sale of military equipment. Steve's brother worked for a large electronics company with substantial sales in the military sector. He had told Steve he could secure a contract to manufacture backpacks for army radios. I was dead against this plan. First, we had no experience in this area of manufacture and the specification was very tight. We did not have the machinery or manufacturing skills to deliver the goods on time. Second, I didn't want to 'taint' the Wild Country brand. Steve asked me what I meant by 'taint'. I tried to explain but he still didn't have any idea what I was talking about – but I was adamant. Any such change would be over my dead body. It wasn't going to happen.

Steve told me that I was holding the company back. When it came to decision making we had always been equal, but the circumstances of our relationship conspired to make Steve the junior partner whatever the law might say. I had appointed Steve as my deputy in the Antarctic. I had founded the company. I had taken the risk. I had been there from the start, had done the groundwork and found the suppliers, made the contacts and given the business a name. Wild Country was always going to be my baby, whoever owned it. In retrospect it's surprising the schism didn't happen earlier.

The partnership agreement required Steve to offer his shares to me in the first instance and before we could do anything we needed to come to an agreement about the value of the company. I suggested we both write down what we thought the company was worth. Amazingly, we both wrote down the same figure: £800,000. I would have to find half that to buy him out. Our agreement specified that the purchaser would be given time to raise the cash. Two weeks later Steve asked for a meeting to tell me that he had undervalued the company. He now thought it was worth twice our agreed estimate. Under his new valuation, I would have to find £800,000. Without missing a beat, I told him that if he thought the company was worth that much he could have my shares for £400,000.

I don't know what Steve expected but he could hardly have thought I would agree with his new valuation. I suppose he thought I'd pay him an additional hundred thousand or so. He certainly didn't expect my response. It all happened very quickly. Within ten minutes I had a signed document from Steve that he would buy all my shares for £400,000 and we had shaken hands on it. All I could think was that 200 per cent growth per year on my initial capital for seven years was not so bad.

One of Steve's conditions was that I should stay away from the business and not interfere. My conditions were that I would remain on full salary until the deal was completed. There would be board meetings when necessary, which I would attend, but that was the extent of my involvement. I also agreed with Steve there would no objection to my starting an outdoor retail business with no restrictions on location.

I was consulted about the future only once during my 'sabbatical', when the company was offered the Clog brand and its facilities in North Wales. As a director I nodded this through thinking it had little to do with my plans. In retrospect the effect the acquisition of Clog had on Wild Country was neutral, even negative. It should have helped our productivity but it didn't. What it did do was create an opportunity to produce and market a range of budget climbing tools. Why would a company that aspired to make the best climbing equipment on the planet want to produce second-rate gear? Although the acquisition did not cost anything in cash, it did divide our effort and confuse the market.

My contract with Steve specified that for three years I would not be involved in any manufacturing that competed with Wild Country. A clause of this nature was usual in circumstances like this. After three years I could do anything. I felt totally relaxed. For the first time since starting in business I would be properly capitalised. I was confident that with the experience and knowledge I had acquired founding Wild Country, I would enjoy planning and creating a new retail business.

I needed time to think. There was an international climbing festival at Montserrat in Spain I wanted to go to and I persuaded Jan to spend a month touring, something we had never done before. We took the ferry to Santander and explored the Picos de Europa before heading east to Catalonia for the festival. I met a lot of Spanish climbers including the legendary Jordi Pons, who I later got to know when I became the British delegate to the international mountaineering federation, the UIAA. I also had the honour of climbing with Nils Bohigas who in 1984, with Enric Lucas, made an outstanding alpine-style new route on the vast south face of Annapurna, one of the greatest ascents in the history of Himalayan climbing.

Afterwards we stayed with my friend Christino Nart, a communist who had cigarette burn scars on his forearms from being tortured by Franco's men. Christino was a manufacturer of polypropylene fleece and outdoor clothing I thought looked promising. I met Luis Fraga at Christino's house. Luis was an extreme right-wing politician, an aristocrat, mountaineer and leader of the Spanish Everest expedition. He was the nephew of Franco's finance minister. When he learned we would be going to Madrid, Luis insisted that we meet him there and he would take us to the Prado to show us the Goyas. This juxtaposition of politics, commerce and social standing was an extraordinary insight into the complexity of Spain. One day Christino took us for a hike up to the monastery on top of a local mountain in the Parc Natural de Sant Llorenc del Munt. It took us hours to get there and we were famished by the time we got to the top, but when we did we were welcomed by a young man called Lluís Comes i Arderiu who made his living by translating Tom Sharp novels into Catalan. He also made the best aioli I have ever tasted.

We made a pilgrimage to Rioja, and visited the Gallego brothers in Murcia. Miguel Àngel Gallego, the Chris Bonington of Spain, treated us to dinner at El Rincón de Pepe, one of the great restaurants of the region. We visited Granada and the Alhambra with its magnificent backdrop of the Sierra Nevada. We stayed at a wonderful *parador* at Jaén and spent a breathtaking day at the Prado where, true to his word, Luis Fraga guided us round the Goyas and the Velázquez. I felt privileged to have such a guide. There was a familiar painting round every corner. The Hieronymus Bosch triptych was unexpected and the highlight of the day, but I realised I had dropped a clanger when I asked Luis if we could go to the pavilion where Guernica was displayed with an impressive array of Picasso's sketches and paintings leading up to the completion of his most famous work. Luis politely declined. 'If you go to see Guernica, you go without me.' The memory of the civil war was still raw, almost fifty years on.

It felt odd returning to Britain with the prospect of having a lot of money and the freedom to do whatever I wanted in the mountaineering market – a clean sheet of paper on which I could paint my own picture, dream my own dream. I got to work at once to search for a suitable location. I was looking for a large building with enough internal space to be able to replicate the sort of ambience L.L. Bean had, somewhere easily accessible to walkers and climbers visiting the Peak District with good access and parking. There was a large brownfield site in Bakewell backing on to the river that had once been a sawmill. It seemed perfect except for the fact it wasn't for sale. Then Sally Turnbull, Dick's wife, found the building that would become Outside.

It was a former agricultural workshop and filling station on the main road through Hathersage, now being used as an auction house by an estate agent. I knew instinctively I wouldn't find a better location within the national park. I would need planning permission but I could afford it – or rather, I would be able to afford it when the sale of Wild Country had gone through. Climbers and walkers from all over England passed by the building every year, some several times. If I could make it into something like my dream, a magical emporium, then they would be enticed in. My intention was to make it the best climbing and mountaineering shop in the country.

When people make purchases for their sport, recreation, hobbies, or anything else they are passionate about, they will travel, sometimes quite a long way, to get exactly what they want. They will go out of their way to make that purchase in a store that offers a sense of occasion, somewhere that helped to make the day special. For someone to make a decision to buy something expensive they should be relaxed. A feeling of space helps, but they shouldn't feel under pressure from the staff. Not only should sales staff be knowledgeable, they should understand what the buyer wants the equipment for and be able to adjust it and advise on its use, while remembering that a lot of our customers already knew a lot about the equipment they wanted to buy. Being close to Sheffield there were many knowledgeable and enthusiastic students we could train as sales staff. We had one rule above all others. If a customer asks a question about a product and the salesman doesn't know the answer, don't try to wing it. Find someone else who does know.

It was important to have somewhere in the shop where customers could escape. If the sales staff could direct them to a coffee shop to let the customer think about the purchase without pressure they were more likely to make the sale. If customers are relaxed and enjoying the experience, they will probably buy something. But if they feel rushed or under pressure, you just lost the sale. The customer will still reflect on their decision and buy that £300 jacket, but it won't be in your shop.

The space available at Hathersage was substantial but there was an awful lot of work to do. The front of the shop had large shop windows either side of the main entrance. Inside the building there were several yards of what would be prime retail space for clothing the full width of the building. Beyond this was a natural break where the sales counter would be. At the side of the building was a door that would serve as the entrance to a cafe and washrooms on a mezzanine via a curved staircase. Beyond this was a large, high space ideal for selling anything from boots and packs to clothing, sleeping bags and even tents, which we could keep assembled and suspended from the open roof area.

My friend and climbing partner Nick Longland had worked for the National Coal Board for ten years as a geologist, but all that time had been nursing an ambition to run his own restaurant. 'Longland's offered a quid pro quo: the cafe helped shop sales, the shop provided customers. The idea was to have a welcoming eating area that would provide healthy fast food during the day but could be changed into a pleasant country restaurant in the evening.

Nick and I got to work on the building. We took the floorboards out of the first floor at the front and used them to build a wall across the middle of what used to be the auction house. We built a small climbing wall in the back of the building and had a pond in the centre. I designed the curved staircase up to the mezzanine overlooking the main part of the shop. Every aspect was created to emphasise the feeling of space. It was different from L.L. Bean, but that was the inspiration. We divided the upstairs room into three: two-thirds restaurant, one-third kitchen and storage. The restaurant used exposed wooden timber beams and had a high apex so that it would create the sense of space and not be too noisy. Given our budget, I think we achieved our ambition of a big, uncluttered sales area that would provide an unusual, exciting retail experience.

Then in January 1987 everything changed. Steve told me our deal was off and that he couldn't buy my shares. Almost as bad, Wild Country was being sued by Lowe Alpine Systems for breach of copyright. The bank had loaned me the money to buy the Hathersage building and refurbish it on the basis that I would repay it from my sale of Wild Country shares to Steve. Now that wasn't going to happen. In the old days I would have gone to see Mr Rigby, but Mr Rigby had retired. Wild Country had been trading for nine years and had a good track record with the bank. That helped, but not much. The bank had its own formulas, and if you didn't produce the right answers, there was little scope for latitude. I had no more leverage and would have to raise money by finding investors. If I failed, the bank could force me to sell the shop before it had even opened. The important thing now was to get the building finished, get it stocked and get it open. Suddenly I found myself fighting for everything I considered worthwhile.

Steve asked for a meeting to explain what had happened. He told me that Rick White, our distributor in Australia, a climber I knew well, had been distributing Lowe Alpine Systems rucksacks but had lost the contract. Rick had immediately gone to Korea and found a company to make identical packs. Rick was back in the market. The only difference between the rucksacks was that Rick's had different names. Rick then asked Steve if he would market 'his' packs in Britain, under the Wild Country name, and through our distribution company in New Hampshire. Rick was out to get his pound of flesh from Lowe Alpine.

Copyright law in Australia is relaxed compared to Britain where copyright can be applied not only to words and language, but also to designs, including the blueprints and cut-out shapes used in the manufacture of rucksacks. It was all too easy to see that Wild Country was in breach of Lowe Alpine's copyright, and that the designs were the intellectual property of Lowe Alpine Systems. Copyright laws in Britain are also very much in favour of the owner of the design and the penalties are draconian. The infringer not only has to pay a sum equal to the net profit, as in patent law, but a payment equal to turnover.

Steve had done all this quietly, without a board meeting. Now, because of this, I was in big trouble. I owned half of a company being sued for making illegal copies of a product. Having no idea this was happening counted for nothing. Ignorance is no defence. And it was not as though I could sue Steve for breaching our agreement. It was one of those situations where if you lost it would cost a bomb, and if you won, you'd lose a bomb. Anyway, I had been through the legal mill with Yvon Chouinard and knew that being right didn't mean winning. And in this case we weren't in the right.

Mending fences with Steve was not an option; the fences were too badly broken. There was no way back. I owned fifty per cent of a well-respected company whose reputation was about to be threatened. What was required was a stroke of boldness. I told Steve I would buy his shares for £250,000. From this sum I deducted £17,000, the price of Steve's yacht, which he wanted to keep but was technically an asset of the company. Then I told him I would take care of the Lowe Alpine problem. There was no discussion, no bargaining. Steve agreed to my offer knowing it was the best deal he would get. That was the last time I ever talked about business with Steve, and we managed to keep it amicable.

I allowed £50,000 as the cost of settling the copyright dispute and flew out to the Las Vegas Snow Show a couple of days early for a meeting with the Lowe family. My position was one of guilt; my job was damage limitation. George Lowe welcomed me and I said hello to Jeff who I had met several times. George said they knew the problem was not of my making, that they had discussed it, and they had a figure in mind to settle the problem. I waited, holding my breath: $15,000. I tried not to show any feelings. I thought my mind was playing tricks. Did he really mean 15, or had he really said 150? I told George his offer was very rea-sonable but what about the packs that had already been manufactured? George said that because there weren't many, about 2,000, Wild Country could sell them off and agree not to take any liberties with Lowe in the future. I had to pinch myself to make sure I wasn't dreaming. Jeff even gave me one of his new Latok fleeces that I'd admired.

At the time, I wanted Steve out of the way and to get into the driving seat again. But the impact of these events, which had left me seriously undercapitalised again, would continue to create problems long into the future. When the London-based retailer Alpine Sports went into recei-vership in 1984, I had given the climbing manager, Dick Turnbull, the job of sales manager at Wild Country. During the fifteen months I had been absent from Wild Country, Dick and I would meet most Tuesday even-ings as members of an informal climbing group. I asked him if he would be interested in being a part of the new shop. Dick seemed interested, enthusiastic even, so a few months later I was surprised and disappointed when he told me that he was no longer interested. Steve needed a product person and I assumed Steve had offered Dick a deal to keep him at Wild Country to cover the gap I had left.

With Steve gone and having taken back the reins, my options were to make him redundant, keep him on as sales manager at Tideswell or move him to the new shop in Hathersage. To make Dick redundant would have been stupid. He was a good manager and he had the best knowledge of anyone I knew in the climbing market in Britain. I knew I wouldn't make a good shopkeeper. There were also a lot of balls in the air and although I had proved to be quite adept at catching them, I was now starting to drop a few. I was spreading myself too thinly. I was the owner of a climbing hardware company in Tideswell and another in North Wales. I also had a tent production company in Alfreton and a small distribution company in the USA. I employed over a hundred people. The company was maturing and it needed more management. Gone were the days of watching the orders come in and doubling turnover every year. Wild Country was now in the real world.

The obvious place for Dick was in the new shop but his lack of enthusiasm for my project was a concern. I was also making the assumption that he still wanted to work for me. I also faced the pressing need to find new capital. I decided to invite the company's three senior managers to invest in the business.

Wild Country's accountant Mike Longden agreed to purchase thirteen and a half per cent of Wild Country and become managing director. Hugh Banner, general manager of Clog, bought three and a half per cent. Dick would purchase ten per cent of Outside and move to the shop as its managing director. On 30 April 1987, I completed the purchase of Steve Bean's shares in Wild Country and ten days later we opened the doors of Outside to the public. I did not spend much time worrying about Outside. Right from the start I knew it was going to be a success.

It took off like a rocket, attracting young and old, climbers and hill walkers and passers-by off the street. Over the course of the first year we kept a record of where our customers lived. Half of them came from the south-east and about thirty per cent came from London. Finding highly motivated, knowledgeable shop staff was straightforward. The location was even better than I had anticipated with climbers and walkers using the cafe as a meeting place. There were a few hiccups. I walked into the climbing section one day and found a delivery of harnesses made especially for Outside. I recognised the webbing as one used by Troll. It wasn't the fact that Dick had placed an order with one of my competitors that hurt, more that he had not given me the opportunity to compete.

The business plan required Outside to achieve a turnover of £350,000 in the first year. It was very quickly apparent we would exceed that figure.

Within a few years we were turning over £1.5 million. The editor of one of the climbing magazines, a well-known commentator on the English climbing scene, had scoffed when I had suggested – half-jokingly – that Outside would move the centre of gravity of Peak District climbing away from Stoney Middleton to Hathersage. Now I felt as though I was flying rather than fighting gravity.

On the summit of Shishapangma (8,027 metres) on 26 May 1990.
Photo: Russell Brice.

13 THREE BIG MOUNTAINS AND A SMALLER ONE

I had always wanted to climb a big mountain but it wasn't until 1989 that I felt relaxed enough about the business to take several weeks off. Time was passing and I wasn't getting any younger. If I didn't get on with it, my dream would remain just that – a dream. One expedition was all I wanted. One summit would satisfy my urge. It didn't have to be Everest. Though it is very big, it is also very expensive, and even then was getting overcrowded. A smaller objective would be fine, so long as it was the real deal. As it turned out, one mountain did not feed the rat, it just whetted its appetite. Over the course of the next three years I went first to Nepal, then to Tibet and finally the Karakoram.

A Himalayan trip should not be taken lightly. In the fifties, some mountaineers talked about conquering mountains. I don't know of any mountain that has been conquered, but I know of many mountaineers for whom the reverse is true. It is a matter of complete indifference to a mountain whether or not a mountaineer sets foot on its summit or not.

When I was a young climber, 8,000-metre peaks were invitation only. They were expensive, required sophisticated logistics and participants needed to take a couple of months off work. To get on a team, you needed an extensive mountaineering track record. I did not have the time or experience to organise my own expedition, but by the time I got around to realising my ambition, the commercial expedition business had burst into life. The more ambitious trekking companies had started by climbing straightforward lower-altitude peaks. It was only a matter of time before guiding services began on big mountains.

I saw an advertisement in one of the climbing magazines that a company in Bristol was offering an expedition to Changtse, the northern peak of the Everest group. It was over 7,500 metres high and approached from Tibet like the early British expeditions to Everest in the twenties and thirties. It was among the very first commercial expeditions organised and marketed by a British company. I picked up the phone and talked to Steve Bell, one of the owners of Himalayan Kingdoms, later Jagged Globe, and leader of the expedition. It was just what I was looking for: no time-consuming logistics, no finding a team. All I had to do was get to the airport with a rucksack full of high-altitude climbing kit.

The make-up of our team was diverse. Two Norwegians, a Finn and two Brits, a BBC producer called Graham Hoyland and me, flew from Europe. In Kathmandu Steve introduced us to those members of the team from the southern hemisphere: two Aussies, the New Zealand guide Russell Brice and a chap from Hong Kong. I had assumed I would be one of the older members but as it turned out I was about in the middle. Russell was supplying most of the logistics for our trip. He had a lock-up in Kathmandu and a rather motley selection of tents and shelters. Russell also had his own team of Sherpas who worked as a sort of cooperative.

Our first problem was that the border between Nepal and Tibet had closed as a consequence of the demonstrations and massacre in Tiananmen Square in Beijing. Changtse was off the menu. Steve Bell immediately sought permission from the Nepali authorities to climb an outlier of Himalchuli, a mountain south of Manaslu and similar in altitude to Changtse. Even better, it had only had one previous ascent.

There was much work to do before we left, checking equipment and buying fresh food that would survive the trek to Base Camp. We explored the city on bikes from the Summit Hotel, a quiet oasis on the fringe of town. In the evenings we ate steaks at Rum Doodle, or great Thai food at Yin Yang in the garish tourist district of Thamel. I had expected Kathmandu to be like a bigger Darjeeling, but I could not have been more wrong. Darjeeling is a spacious town, at least in my memory, clean by Indian standards and at 7,000 feet relatively cool. Kathmandu, at 3,000 feet, is hot, dusty and dirty.

We went to Dumre by minibus and hired a beaten-up old truck to take us on to Bhotewodar where we spent the night. We had maps, but they were inaccurate, and though we had a vague idea of the way to the bottom of the mountain, the Japanese, who had made the first ascent, had approached from the other side. We faced six days of trekking uphill to get us to where we thought we could make our base camp at about

14,500 feet. On the third day we came to a small village where the children ran away from us. I think we must have been among the first Europeans they had seen.

Climbing at high altitude is very different from Alpine climbing. I cannot think of any other activity to which it equates, except maybe ocean sailing. It is committing, debilitating and dangerous. Most of the climbers who grasp this particular nettle do not spend much time, if any, on technical rock, or even technical ice. They are more often trudging up a trail carrying a huge pack, hoping the next camp is not too far away.

The three-kilometre ridge on Himalchuli, between the small summit at the start of the ridge, first climbed on Graham's birthday and consequently dubbed Graham's Knob, and the top was a Himalayan version of the Cuillins with technical sections that Russell and I had to equip so we could all carry loads safely. I could not believe how hard Russell worked, or how conscientious he was. I had brought the prototype Terra Nova four-person tent that I had been working on with a view to using it on the mountain to get feedback on the size and design and to photograph it. We pitched this tent about halfway along the ridge as Camp 2.

The last thing I had done before making my way to the boarding gate at Heathrow was pop into WH Smith to buy a paperback. I had a couple of books already but I felt a bit light on reading material. I didn't have much time so I picked up the thickest paperback I could see: *Rivals* by Jilly Cooper. Five weeks later, high on Himalchuli, four of us lay in the prototype tent in our sleeping bags, waiting for a storm to blow itself out. I had read 600 pages of *Rivals*; the other three had finished their books. Carefully I divided my book into four pieces, keeping the last part for myself and distributing the remaining three. It didn't really matter that you read the sections in the correct order. Everybody enjoyed what they had and we were still swapping individual chapters for a pint of beer when we finally got back to the Summit Hotel in Kathmandu.

The other team members insisted I write to Jilly Cooper to tell her how much we had enjoyed her book so I did, telling the story of how I had carved up her book. My letter would have arrived at her publisher the following Monday morning. On Wednesday her reply popped through our letterbox and was immediately pinned up on the corkboard in our kitchen, where we left it for months:

*Dear Mark, Life is very bleak, sometimes, even for writers living in
beautiful parts of Gloucestershire, and I cannot tell you how your
wonderful, wonderful letter absolutely cheered me up to the sky,
as high as your mountain.*

*It was a wonderful letter and a wonderful testament to a writer
to think of you all reading bits of me so high up. You have made me very,
very happy. I feel warm and cherished and I am very glad that I made
you laugh. Will you give my love to everybody and say thank you so
much for such a wonderful tribute. I'm in the middle of writing a sort
of semi-sequel to Rivals at the moment, on polo; I'm very stuck on it
but letters like yours certainly help to break the block.*

Much love to you all, Jilly.

I don't make a habit of writing to authors, but in a similar vein, I wrote to
Philip Pullman regarding a reference to Friends in the trilogy *His Dark
Materials*. He had spelled Friend with a lower-case 'f', assuming that
Friends was a generic name, rather like hoover, which to some extent it is.
He also responded to my letter within a few days, though not as quickly
as Jilly and with fewer 'wonderfuls'.

Himalchuli turned out to have the hardest climbing of any of my
Himalayan trips, most of which were, from a technical point of view, just
high-altitude hiking. Graham and I carried more loads than the others, eight
from Base to Camp 2. We also found ourselves above of all the difficulties
at about 7,000 metres, but we were so tired that we left food, fuel and
bivouac equipment above the last steep climbing and then went down to
Camp 2 hoping to recover to give it another shot. Unfortunately we were
chased off the mountain by the onset of the monsoon.

In 1990 I was invited to go to Russia by a young chap called Mark Raggett
who specialised in finding production companies in Russia and putting
them in touch with specialist British companies for their mutual benefit.
It was part of Mikhail Gorbachev's plan for making Russian manufacturing more accessible to Western markets. One of Raggett's initiatives
was putting the first British astronaut into space: Helen Sharman, a woman
from Sheffield who spent eight and a half days on Mir space station.
One of his tasks on this trip was to create the infrastructure necessary
for Russian satellite photographs to be marketed in the West. The only
satellite photographs available at that time were from NASA, and they

were very expensive. It would not be difficult to undercut the American photographs and it was a rapidly expanding market.

My trip was heavily subsidised. All I had to do was turn up at the airport with a list of products the Russians might manufacture for Wild Country. But I wasn't altogether comfortable about the venture. All the other companies were huge, much bigger than Wild Country. I had a feeling that Mark Raggett hadn't told me everything. When I challenged him about it I discovered that he did have another agenda. Someone had told him that Elbrus, the highest mountain in Europe, was easy to climb and he wanted to climb it. He hadn't figured out a plan, but I told him I was interested, on both counts: manufacturing and Elbrus. We would go twice, the first time just for business.

I knew the Russians had some very advanced aluminium alloys that might be suitable for use in a variety of mountaineering tools and possibly karabiners. I had heard that they had some sophisticated composites, combining 7000-series alloys with both carbon and boron fibre to make super-lightweight forgings for their aerospace industry. The components were between fifteen and eighteen per cent stronger than the basic 7000 alloy. This was a significant improvement, but the added cost was substantial, four or maybe even five times more expensive, but my information was limited and I wasn't sure about its reliability.

I found it very difficult to discuss costs and prices in Russia. The command economy had created a culture in which the price of anything was immaterial. If the powers that be thought something was necessary it would be produced, whatever the cost. The job of producing the goods would be allocated to a suitable factory, which would manufacture the product for the whole of Russia. With a price tag decided by committee, the item might sell at a profit or might not. Profitability was not a dirty word exactly, but it was strongly tainted and of little interest to anybody. Marketing was another taboo term, not used in polite society.

Another problem was consistency. I had brought a few sample karabiners – our top-end models – with a view to having samples manufactured in Russia. They copied them faithfully, but when I tested them the scatter of results was not merely excessive, it was simply awful. Karabiners that should be breaking consistently at 2.5-plus kN were breaking at loads varying between 1.1 kN and 2.5 kN. But it wasn't the inconsistency that concerned me most. It was the inability of the Russians to accept there was a problem.

Raggett told me that some friends of his, a couple from south London, wanted to join us for our return visit to climb Elbrus. What did I think? The more the merrier was my reply. At this stage I still had hopes the Russians would produce something special and I had an ulterior purpose. I was flying out to Kathmandu soon after to attempt Shishapangma, the highest mountain wholly in Tibet. A few days at 5,000 metres in the Caucasus would kick-start acclimatisation. After a few days, business in Moscow we flew down to Mineralnye Vody in a huge Ilyushin IL-86, a Russian jumbo jet. It was massive. To get on board you walked up a stairway that folded from underneath the fuselage. Six people could walk up side by side. At the top there was a bulkhead where you could turn left or right. We were ushered to the left and what I think was first class. Looking at the sea of faces stretching back into the fuselage, I think they had held the flight especially for us.

Terskol, the ski resort at the foot of Elbrus, was a two-hour drive. It was like going back in time to the fifties. Our accommodation was a Bauhaus dacha built by the Germans during the war, two miles north of town. We had this to ourselves. Our meals were taken at a rather institutional hotel. My memory is of grey meat, grey potatoes and grey vegetables covered in grey gravy. This was in gloomy contrast to Moscow, where we had gone out one evening with some Russians Mark knew. We seemed to wander round aimlessly for a while, looking for a restaurant. Then one of the Russians asked if we had any dollars or sterling. I offered him a £10 note and Mark matched it. We went down a stone staircase and knocked on a solid-looking door, which opened grudgingly. A short conversation resulted in the door opening wider and soon we found ourselves sitting round a table in what was obviously a popular eating-place. A bottle of Russian champagne appeared, followed by another. A bowl of black caviar arrived. I wondered how many more £10 notes we would need to make it back on to the street. The caviar was soon disposed of but as the empty bowl was removed a large plate of smoked salmon arrived, then a platter of cold meats, salami and finely sliced smoked ham and finally a plate of ice cream. The empty bottles were replaced by a bottle of vodka and a bottle of brandy. I opted for the brandy.

There didn't appear to be the same black-market options in Terskol but we enjoyed skiing in fabulous weather for a couple of days and then took the cable car up to begin our ascent. We spent the night in a series of nine tubular, or 'barrel', huts at 3,800 metres. These accommodate six people each and are usually quite crowded although in April we were the only people staying there. Mark Raggett had hired a guide, a mullah called Ybu, and the following day we climbed up 600 metres but it was obvious the others were having a hard time.

Next day we set off at four in the morning, reaching the previous day's high point three hours later. It was desperately cold with a steady katabatic wind flowing directly down the mountain. My face and chest were freezing despite wearing a Gore-Tex suit. At least the climbing was easy, except for one thing. We were walking up smooth, hard ice. The ice was so hard that our crampons, which were essential, left no mark on the ice whatsoever. The others did not go much higher. They had no experience of altitude and had never worn crampons before; they weren't enjoying themselves. Ybu and I reached the lower east summit soon after eleven o'clock and traversed round to reach the main summit soon after midday. Now the snow was softening and we were able to descend the north face directly and very quickly to the huts. We collected our gear and had a magnificent ski down to the valley.

That night we celebrated in the unusual surroundings of an elaborate sauna, complete with library, television lounge, various heated rooms and a stream supplying ice-cold water into a plunge pool. When we were done, I turned off all the electrics, as per instructed. We were woken up at three by the noise of the sauna building burning down. Rushing to the window I saw flames leaping high into the sky and setting the neighbouring pine trees on fire. By the time the fire engine arrived the sauna was gone.

No one talked to us. No one even looked at us. We had become invisible. All that day we were guilty until proven innocent. I prepared myself for the salt mines. Then, at teatime, along with the cakes came smiles. It turned out the caretaker had seen us leaving the sauna and phoned round her friends. They had been waiting for us to vacate the sauna so they could have their own party. It must have been a good deal more out of control than ours had been. I was off the hook.

Much to the confusion of the Russians, who seemed to think we were mad, we took the night train back to Moscow. We made a quick trip to the market in Mineralnye Vody and bought fantastic bread, fresh butter, various cheeses, salami and dried meat, red wine, brandy and a variety of pickles. We were back in Moscow early next morning.

———

When I was at primary school I used to pore over my Philip's *Atlas of the World*. I had always liked maps and particularly liked maps of mountain areas. There was one mountain in this atlas that winked at me. It was in Tibet, standing alone on the Tibetan plateau unlike the other high peaks that made up the Himalaya. This mountain was called Gosainthan. It was huge, over 8,000 metres and I wondered why I had never come across any mention of it. No one seemed to have climbed it and there was no expedition book. It seemed that no one apart from the cartographer and me knew anything about it.

The mountain, it turned out, was more usually known as Shishapangma, and wasn't climbed until 1964, after I'd gone to university, thanks in part to the mountain's isolated position within communist China. It was the last of the 8,000ers to be climbed. Of the several expeditions I went on, this was the most memorable and the most enjoyable. It was small, only six climbers, well run with no mistakes and deeply satisfying. Our leader was Russell Brice, our guide from Himalchuli the year before, now running his own company, Himalayan Experience. Our team comprised two Norwegians, an Australian dentist called Barry and a New Zealander.

There were no tours of Kathmandu this time; the people of Nepal had recently overthrown the country's absolute monarchy and the streets were still tense. A curfew required us to be back at the Hotel Tibet by eight o'clock in the evening. Base Camp was just across the border, across the Friendship Bridge, and you could in theory drive there in a day depending on the mood of the Chinese border authorities.

We were a little ahead of our schedule so we took our time and spent a couple of days hanging out at 5,000 metres to acclimatise and stay clear of Base Camp, where a large Japanese expedition was coming to its end. There were also some Swiss, and an international expedition sponsored by the French computer company Bull who were trying to climb all fourteen 8,000ers within a year. Russell had a reputation for being generous with provisions but not even he could match the opulence of the Bull team. Alan Hinkes, who went on to be the first Brit to climb the fourteen, was part of the expedition and gave me a huge slice of their Beaufort cheese, my favourite, which was the size of a car wheel.

It took a week to adapt to the thin air of the Tibet plateau and we needed to be fit; the hike up to Advance Base Camp (ABC) was a long one: thirty-six kilometres. To carry our equipment up to ABC we had five yaks, admirable animals that seemed able to go anywhere. Mark, the New

Zealand climber, and I spent an afternoon fossil hunting in a dry riverbed near Base Camp. We found a few scraps and then gave up, but returning to Base Camp I noticed a smooth oval stone and casually prodded it with the toe of my boot. The stone was about four inches across and fell apart to reveal a beautiful ammonite, which fitted together like a three-dimensional jigsaw, a powerful reminder that the high plateau was once below the sea.

It was a relief to be on such a compact expedition, and happily the vast Japanese pulled out. By the time we got to ABC we had the mountain to ourselves, apart from two Czechoslovakians, husband and wife, who turned up without a permit from I don't know where. They spent two days resting and then said goodbye, asking us not to tell anyone we had seen them, heading off up the mountain. We never saw them again. I have no idea what happened to them.

Then it was our turn. We set off with heavy loads up a long glacier approach but were pinned down for three days in our Quasar tents. By the time the storm passed, there was half a metre of new snow and we had eaten most of our food. We had no choice than to leave the tents where they were and return to ABC to rest for a few days to recuperate. When we set off again we had lots of food, the sun was shining and we were feeling restored. We picked up the Quasars and continued climbing, pitching the Terra Nova I had used the year before on Himalchuli at 7,000 metres. Next morning we took the Quasars up to the foot of the summit ridge and pitched those at 7,400 metres – our high camp. We had a perfect night with no wind, got up early and set off up easy-angled but firm snow. Russell and the younger members of the team got to the summit at about ten o'clock. I got there at eleven. Barry the dentist from Australia – and the old man of the team – slowly ground to a halt. He gave up about a hundred metres from the top. It was heartbreaking, watching from a distance, but the wind was getting up and we had to get down.

After Shishapangma, I intended to call it a day as far as the Greater Ranges were concerned but then Steve Bell asked me if I would be interested in a trip to Broad Peak. Having climbed in Nepal and Tibet, I thought it would round things out nicely to climb a big mountain in the Karakoram before finally hanging up my boots.

The Karakoram is a broad jumble of peaks separating Pakistan from Tibet. Arid and broken, it is complicated compared to the thin line of Himalayan peaks that separates Tibet from South Asia. In the centre of this mass of peaks stands the most beautiful and the highest of all: K2. The mighty Baltoro Glacier sweeps down from the north, joined by the Godwin-Austen Glacier at Concordia from where you can see more 8,000-metre peaks than anywhere else on earth: K2, dominating everything, Broad Peak and the two Gasherbrum summits, and two near-misses, Chogolisa and Masherbrum, all of them packed together within a few hours walk of one other.

Technically speaking, K2 is probably the hardest of all the 8,000ers and the lack of any satellite peaks enhances its grandeur. Broad Peak, on the other hand, is not such a beautiful mountain. In fact, it's downright ugly. I couldn't help but compare this trip to the others I had been on. Kathmandu is a fun place and lots of expeditions are arriving in late spring. We were busy during the day and partied in the evenings. In Islamabad we were required to attend an Islamic briefing and finding a beer required serious research. Our team was bigger too: fifteen men, including Alan Hinkes, and Flor, our female Venezuelan doctor. It was too many. The photographs taken on the way to Concordia looked more like an army on its way to war than the lightweight trip to Tibet the year before. I spent a lot of time ferrying loads but at our high camp at 7,000 metres we were pinned down in a sixty-hour storm. Flor developed what appeared to be pulmonary oedema and I escorted her off the mountain. Three members of the team, including Ramone, Flor's sixty-year-old husband, stuck it out and reached the summit.

I felt it was time to get back to business.

The Foundry during a busy session in February 1991.

14 CLIMBING THE WALLS

The Leeds University climbing wall is often cited as Britain's first, but the educationalist Colin Mortlock created one in 1961, three years before Leeds, on a brick wall at one end of a gymnasium at the Royal School. Holds were made from rectangular blocks cut from sheets of plywood of various thicknesses and attached to a brick wall. This was long before battery-powered hammer drills. Bigger holds, cut from one-inch ply, were screwed into holes drilled with a manual hammer and a star drill. Smaller holds were cut from quarter-inch ply and held by masonry pins. I climbed on this wall in 1961 and it was way ahead of its time. Mortlock should be congratulated for his vision and hard work. But before 1990 there were no dedicated climbing walls. Those walls that did exist were often built in existing local authority sports facilities, turning something like a disused squash court into what today would be called a bouldering wall.

In 1989, Dick Turnbull and I visited some of the new climbing walls in Belgium, a country somewhat starved of steep rock. We were impressed with their size – up to eighteen metres high – but they were just walls and lacked character. We were thinking of opening a climbing shop in Sheffield, but rather than find expensive premises in the centre, we thought we could find a big building in a run-down part of the city and build a really good climbing wall, not so much a climbing gym as an indoor crag, with corners, overhangs and slabs, a much more realistic climbing experience than what we'd found in Belgium. We had moved Peak District climbing's centre of gravity from Stoney Middleton to Hathersage. Could we create a bit of Peak District magic on the wrong side of the tracks, on the left bank of River Don? Location would be everything: accessible from the city centre with good parking and a good pub with decent beer nearby.

The concept was beginning to grow on me.

We started looking around the industrial district of Sheffield for a tall, disused building that was waterproof and cheap, without much success. Then we found Jerry and Paul, or rather they found us. I had not met Paul Reeve before but I knew Jerry Moffatt very well from our time together developing Boreal rock shoes in Spain. Jerry had also seen the Belgian climbing walls and was looking to invest in a business venture in which he could involve himself personally. After all, what does a retired world champion climber do all day? Paul Reeve worked for BT and was looking to move on; he had already decided that a wall in Sheffield would be a winner. In the end it was Paul who found the building on Mowbray Street in the old metal-bashing heart of the city. Although it was strong, it looked a bit of a wreck and needed a new roof, something we couldn't afford. That would have to wait. Anyway, a few puddles on the floor added a little verisimilitude to the notion of the wall being an indoor crag. The apex of the central ridge was fourteen metres high in the middle, sloping to twelve metres at the sides. It even had character.

I have been involved with a number of businesses, but when it came to excitement and fun, the Foundry was the most exciting and the most fun. Nobody in Britain had tried to build a wall on this scale. I thought that if we provided Sheffield with a facility that was interesting and challenging, we would be able to attract the younger end of the climbing spectrum; little did we know that the Foundry would attract kids of all ages, from seven to seventy.

I used a large cardboard box to make a scaled down model of the building and used sheets of polystyrene to visualise what the wall would look like inside. The wall would be big, 500 square metres with a flat concrete floor – and puddles. Although the roof only reached fourteen metres, with overhanging panels we could make routes fifteen metres in length. We needed washrooms, showers, changing rooms and toilets. We needed a cafe and retail space. I wanted to have a state-of-the-art bouldering wall and made a polystyrene model of that, too. The Wave, as the bouldering wall is called, has proven to be the most-used feature of its type and attracts people now as much as it did when we opened twenty-five years ago.

Not only would the Foundry become the first and best new-generation climbing wall in Britain, it was also one of the cheapest. We didn't have a big budget. The total spend was £250,000 and that was after we were forced to make expensive alterations to meet fire regulations, something I hadn't taken into account. The work went well enough, but the footings for the Wave used vast amounts of concrete and took us fourteen feet down into the silt and gravel of the riverbank, which also added to the cost. We had hoped to open in October but in the end it was December 1991. Nobody knew what to expect. It was fascinating to watch climbers walking in for the first time. They would stop, and you'd hear gasps and expletives that we took as tributes to our investment. One of our competitors, when he first saw the Foundry, said: 'In future all climbing walls should be like this.' We were wrong on one count. Dick and I thought the Foundry would be a sideline. It turned out to be the main event.

The opening of the Foundry was not without controversy. One of the problems with subcommittees is that they attract people more interested in the committee than the work of the committee. The BMC's climbing-wall committee had come up with a set of guidelines that local councils could refer to when building new walls or converting old ones. One of the recommendations was that climbing walls should have holds made from real rock and that they should be cemented into the wall. This was not a good idea. The inability to change or move holds was a recipe for boring walls: from a commercial standpoint that would be a disaster. It was obvious to our management team that routes needed to be changed to maintain public interest. We had no intention of building a wall with fixed holds.

While we were designing and building the Foundry we discovered Sport England was making a grant available for an international competition-climbing venue. The Foundry was the only facility that could house such a wall, although the BMC led us to believe there was another site in the Sheffield area that had also registered interest. We were summoned to Leeds for a meeting with the BMC and Sport England. We refused point-blank to follow BMC guidelines, pointing out that a competition wall would have to have changeable holds. We had no faith in a subcommittee that had recognised local authority gymnasiums and leisure centres, often designed by architects, that were, almost without exception, a waste of time and public money. We didn't get the grant.

Our spat resulted in a discussion about what climbing walls were for. It was obvious that the BMC wasn't properly representing the needs of indoor climbers or the future of indoor climbing. Their subcommittee had little knowledge of what was happening in the real world. It had lost the right to influence design or construction. We weren't trying to mimic reality but create something that was both familiar and new, a climbing facility where climbers and non-climbers could have a few hours of fun. Fitness was a bonus, but we were really in the business of offering climbers something entertaining and innovative, which fitted in with their lives – not an idealised version of whatever someone on a committee thought climbing should be.

When the Foundry opened it was fantastically popular. There were 90,000 user-visits in the first year. That's an average of 250 climbers per day. Four hundred people a day came at the weekends. Unfortunately this popularity created a real danger. It could get so crowded there was the possibility of climbers falling on to other climbers. We had no alternative but to insist on climbers top-roping at peak times for the first few months. By the time summer arrived the novelty had worn off and we were able to open another leading wall.

It was obvious that the Foundry had hit the spot, and within a year new walls were opening on a regular basis. They had a huge impact, much bigger than I thought they would. There is now a new generation of climbers that only ever climbs on walls and never climbs outside. I don't see this as a problem; climbing on walls is simply a new game many people enjoy. If they only ever climb indoors, that's up to them. Walls have obviously led to higher standards of free climbing, both bolted and 'trad'. Because so many youngsters now start climbing on walls, the switch from bolts to trad has created its own risks. Those have to be managed and supervised. The advent of walls changed my view of teaching young children to climb. I used to think climbing was an activity best confined to consenting adults, because of the inherent danger. It wasn't something to be encouraged. With the levels of safety and control possible in climbing gyms, it's become possible for even very young children to climb in safety and have a whale of a time.

The success of the Foundry brought many prospective businesses to my door. A London architect asked for my advice in creating a climbing wall inside a group of grain silos on the River Thames on the Isle of Dogs. There were fifteen silos, about twenty feet in diameter and 120 feet high. I suggested they made an easy silo, a medium silo and an X-rated silo, with another for abseiling and rope-work, like the shaft in the ice shelf we dug in Antarctica. I suggested a zip wire and a flume for kayaks that ended in the Thames – and a powerful fan that you could fly above in a wingsuit.

My own fantasy climbing wall would be at least 300 feet high, with dihe-drals, cracks, overhanging walls, slabs, all outside. Inside would be a national climbing centre, with offices for the BMC, a large lecture hall, a museum, a national archive facility, accommodation, a training gym and a large indoor climbing wall.

If the Foundry was prospering, other parts of the business were becoming more difficult. After I bought Steve Bean's shares, ownership of the Wild Country group had become broader and more complex. I had need-ed to bring in investors. Dick Turnbull used a timely legacy to buy ten per cent of Wild Country and Outside; Mike Longden had taken out a second mortgage to invest a similar amount. From having been in a position of calling the shots, all the shots, I found myself being challenged by the now quite large management team. I became critical of the work of younger managers and irritated by their failure to see obvious solutions. In the shop Dick kept referring to 'us' and 'we': 'we want to do this', or 'we want to do such and such'. When I asked him who 'we' were he looked surprised – him and his staff of course.

'What about me?' I asked. Dick gave me a blank look as though I was being awkward. 'I only own three-quarters of the company.'

Another argument was over the Wild Country logo. After launching the company it took me three years to come up with a logo I liked. I got the inspiration while driving from Las Vegas to Snowbird to go skiing with friends. I'd left a motel north of St George before dawn, and as the sun came up, there was my logo. The sun cut by two thin bands of cloud, yellow at the top, orange in the middle and red at the bottom. The Wild Country USA team said there was a similarity to the logo of Comfort Inn Hotels and used to joke about it. When I found that the UK team thought we needed something new I disagreed, but did not fight the consensus, though in my own mind I was proud of the design and still thought it shouldn't change. The current management have readopted the setting sun and made it simpler and stronger. I was pleased as punch when I saw the logo on T-shirts made for Pete Whittaker and Tom Randall – the Wide Boyz – before they made their historic ascent of *Century Crack*, the 120-foot horizontal off-width in Canyonlands.

Most significantly, I was finding it increasingly difficult to work with Mike Longden, CEO of Wild Country. In July 1992, I reached breaking point. Two of my key sales staff, Andy Bowman and Steve Foster, had already left. Both of them were good friends – and still are. Steve in particular had been a fan of Wild Country from its earliest days. But neither of them could get on with Mike. My fear was that Dave Shaw, Wild Country's shop-floor manager, might also leave.

Then the owner of the Tideswell factory suggested we buy the property from him. It seemed to me a no-brainer. The cost of buying the factory was actually less than the cost of renting it. We could get a mortgage and in fifteen years the company would own a valuable and appreciating asset. Mike took the view that we were a manufacturing business, not a property company, and refused to discuss it further. It was this more than anything that prompted me to hive off the tent business and Mike with it. Wild Country would continue to manufacture mountaineering equipment and to this end we took a lease on a new workshop to make karabiners on an industrial estate in Chesterfield. The new company would be called Terra Nova Ltd and continue to make tents. Negotiations for the divorce got underway.

There had been other problems. When Steve Bean hold sold out, Hugh Banner bought a small shareholding. Hugh had previously made a range of small brass nuts, used for the thinnest cracks, to challenge the market leader RP – made by Roland Pauligk in Australia. I had taken a set of these nuts and used the high-speed belt sander to round off their sharp corners. I found they were particularly good on gritstone and granite but when I asked Hugh to make some prototypes, he refused point blank. I was surprised, and not sure what to do so backed off, feeling a little irritated. I soon found out the problem wasn't my design – I was the problem. He would have preferred it if Steve had taken over the business. What Hugh wanted was his own company, and now Steve Bean was out of the picture there was no reason to stay. Shortly after our exchange about the nuts, he resigned from the Wild Country board and set up HB Climbing Equipment in Llanberis. My rounded nuts went into production as Stones – small Rocks. I still prefer them to any other micro-nuts.

Hugh started by manufacturing TCUs: three-cam units. To do this he purchased lengths of Wild Country cams from our aluminium extruders but without consultation or permission. Whichever way I looked at this I couldn't see his actions as being anything other than a betrayal. I was also irritated that he thought I wouldn't notice what he was doing. I was tired of lawsuits and legal battles but we couldn't stand aside and let Hugh steal our cams, so we sued HB for the value of the extrusions, £14,000. I was surprised when Hugh countersued for the same amount for Wild Country's use of some of his lost-wax casts, whose value was a tenth of the extrusions.

It was soon obvious this was a tactic that Hugh, an ardent chess player all his life, was using to avoid a fast legal decision. Sure enough the case rumbled on and on, and by the time anybody got round to preparing the case we had all more or less forgotten what it was about. We settled out of court for our costs. I didn't mind that Hugh had left Wild Country to compete against me. That was just business. What hurt was the friendship I had shown him didn't seem to count for much. He showed me an approach to business unusual in the mountaineering market. It wasn't one I chose to emulate.

In the midst of this trauma, the demerger of Wild Country from its tent business was plodding on. Mike had shares in Outside that he did not want, and Dick had shares in Wild Country that Mike needed. There needed to be a share swap. We told Mike he would have to start paying for the use of the Wild Country name from January 1994, Mike said he wouldn't accept the 1992 valuation of the tent business for his share swap with Dick. That's how it went, tit for tat, like an argument between children.

On a Monday in mid February I arrived at the office of our solicitor, Andrew Hartley, to discuss tactics. Over the weekend I had picked up the tent catalogue Mike had just produced for his new company Terra Nova. I put this on the table for our lawyers to examine. There was a gasp of disbelief. The catalogue claimed Terra Nova was using the name Wild Country under licence. This wasn't just a lie; it broke the terms of our agreement with him. I wondered if Mike thought no one would notice. From being in a position of strength, Mike had handed us what he himself referred to as a 'loaded shotgun'.

The following Wednesday we had a scheduled meeting with Mike, Dick and Jonathan Hunt, the lawyer Dick and Mike had hired to oversee the demerger and the sale of Mike's shares in Outside. Andrew explained the significance of the catalogue and we immediately convened a board meeting to suspend Mike pending an investigation. Wild Country accountant Garry Walker and I went down to Alfreton and found more evidence Mike had been breaking our agreement. He'd even produced invoices with two VAT numbers, something that is illegal and could have risked his status as a chartered accountant. The new company had also been answering the phone as Wild Country. This in itself was action-able. Mike then tried to convince us that the catalogue had just been a sample for my approval and didn't know it had been widely circulated. It was a transparent lie.

We faced a simple choice. Either dismiss Mike or offer him six months' notice while we completed the demerger. We held another board meeting for the following Tuesday to review the evidence and reach a decision: we could continue the demerger swiftly and on our own terms. Negotiations were over. When I gave Mike his notice, he responded bitterly: was that all the thanks he got for all the work he'd done over the years? Even then he couldn't grasp the reasons we were getting rid of him.

The demerger went ahead a month later. I spent a wearisome day in Andrew Hartley's office dealing with a string of concessions. There was a certain amount of brinkmanship by both Mike and Dick. At seven o'clock in the evening I was asked to concede yet another point. I told Andrew I'd had enough. Andrew phoned Jonathan Hunt and told him there would be no more changes. We could hear Jonathan Hunt and the others laughing. Andrew said: 'No one's laughing here.' That was the end of it. We walked over to Jonathan Hunt's office at nine o'clock after a very long day and got through the signing by about ten-thirty. There was no sense of euphoria or even pleasure. There was no bottle of champagne. I simply thought: 'Thank God that's over.' I could not even bring myself to shake Mike's hand. I imagine he felt the same about me.

More problems piled up. In the spring and early summer of 1995 the climbing market in the USA was flat and sterling was strengthening, damaging exports. This made our trading position difficult. I was aware of the deteriorating situation so in the spring asked our accountant Garry Walker for a detailed cash-flow forecast. Garry nodded and I waited – in vain. I only have myself to blame. I should have put more pressure on Garry but time passed and no forecast was forthcoming. I asked again, indicating a degree of urgency. Still nothing. Garry said he was busy, but I failed to see to what extent he had taken his eye off the ball. Wild Country, always undercapitalised, was constantly at risk of overtrading, essentially selling more than our cash flow would allow us to manufacture.

In September 1995 Garry told me that we had a problem. We didn't have enough money coming in to get through the next month. I had suspected we were sailing close to the wind, but as I had asked Garry for a forecast back in March and repeated the request several times since, I assumed he had things under control. I wasn't prepared for the disaster the company now faced. We were at the limit of our borrowing. I was personally guaranteeing the whole of our overdraft facility at the bank. It was far too late to have a fire sale; we needed the money now. I didn't have much in the way of options. I asked the bank how much I could borrow against my share of Outside. The answer was: not a lot. I asked if I could remortgage the house: it was already mortgaged up to the hilt. The sensible thing to do was let Wild Country go into receivership and fall back on Outside. But that was impossible. I would be selling my soul. Now it had come to the crunch I couldn't pull the plug on Wild Country. The cost could not be measured. If I could sell my holding in Outside and get through the next few months then maybe Wild Country would survive. Dick had already expressed a wish to take control of the shop and we'd been discussing terms.

Those were black days. I was surprised by how many people knew about my problem and took an interest. I even got a call from Chris Brasher, the Olympic runner, journalist and founder of Brasher boots, expressing an interest in the tent business. He was far too late.

My meeting with Dick was tough. He said he was only interested in acquiring a controlling interest in the shop. I told him it was all or nothing; he had to buy the whole lot. I was not going to jeopardise Wild Country's chance of survival by not giving it my best shot. It is always difficult to value a private company but a starting point was the value of Outside's assets, most of which was the five years we'd spent paying off the mortgage and improvements to the building. I didn't know what Outside was worth, but it must have had verifiable assets of well over £100,000. Add to that the fact that it was now a well-established business. In an open sale the growth of turnover and growth in profits and the company's goodwill could well be worth double its asset value, or three times, or even four times. But this wasn't an open sale and the chance of finding another buyer at such short notice was too small to waste any time on it. Dick was the only buyer.

I had to do a deal very soon. It was as though there was a time bomb under my office desk. If I didn't find agreement with Dick, Wild Country would go into receivership, putting the jobs of fifty employees, colleagues and friends in jeopardy. I felt a realistic value could be well into six figures, but under the circumstances – a forced sale – my asset value might be halved. If I valued my holding at cost, surely I could find a buyer who would snap it up? Would 150 grand be enough to pull Wild Country through? The bomb was still ticking.

Dick made me an offer. At first I thought he was joking. Then I realised he was serious. My guts began to tie themselves in knots. I felt sick. I didn't know what to say. I couldn't say anything. I couldn't trust my voice not to give me away. I was close to tears. I thought about what Jan had told me the previous evening: 'Why not let Wild Country go down? You and Nick could run the shop together.' The sensible option, to let Wild Country fail, was unthinkable. I have to hand it to Dick. He knew me better than I knew myself. He knew I would put Wild Country before the shop. The day I sold Outside was the blackest of my life. But at least I could still look at myself in the mirror.

I had been working hard for twenty years and was getting tired. I felt personally under siege. If you own a small business, one of the most important things you have to do is to develop an exit strategy. Who might buy the company? How much are they going to pay you? What will your role be in the new regime? I had first discussed the idea of merging Wild Country and DMM in the early nineties. They were the obvious people and I was on good terms with DMM directors Richard Cuthbertson and Fred Hall. Now, with the short-term future of Wild Country in the balance, I wanted to get out. While I concluded my deal to sell Outside and secure the future of Wild Country, I continued negotiations with DMM. Our accountant Garry had visions of a management buyout and tried to persuade the workforce I was threatening their future. Nothing could have been further from the truth; I simply wanted the company to remain part of the climbing community. In early 1996, the deal for the merger of DMM and Wild Country went ahead. After almost twenty years in business, I was suddenly retired.

Aerial photo of Stanage Edge, August 1973.

15 INFINITY ON TRIAL

Two years after selling Wild Country, I came home from a climbing trip to Spain to discover I had Parkinson's disease. Any plans I might have had for a long and happy retirement disappeared overnight. Jan said I was in denial. I certainly didn't want to believe it. I was expecting to wake up and find it was all a bad dream. A friend in my local Parkinson's group, newly diagnosed, described his feelings on being told he had the disease as 'helpless rage'. That seemed wholly understandable to me.

I cast my mind back to my own reaction. It was a lovely summer day. Jan was outside in the garden when I got home; she asked me how I had got on. I told her I had Parkinson's and laughed. I really had no idea what was wrong with me. Friends tell me I became very quiet, not myself, withdrawn. I think that for a couple of months I was clinically depressed. If that's true, it's hardly surprising. Parkinson's is a failure of the brain to make the neurotransmitter dopamine, essential for sending nerve signals round the body. For someone whose life revolved around physical activity, this was a disaster.

Earlier that year I had agreed with a friend to walk the GR20, the justly celebrated route through the mountains of Corsica. Jan and I had met John and his family on Corsica several years before and we'd stayed in touch. John was an ex-paratrooper who had done a business degree and now had a senior job in the oil industry. We often talked about the GR20, considered by many to be the best walk in Europe, 180 kilometres down the spine of the island. October seemed like the best month.

Despite the Parkinson's diagnosis I could see no reason to cancel, although my right knee was beginning to give me some arthritic pain. John and I agreed we would go as lightweight as possible, but because we would be doing this in October when there was little or no chance of getting food without a long detour, we would have quite big packs when we set off. When I saw the size of John's pack I wondered what I had forgotten. Being an ex-soldier, John had a Bergen rucksack that weighed considerably more than my stripped-down pack. John's load was a third heavier than mine.

We agreed we would take turns to cook, but had not discussed menus. My bag of food was smaller than John's. I had organised my breakfast food into twelve poly bags.

'What's that?' John asked, nodding at my bags of home-made granola.

'Granola.'

'What's granola?'

I explained it was a mixture of cereals and nuts, baked in oil and honey.

John gave my breakfast bag a disparaging look. 'Like cornflakes you mean? I always have porridge.' There was no room for argument about which was superior.

Before setting out I had made more than enough granola and packed the extra into each of the bags that held my daily quota as a sort of emergency stash that could be used as trail food. I knew that an army marches on its stomach but John's choice of food was not state of the art. His soup took twelve minutes to boil. Next morning John was still heating water to clean his porridge bowl when I was packed up and ready to go. We had agreed to make our own lunch but I thought I detected a covetous glance towards my pumpernickel and salami sandwich, dried apricots, marzipan and date layer-cake. That evening I had a steaming cup of broccoli and Stilton Cup a Soup in John's hand within three minutes of arriving at the hut.

At breakfast on the third day it was obvious I had overdone the granola. I had only just opened the second of my one-per-day bags. John asked me if he could try some. I could see he liked it. We abandoned the porridge oats as an offering to the Corsican mountain gods, one they promptly passed on to the birds, a little way from the hut.

Our trip was a great success. Apart from one day of mist and drizzle we enjoyed beautiful, crisp, autumn weather, camping out with just a Gore-Tex bivvy bag for several nights. The walking was unrivalled and there were remarkably few people on the route. We shared a hut for two nights with a platoon of French solders; John was very impressed with their charcoal fleece jackets. We also met an Egyptian woman of a certain age crossing the Cirque de la Solitude, a strenuous, technical, exposed and, in places, steep section of slabs with ladders and cables to encourage the less experienced. By the time I got home I knew that there was life after Parkinson's.

To begin with, after my diagnosis in August 1998, I had few problems from Parkinson's. I was very fit and I made an effort to remain fit. I sometimes felt a lack of confidence, but I had always had more of that than was good for me. The effects are variable. There are twenty-eight recognised symptoms and you can suffer from some of them or all of them, though not usually at the same time. Most are physical disabilities like not being able to do up shoelaces and buttons, but there is a general feeling of malaise that I call 'feeling Parkinsony'. This will vary from day to day or even hour to hour. The closest comparison I can make is with jet lag.

For a time I went climbing as usual except I would only lead climbs I had done before. I remember doing *Rubberneck* at the Roaches and burning off my regular group, the Tuesday night team. Another Tuesday night I held the ropes of Colin Foord, a good friend with whom I had done countless climbs, as he tried *Bachelor's Left-hand* at Hen Cloud. Colin must have been having a bad day because he bailed out. Almost without thinking I said I would have a go. There is an awkward, teetering start followed by a strenuous finger-pocket pull on the crux. Then an easy slab, a steep crack on good hand jams and a little grovel gets you to the top. Much to my surprise I did it, not with ease, but competently. I was not aware that the legendary Martin Boysen had been watching me, but I glowed with pride when later he patted my shoulder and said: 'Good lead.'

The last Extreme I led was *Visions of Johanna* at Bosigran on the Cornish coast – an old favourite. I usually combined it with the top pitch of *Little Brown Jug*, my favourite way up the crag. I had been there in April 1968 when Mark Springett, Frank Cannings and Peter Biven made the first ascent of *Visions*, playing Bob Dylan on a tape deck at the foot of the cliff. Thirty-seven years later I climbed it again with my daughter Jody. I led the first pitch, which is quite technical, fingery and not easy to protect. This takes you up to the slabby crux pitch of *Little Brown Jug* and the final overhanging crack where I was glad to have the rope above me. It was a hard struggle and I knew it was my last time.

Sheffield is a good place to have Parkinson's. There are several neurologists who specialise in it, and three specialist nurses. I have a checkup every six to twelve months. The nurses put you through the same set of tests every year. One of the tests is about short-term memory. One time I was asked to remember an address that they gave me soon after

I checked in. When the nurse told me she was going to ask me to remember an address, I was ready.

'42 West Street.'

It was the same address I'd been given the year before. At least my long-term memory was fine. My new neurologist, Dr Aijaz Khan, asked me what I would ask for if he could give me one wish. When I said I would like to be able to continue to climb he thought I was joking and was quite amused when I told him I was being serious.

When I was diagnosed eighteen years ago I was told that there would be a cure within five years. I don't know where this optimistic piece of information originated, but it was not true then and when I read some of the literature, which I don't do very often, I am not persuaded it has changed very much now. There have been many improvements, like the clever use of medication cocktails that improve the take-up of the main drug. There are two main types of Parkinson's drug: Levodopa, or artificial dopamine, and a group of drugs called dopamine agonists, which prompt the body to produce more of its own. At the moment I take the maximum dose of a particular dopamine agonist, which comes in a prolonged-release pill. I also take four or five, depending how I feel, of a cocktail of three types of Levodopa pill. Add to that Co-codamol, Naproxen and Tramadol, three painkillers that give me relief from back surgery and the insertion of a titanium cage. This is topped off with Omeprazole to stop the other drugs from rotting my stomach. Listen carefully and after breakfast you will hear me rattle.

It may sound daft when I say I am lucky, but people I know, who were diagnosed around the same time as me, are in a worse state. I have good days and bad days, and if you were to meet me on my best days you might not know I had a problem. I seem to be fortunate in the way I respond to drugs. If the neurologist tells me that such and such a drug will do something specific, it usually does. Moreover, it does so, by and large, with the minimum of side effects. People say I have a good attitude, but the fact is I'm stubborn.

In 2002, the president of the British Mountaineering Council, Dave Musgrove, announced he wasn't going to offer himself for re-election. He had taken over with the BMC in a state of financial crisis and had devoted more time than a president would normally. He needed to get back to his life. I was the only person willing to accept the nomination. My reason for doing so was half selfish, half altruistic. Parkinson's was causing a slow, but steady deterioration in my ability to climb, and I was glad to have the opportunity to do a job that kept me involved in the mountaineering world. The job would be both a challenge and also an opportunity to contribute something. I like to think that my loss was the BMC's gain, but not everyone would agree with that.

I had been outspoken with my views on the BMC, not least over the Foundry. I had even offered my shares to the BMC if it relocated, a cat among some startled pigeons that was welcomed by some volunteers but met with stony silence from the paid staff. Yet if I seemed critical or subversive, I believe I had earned the right. I was no stranger to the BMC, having volunteered in a number of roles over the years. During the seventies I had been secretary of the Peak Area committee and in that role attended the BMC's management committee. I had been a founder member and first secretary of the access and conservation committee, organising a mountain conservation symposium at Plas y Brenin in 1977. With Pete Livesey, I was one of two BMC nominees on the mountain training committee during the difficult period of bad relations with the Sports Council. I had also been the BMC nominee on the board of the Peak District National Park for six years. Although I had not been so involved since founding Wild Country, I still attended area meetings and the BMC's annual general meeting.

So if I was not the most popular elected officer of the BMC, I hoped I was equally known for my willingness to get stuck in and, where necessary, make changes. I was very clear in my mind about what was required and how it should be done. The senior personnel needed to stop thinking of themselves as masters and to think of themselves as servants. The management committee, made up of volunteers, was mistrustful of the management team, and the senior managers lacked respect for the management committee. The previous CEO had left at short notice. The financial controls that should have been in place were inadequate. The financial controller had just been sacked. The BMC was paying for an expensive mountaineering exhibition at Rheged in the Lake District. A £3,000 grant authorised by the management committee had somehow mushroomed into debts more than fifty times that amount.

My ability to make changes was limited. If I were to make any kind of contribution I would need the help of the new CEO, Dave Turnbull.

Fortunately Dave had an open mind and we quickly developed a good working relationship. I was also lucky in having a newly elected treasurer, Gordon Adshead, who had put in place new financial controls. But changing the BMC's course was like steering the proverbial oil tanker.

Among the issues that concerned me most were policy making and the lack of opportunity for members to debate issues. The former was structural. The management committee – known as ManCom – wasn't actually there to manage the BMC, although some of its members thought so. ManCom was in reality the senior committee overseeing policy. The finance committee oversaw major expenditure. Some of the senior paid staff thought it was their job to make policy and ignored ManCom. My intention was to rewrite the articles of association and change both the culture and the voting system. ManCom finally agreed to change its name to National Council.

Getting rid of the block vote was harder. The BMC had been founded in 1944 as a way for the great and the good of the Alpine Club to give climbers national representation without needing to open its doors to the great unwashed, thus preserving the club's elitism. However, just to be on the safe side, the Alpine Club also gave itself the right to veto the BMC's choice of president and secretary. Member clubs might have one vote for each member, but at the BMC's AGM each club could only cast its vote as a block. Were a vote necessary, a phone call between the secretaries of the AC, the Climbers' Club and the Fell and Rock Climbing Club would dictate the result.

During the eighties the BMC began allowing individuals to join so they could buy insurance. This became a nice little earner for the BMC and, over time, the number of individual members gradually overtook the club membership. But these individual members did not have a vote at the BMC's annual general meetings. Changing that was a major achievement, akin, according to Ivor Delafield, sitting on the competition committee, to persuading turkeys to vote for Christmas.

Curiously, even though the big clubs had all the power, they offered the least opportunity to discuss policy. Small clubs meeting in pubs on a Thursday evening to make arrangements for the weekend would inevitably discuss important issues. But the members of the bigger clubs didn't meet in this way. And yet their secretaries could go to the BMC's AGM and cast a thousand votes for a policy that had not been the subject of debate.

My own club, the Climbers' Club, had massive voting power but never discussed the BMC, not even at their AGM. When I was president of the CC, I introduced a new, informal meeting that took place before the CC's AGM where any subject could be discussed. The only proviso was that the BMC should always be the first item on the agenda. This worked well. It created a more relaxed atmosphere, helped sort out minor problems and had the excellent effect of speeding up the AGM.

────────

I didn't have long to wait for my first crisis at the BMC. During my first week in office, an email arrived from Sport England telling the BMC to prepare for a substantial cut in funding. The CEO would normally have dealt with this, but Dave Turnbull was having a few days off after working long hours over the AGM weekend. I could have waited for Dave to get back, but that would have been a cop-out. Anyway, crises are an opportunity, and I needed to stamp some authority. I phoned Zoe, the liaison officer at Sport England who normally handled BMC matters, with a request for a meeting with Richard Caldicott, chief executive of UK Sport, but was told there was a waiting time of six months: so join the queue.

By coincidence, it was the fiftieth anniversary of the coronation of the Queen, and, of course, the first ascent of Everest. A big jamboree was being held at the Leicester Square Odeon at which the Queen and the Duke of Edinburgh would be honoured guests. Anybody who was anybody in the climbing world would be present. I phoned Chris Bonington and asked if he could get me an extra ticket and another for the drinks party at St James's Palace afterwards, explaining who the extra ticket was for and giving him an outline of my plan. Chris got back to me very quickly promising a ticket.

I got hold of Zoe again and asked her if she thought her boss would appreciate an invitation to the Leicester Square event. The response was positive and fast. I then asked if we could have a meeting with her on the morning of the event, to which she agreed. Then we emailed Richard Caldicott telling him that we were going to be at a meeting in the Sport England offices on the morning of the event and would he like us to escort him to Leicester Square afterwards? We had the undivided attention of the chief executive for fifty minutes and the problem was solved.

Other problems were less tractable. Access was and always will be a major part of the BMC's work, and a burning issue nationally. While I was president I found myself caught between opposing views. There was an on-going and occasionally heated exchange between members of the access committee on the one hand and Alan Blackshaw, a patron of the BMC, who had successfully made the case for new access laws in Scotland. He had been critical of the way in which the landmark Countryside and Rights of Way Act was being implemented. Blackshaw argued the right of access the new law would give us was not as advantageous as it appeared and a waste of resources. As the newly elected BMC president I found myself piggy in the middle. I wanted to get the two sides together to explore the common ground, but the argument had become personal.

The more I became involved and examined the arguments, the more compelling I found Blackshaw's arguments. In fact the logic of Blackshaw's case seemed to me irrefutable. What I found difficult was his refusal to meet his critics halfway. One cannot blame him for that. He had done more research than anyone else and painstakingly responded to all the objections to his arguments. He said he would not meet with anyone from the access committee until his questions had been answered.

Blackshaw relied on a series of statements from weighty jurists that supported his argument that there was an existing common law right of access in England and Wales, like this statement made on 4 March 1892 by the famous lawyer and president of the Alpine Club James Bryce who made concerted efforts to make such rights statutory – without success: 'There is no such thing in the old customs of this country, as the right of exclusion for the purposes of the mere pleasure of the individual; and there is no ground in law, or reason for excluding persons from a mountain, the right having there no value except to prevent other people enjoying themselves.' There were similar statements from people like Sir Arthur Hobhouse, educated at Eton and Trinity, Cambridge, whose 1947 report formed the basis of the national park system: 'The right to wander has not been contested to any serious extent.' And Lord Denning, later Master of the Rolls, who two years after the Hobhouse Report could say: 'Despite all the great changes that have come about in the other freedoms, this freedom has in our country remained intact.'

Kevin Gray, professor of law at Cambridge University and himself a keen hillwalker, was asked to write a paper for the BMC access committee, clarifying the law with respect to access. In his paper he wrote that common law customary freedoms were 'almost uniformly restrictive and prohibitory'. As a layman, I couldn't see how Professor Gray could maintain 'there has been no general common law right of access', after reading opinions like those Blackshaw had marshalled. He continued: 'English Law has traditionally refused to accept that members of the public can ever acquire the right to wander at large over land in the proprietorship of another person.' I felt he had missed the point. The public is not attempting to acquire a new right, but exercising a customary freedom that has existed from time immemorial.

The law of trespass has not been successfully invoked in living memory. In order to break the law, one has to do damage, or something that is illegal. It seems that to all intents and purposes, the activity of trespassing in the countryside has no legal implications, and the old 'wooden lie', that trespassers will be prosecuted, remains just that – a lie.

I had some evidence for this from my own experience. Towards the end of my time as a member of the national park board, I attended meetings with the Country Landowners Association to negotiate new terms of compensation for landowners who had signed access agreements. These agreements gave the public access to a large area of moorland, for which the national park deserved and got considerable credit. In return for access the landowners were paid an agreed fee per acre of land and per mile of drystone wall.

After twenty years the original agreements were coming to an end and everybody wanted to make sure the new agreements were in place when the old agreements lapsed. The landowners wanted an increase of 100 per cent plus inflation. This was unrealistic: the Peak Park had no money. The best they could do was to offer the original terms plus inflation.

We spent the whole afternoon going nowhere. The time was approaching five o'clock and everyone was resigned to having to call another meeting. I was wondering what would happen if there was no new agreement. This was something that, rather surprisingly, had not been discussed prior to the meeting. It struck me as odd that nobody from the landowners' side had threatened to take this line. It would be difficult for the national park to suggest the possibility. Then it struck me, like a powerful light being turned on, that such an outcome would be the last thing the landowners wanted. If there was no new agreement, they would forego all their compensation, and the public, having got used to going where they liked over the moors for twenty years, would just continue to go walking. The national park would no longer be required to provide a ranger service to police the access land.

I caught the chairman's eye. 'As we seem to be as far from an agreement as we have ever been, what arrangements will the landowners put in place to deter the public from walking on their land?'

There was a long silence, which emphasised the reluctance of anyone to answer the question. A couple of board members put their hands up to speak, but the lawyer for the landowners asked the chairman if they could take a few minutes to discuss my question in private. Four minutes later they returned and the lawyer agreed that they would accept the Peak Park's offer. I don't know what transpired in those four minutes, but suddenly the meeting was over. The details could be sorted out later. Briefcase in hand I headed for the door, only to be waylaid by the Country Landowners Association lawyer who, with an amused smile, said: 'Your timing was impeccable.'

Having been involved in the Peak District National Park in several capacities over the years, it gives me no pleasure to conclude that there are in fact no national parks in Britain. No doubt this will come as something of a surprise. Our so-called national parks were designated in the early fifties to do three things, principles that were updated in the 1995 Environment Act. There are two statutory requirements: conserve and enhance the natural beauty, wildlife and cultural heritage of the parks; and promote opportunities for the understanding and enjoyment of the special qualities of national parks by the public. They also have the duty to seek to foster the economic and social wellbeing of local communities within the national parks.

Even a cursory study of these objectives shows they are mutually exclusive. Take conservation of the landscape. Large parts of our national parks have been laid waste for the extraction of limestone and minerals – and to provide jobs. This indicates a total lack of understanding of what a national park should be – or else a lack of commitment to their ideals. In real national parks, you don't get permission to dig up large chunks of land. Some of the Peak District has been dug up twice, to make sure every last bit of economic value has been stripped from the rocks. By comparison, little has been done to provide for the enjoyment of the landscape.

The word 'national' suggests the land belongs to the nation, which of course it doesn't. The total area designated as national park amounts to ten per cent of the surface area of England and Wales, yet the nation owns less than one per cent of this land. Park boundaries were instead decided by a small committee driving around the countryside drawing lines on a map.

These lines were as effective at protecting landscape and enhancing nature as, well, a line drawn on a map. National parks remain one of the biggest con tricks played on the people of this country.

If we are serious about protecting what remains of our natural heritage, if we want to take national parks seriously, then there should be a national organisation implementing a statutory plan with long-term objectives and a staff that are trained to national standards. The land included should no longer be the consequence of an arbitrary line on a map, but surveyed and assessed, with new ideas about the scale of landscape conservation taken into account. There should be decisions taken to give land back to the wild rather than persisting in uneconomic forms of farming and the widespread degrading of a landscape to maximise numbers of grouse.

The purchase of land covered by this survey will give a projected price, a formula for valuing land for purchase in the future. The timescale for this purchase can be as long as the nation wishes, perhaps as long as 250 years with the necessary tax breaks for those who are cooperative in implementing this purchase, particularly at the outset. Only then will we get national parks that are truly national.

———

The initiative at the BMC that gave me the greatest pleasure was the development of British Mountain Maps, one of those happy accidents that solve a problem. I was invited to the opening of an exhibition at Rheged in Cumbria on the history of the Ordnance Survey and after the formalities found myself eating lunch at the same table as Vanessa Lawrence, the Ordnance Survey's longest-serving director general in a hundred years. During the course of the meal I asked her why her organisation didn't print maps on plastic as other map producers do. Her answer was that they would be too expensive. I was surprised. I already had several plastic maps: one of Killarney in Ireland, a French map, a very useful Lonely Planet map of London and best of all a plastic map of Yosemite National Park published by National Geographic that cost me $8.50, considerably less than the price of a standard OS 1:50,000 paper map. And it didn't fall apart when wet.

Being familiar with price structures in America, I could not let this go. If the Americans could put a plastic map on the market for $8.50, surely the Ordnance Survey could do it for £8.50? We were sitting at a round table set for ten people so it was possible for all of them to hear our conversation. I became aware that the ears of the others at the table were swivelling in my direction to listen in. I also detected a hint of irritation in her voice. It was quite clear she didn't want to pursue the conversation.

'Mountaineers rely for their lives on the integrity of their – your – maps.'

I hoped for some minor concession or even an expression of sympathy but she seemed wholly dismissive.

I was somewhat taken aback by her refusal to meet me halfway, but any further discussion was clearly pointless and would only exacerbate an already uncomfortable situation. I decided then and there I would make it her problem. The map project was highly suitable for the BMC. If we could come up with a set of maps designed specifically for mountaineers and hillwalkers it would help address the criticism that the BMC never did anything for hillwalkers and promote the BMC's brand. I have always liked the 1:40,000 scale for walking and running on British hills but there was an additional bonus I had not anticipated. This scale means that the kilometre squares on the map are also one-inch square, making estimating distances that little bit easier. And by using plastic, we could use the reverse side to print useful safety information and enlarge key areas.

The Ordnance Survey used to be a national institution, part of Britain's military defence. When it was privatised new articles of association required it to make maps for anyone with a legitimate requirement. I got in touch with them and told them what I wanted: a 1:40,000-scale map printed on plastic that had none of the usual boundaries, parish, county, national park, country or constituency. I was told I had to have bounda-ries. I asked them why. 'That's our policy,' they said. After that I gave up on the Ordnance Survey. Next day I got in touch with Sue Harvey of Harvey Maps in Scotland. Harvey had pioneered the 1:40,000 scale I liked so much. I found them far more receptive and easy to work with.

One of my particular dislikes on OS maps is their use of shading. The Swiss do it well, but their mountains lend themselves to this treatment. I wanted to use layered colouring on BMC maps. This is where the various bands of contour lines become darker the higher the area depicted. The problem with this is that the ridges and the summits tend to be much darker than the valleys and lowland. As most of the main features, paths and names are on the high ground I wanted light colours on the high ground. I spent a lot of time with watercolour washes, trying to find the right colour combinations to give an impression of height but on which we could print paths and names. I ended up with a solution that was unexpected and counterintuitive. I found that by starting with light colours in the valleys, getting darker up to halfway height and then becoming lighter from midway upwards to the ridges and summits was the best solution. The ridges were printed light grey.

For the reverse side of the map, I asked the British Geological Survey if they would be interested in providing graphics for a simple, educative geological map on the reverse side. They invited me down to Nottingham to discuss the project. I was a little disappointed by the first map: the colours seemed muddy. However, within a few days I received an enthusiastic letter from the head of the BGS in Edinburgh. He really liked the project and promised improved artwork and drawings of the geomorphology relevant to the area of the main map.

My main concern was that the maps might not be as durable as we were claiming so I embarked on a series of tests. I cut an A4-sized section out of a map and kept it on the dashboard of my car to see if the sun would bleach it. After three summer months the map seemed unaffected. I cut two footbed shapes out of a map and inserted them inside my shoes, and another pair in my trainers. I wanted to see if the print would wear off. After a month they were a bit creased, but still quite readable.

The BMC finance committee was wary of getting involved with a project requiring quite a substantial outlay. I was a little bit miffed when one of its members asked what experience I had to make me so certain the maps would be profitable. I thought my track record spoke for itself but let that pass.

We planned to launch the map at the Kendal Mountain Festival. Andy Gowland, marketing manager of the BMC, suggested we print off some sample maps on plastic and put them in *Trail* magazine. It would illustrate their strength, and indicate our commitment to the product. We could invite the readers to mutilate, tear and generally abuse the samples. The idea worked very well.

Our first map, of the Lake District, launched at the Kendal Mountain Festival in 2006. Doug Scott did the honours, carrying a bucket of water on to the stage, setting it down and pulling a plastic map out of the bucket. He shook the water off the map before laying it on the floor. Doug's twelve-year-old son stood in the middle of the map while four of us grabbed a corner each and lifted him up. The audience rose to its feet and gave the map a standing ovation. Now, eight years later, there are sixteen in the series and I am told that the Lake District edition out-sells the equivalent from the Ordnance Survey. Of all the items that the BMC markets, the maps are the runaway bestseller. Next day an angry lady tackled me, complaining that if a map were to blow away in the wind, it would take many years to decay. I did not have an immediate answer to this criticism but it struck me later that if a walker or climber were to find one of these maps all they would have to do would be to wash the mud off in a stream, shake it out and fold it up for future use.

When the Lakes map had proved itself, the BMC executive committee negotiated with Harvey Maps, giving them the publishing rights. The BMC would get a special wholesale price linked to the purchase volume. Snowdonia North came next followed by the Dark Peak. Then came Ben Nevis and Glencoe followed by the Cairngorms and Lochnagar. My favourite is still the Lakes followed by Ben Nevis and Glencoe. There are a few gaps I would like to see filled, mainly in Scotland. I have been trying to fit the mountainous islands, Arran, Mull and the Black and Red Cuillins of Skye, on to a single sheet. It would have been nice also to include the Black Mountains on the back of the Brecon Beacons map as we did with Lochnagar on the Cairngorms map.

I never intended for there to be a White Peak map, since this isn't really a mountain area, but such was the demand that Harvey Maps felt obliged to print it. They discussed it with me and I suggested that if they did print it, they should include all the drystone walls. This involved a lot of new cartography, but the map is the better for it. Some day, maybe, the Ordnance Survey will print some of its maps on polyethylene, but if it does, I hope it reviews its policy of printing all those unwanted boundaries that make route finding more difficult. In the meantime I commend the BMC Mountain Maps for their excellence and good value.

Going for it in the one-kilometre time trial at Morzine in 1988.
I was third-fastest in the morning session.

16 SWANSONG

We woke early to an immense roar. I stuck my head out of the tent. Brightly coloured hot-air balloons were lifting into a flawless blue sky all around us, gas burners at full throttle. I pinched myself to make sure I wasn't dreaming. We had left Derbyshire the day before during one of the wettest summers on record, determined to find something dry to climb. We had arrived in the Lauterbrunnen valley in the same dismal conditions, rain hammering down, happy to settle for somewhere to camp. But I knew because of Parkinson's this would probably be my last Alpine holiday and I wanted to do more than dream. I stuck my head further out of the tent and saw the Lauterbrunnen Wall covered in fresh snow. That looked real enough.

Over coffee we looked at the guidebook. I had done a lot of climbing in Britain with Colin Foord but had never climbed with him in the Alps. For the next eleven days the weather became miraculous; we were grilled by the sun and bagged a clutch of high Bernese Oberland summits that would gladden the heart of any fifty-six-year-old. It seemed everything we tried came off. When I asked how much it would cost to park our car at the Hotel Wetterhorn, the receptionist told us we should just buy a beer when we came back. I had to pinch myself again.

I can recommend the path to the Gleckstein Hut; it's one of the truly great Alpine hikes. Clinging to the side of limestone cliffs, it offers a degree of exposure that concentrates the mind, until, rounding a corner, you get superb views up to the Schreckhorn and across to the Mittellegi Ridge of the Eiger. The higher you climb the wider the views across Grindelwald expand before the path takes you through a waterfall and up some zigzags to a magnificent hut with a warm welcome.

Hut food seemed to have improved since my last Alpine season and the red wine I had smuggled into my pack, unknown to Colin, made it a feast. I suspected he might not approve of alcohol on the mountain so I had judiciously limited our supply to a single litre. Frown he did. For a full five seconds he refused all offers. Then he relaxed. 'Okay then, just a drop.' A tense moment was over.

We had chosen to climb the Wetterhorn because it was comparatively low at 3,700 metres, and via the route taken by Sir Alfred Wills, since the guidebook recommended it as a good warm-up and the historical link – Wills being the judge who sentenced Oscar Wilde to Reading jail. Somehow we failed to notice that the climb was 1,400 metres long, so that turned into a bit of a trial as well.

Thanks to the bad weather the route hadn't been climbed that month and remained buried in masses of soft snow. Our lack of mountain fitness and the altitude would have been challenge enough given the conditions, but just to add complexity, my right knee had grown resentful of a lifetime of going downhill and hurt like hell. Colin looked after me like a professional but the descent consequently took as long as the ascent. At least we reached the summit, the only party to do so that day. The couloir crossing at the bottom of the long ridge provides the meat of the climb, but while it was thoroughly frozen in the morning, it proved exciting on the return, with regular avalanches of wet snow, water and big rocks firing down from the walls above. We got back to the hut in total darkness, seventeen hours after leaving it, a tribute to our perseverance and endurance if not our fitness. We received an extravagant welcome from the hut guardian who fed us and showed us into the guides' room to sleep. We descended to the valley next day.

In my experience, at this stage of an Alpine season, just as you've warmed up, the weather breaks and you get a fortnight's enforced rest. No such luck in this 'worst-of-all seasons'. The pressure remained high and the weather fair so in the morning we caught the train up to Kleine Scheidegg for the impressively serious scramble up to the Guggi Hut. Our packs were pared down to the minimum of ice gear and a litre of red wine.

The Nollen route on the Mönch, with its famous 'ice nose', is as long as the Wills but substantially harder. My heart was in my mouth at the start, soloing up loose sloping ledges like a cat on an old tiled roof. In the light of our headlamps, the exposure seemed incredible. Finally we put crampons on and began soloing up to the two long and steep pitches of the ice nose. These Colin disposed of very quickly. An easy snow slope led up to a harder mixed ridge and we were then traversing the summit snow ridge to join the hordes, who had arrived via the much shorter regular route on the other side.

The Mönchsjoch Hut was seriously crowded so despite arriving in time for tea – an appreciable improvement on our last adventure – we had to wait for the second serving and then had to sleep on the dining-room floor. This meant we had an early start for the regular route on the Jungfrau, which requires a long hike before you get to do any climbing. At least there was lots of firm snow covering the route's loose rock. Unhappily, we caught up a large party of Belgians, and thanks to age and condition, weren't quite strong enough to break out of their tracks and overtake them. There was some compensation at the end of the day. The train down from the Jungfraujoch was so crowded there was no time for the guard to check the tickets we didn't have.

With three routes in the bag, we ate rösti, slept late and spent the day writing postcards and having afternoon tea. Annoyingly, next day the elements were against us: more blue sky and fine weather. We set out for the Finsteraarhorn, a properly remote mountain, at half past five in the morning, taking the cheap early train – called, rather breezily, the 'Good Morning!' – to the Jungfraujoch and then marching downhill for two hours to Concordia. From there we hiked up the Grüneggfirn, over the Grünhornlücke and down to the Fieschergletscher, reaching the Finsteraarhorn Hut at teatime.

Having been dogged persistently by good weather we ran into some luck early next morning. Half an hour after setting out, thunder heralded the start of an unexpected storm and we scuttled back in time to avoid the rain and went back to bed for the sheer luxury of sleeping till noon. Next day we were first to the summit but as a result of my reluctant right knee last back to the hut. Nursing my knee that evening while reading about our next objective, the Fiescherhorn, I discovered our descent route was the work of my great uncle Hermann way back in 1887. Thanks to yet more damnably perfect weather, we had no choice but to climb both Fiescherhorns – the Hinter and the Grosser. And Uncle Hermann's route wasn't quite so easy in descent, starting as it did straight down the 3,000-foot ice-slope of the Fiescherwand which we forsook for the tedious North Ridge and a long slog up the aptly named 'Eternal Snow' to the Mönchsjoch and back just in time for the last train.

We could see the chiselled features of the young blond Teutonic ticket inspector making a minute inspection of each ticket as it was presented to him. Honesty was clearly going to be the best policy. When it came to our turn, we pointed out that our tickets had expired and could we pay for an upgrade? Instead of handcuffing us and phoning the police, he smiled.

'Never mind mate,' he said with a strong New Zealand accent. 'Looks like the mountains gave you a hard enough time already!' We pinched ourselves yet again, but, yes, we were awake and this was still Switzerland.

So ended what some might call our holiday. We got back to our tent, showered, and dined that evening in considerable style. During the night, a violent thunderstorm interrupted our well-earned sleep and when we woke again the mountains were covered in fresh snow.

My last trip to the Himalaya came in 2000. Russell Brice invited me on a commercial expedition to the north side of Everest, at the time very much Russ's domain. He had been working with the Chinese mountaineering authorities to build a climbers' hut in the Rongbuk valley. Only later would he give up on Tibet in despair at Chinese interference and move to the Nepal side.

That year the Chinese had given him permission to take trekkers up to the North Col and he thought I would make a good guinea pig. I imagine he thought that if a fifty-six-year-old with Parkinson's could do it then anyone could. For me it was the chance to participate in an expedition that would take us back in history to the expeditions of 1922 and 1924, to the time of George Mallory and Andrew Irvine. If Russ thought I was fit enough to get to the North Col and see the upper slopes of the north side of Everest, despite Parkinson's, I certainly wasn't going to turn him down. It was a generous offer but I was unsure what he wanted from me. If there's no such thing as a free lunch, then what was a free Everest trip? When I asked him he simply said I had done him some favours when he first moved to Europe and he was returning them. All I had to do was get to Kathmandu, where the streets were more crowded and more polluted than ten years before, but the welcome in the Hotel Tibet was just as warm.

We flew to Lhasa, a spectacular flight past Everest and then banking left before Makalu. In Lhasa, now a modern Chinese city of a million people, we spent the day exploring the thousand rooms of the Potala Palace, reeking of butter lamps. Graham Hoyland, my television producer friend, was writing a blog for the BBC website and asked me how I would describe it. 'Like a cross between Gormenghast and the Titanic,' I told him.

It took Mallory and Irvine six weeks to reach Base Camp from Darjeeling, but it took us three days in a Land Cruiser. I never did get to the North Col, but I got pretty close. It was a cold season and I found myself struggling, which was something of a shock. I spent a week at the head of the East Rongbuk Glacier, yet even though I'd been in much colder and much higher places, and despite my plush sleeping bag, for the first time in my life I suffered badly. Was it the effects of altitude and unseasonal weather? Or was I simply getting old?

———

By the summer of 2010 I found Parkinson's was forcing me to make bigger compromises with my life and the things that define me, in particular climbing. My balance was deteriorating and I started to have difficulty using small footholds. I was becoming a liability. I continued to go climbing with the Tuesday night team, but I would arrive fashionably late, pick an old favourite climb to say goodbye to and go to the pub early.

I had always given my life direction by tackling big projects. My collection of big days out was as good as many: *Cenotaph Corner* at the age of eighteen, the *Nose*, the Bob Graham Round, the Welsh 3,000ers, Shishapangma. These were not, as T.S. Eliot's Prufrock might have said, coffee-spoon days; these were enormous ladle days. But there seemed so few of them, maybe only a dozen in a lifetime. I was casting about for one more thing of consequence to do, when I received a phone call from David Greaves to become a patron of a charity called Pedal for Parkinson's. I had no hesitation in agreeing and went to London to meet them at a sponsored abseiling event.

During the day I heard a long-distance cycle ride was being planned and made the mistake of showing interest. The idea was to cycle from The Lizard to Dunnet Head, the southernmost and northernmost points on the British mainland, then down the west coast of Scotland to Campbeltown on the Mull of Kintyre, ferry across to Ireland, and continue to Malin Head the northernmost point of Ireland, and Mizen Head, the southernmost. After that it was on to Cork for the ferry to Swansea, and finally the cycle to Hyde Park in London. The whole journey was 2,000 miles. Mike Browell, my friend from so many long-distance projects, asked if

I would like to borrow his second-favourite bike, a Specialized carbon-fibre 'Tarmac' with Campagnolo wheels and a specially assembled rear cassette for the steeper hills. Early in the New Year I flew out to Lanzarote to join Mike for a week of endurance training. This is where I did my first 100-mile day, cycling clockwise round the island.

The team that set out in mid June 2011 was six strong and apart from me all committed cyclists. Dr Chris intended to cycle the section from The Lizard to Dunnet Head. Les, the oldest, fittest and most experienced in the party certainly did not intend to break his collarbone the day after leaving John o'Groats. If I were asked to choose which was the more dangerous, cycling or climbing, it would have to be cycling. I had bad dreams for months about huge trucks overtaking me on roads that were neither designed nor built for them.

My first altercation with the tarmac was an embarrassingly pathetic tumble on a steep hill in Gloucestershire, when I gouged out a lump of flesh from my second finger, losing my balance at zero miles per hour. The second was also at a dead stop. Arriving in Moffat, cold and wet at the end of a long day, I slowed down for a junction. I put my foot down to balance and found that it didn't work and was consequently forced to use my face instead. Then, on the outskirts of Chippenham on the last full day, I flicked the handlebar to the left, intending to ride on the pavement to make room for the thirty-eight-ton truck trying to overtake me. This time, I was moving quite fast. I knew it was going to hurt as I went down, but it could have been worse. The ground broke my fall and I managed to confine most of the damage to those bits of my face that were still recovering from my previous tumble.

There were some great moments. Arriving at John o'Groats ahead of the pack and having my photo taken by a group of OAPs, before realising that's precisely what I had become. There was the osprey I managed to catch on my camera at the moment it caught the trout, the guesthouse at Mizen Point and the sunshine on three of the twenty-eight days. There were also some bad moments: the guesthouse at Stroud, rain on the other twenty-one days and Les breaking his collarbone. There was also the discovery that the left side of my body wouldn't work for more than fifty miles for the nine days between Dunnet Head and Limerick.

The others completed 2,100 miles. As the only non-recreational cyclist I completed 1,600 miles including two consecutive days of ninety-five miles, three of eighty and an average of over sixty per day. I blame the bike for some of this. We raised almost £30,000 for Pedal for Parkinson's. I was humbled by the generosity of people we met on the road, like the lady who gave us £50 at a coffee stop in Devon and the B&B owners who didn't charge us, or rounded their invoices down. Then there was the bike mechanic in Kilmarnock who found what was wrong with my bike and spent two and a half hours fixing it and didn't even charge me for the parts let alone his labour.

I'm glad I did it but I wouldn't do it again, not that way, pre-booking accommodation and adding unnecessary pressure, and not on main roads which quite frankly are very dangerous. Motorists in general are sensitive to cyclists' problems and slow down and give you a bit of room. But there are quite a few who don't. Then there are a tiny minority who are not in the least bit sensitive and don't seem to give a damn. If they are one in a hundred, it's still one too many.

The games climbers play are many and varied. In 1967 Lito Tejada-Flores wrote a celebrated essay on the subject, highlighting the importance of style. Since then, new games have been added to the list. The North Face of the Eiger has been climbed in two hours and twenty-two minutes; the *Nose* of El Capitan has been climbed in two hours and twenty-three minutes. In Yosemite, various combinations of grade-VI climbs have been strung together in twenty-four hours and, similarly, multiple Alpine north faces have been climbed in a day. Apart from holding the Eiger record, Ueli Steck climbed a new route on the south face of Annapurna in less than two days, up and down. It is difficult to say where and how the advances of the future will be made, but they will surely come.

We are privileged in so many ways. We are educated and we have health-care. We have incomes in excess of our needs and spare time in which to enjoy spending it. Is it a reaction to free time, comfort and wealth that cause us to do such unlikely things as climb mountains and rock faces? Do we seek to achieve things that give our existence some sort of meaning?

When I am having a bad Parkinson's day, and feeling a little hard done by, I try to remember 'The Dream'. The Dream is the objective a young person aspires to realise. When you are old, The Dream is what you wish you had done when there was still time. There are many climbs I wish I had climbed but only two that cause me genuine regret. The first is the Lotus Flower Tower in the Northwest Territories of Canada –

one of the most beautiful climbs anywhere. The other is *Right Wall* on Dinas Cromlech, the landmark rock climb for my generation, a route I could and should have done, but didn't. I held the ropes for my old climbing mate Nick Longland. He failed that day but was successful a couple of weeks later. I managed all the routes leading up to it: *Memory Lane*, *Left Wall* and *Resurrection*. But I was never quite ready. The idea of top-roping crossed my mind, but then the route would have been tainted, for me at least, for all time. I had my share of great moments.

Picking my favourite route would be difficult. It would probably have to be the Regular Route on Fairview Dome, which I first climbed with Jody, again with Tom Briggs, and later with his dad, Roger. Anyway, my list would be very similar to yours, especially if you like grit. The biggest kick I got from a route was climbing *Cenotaph Corner* when I was still at school in 1963, when it was still considered to be difficult. If I were tempted, I would not chose to sell my soul for a climb, but I would sell my soul to all the devils in hell to play Bach's 'Chaconne'. I started having violin lessons at the age of five but was never much good. The high point of my musical career was playing one of the leads in Bach's double violin concerto when I was seventeen. I would like to play more, but now I have lots of free time to practise, Parkinson's has chosen to mock me.

The Dream is only an illusion. You reach out and it slips through your fingers. Some people appear to have a firm grip on theirs, but as you get to know them, you find their dreams are as ephemeral as yours. Mountains are just as illusory. Seductive in their beauty, mountains are, in reality, a narcotic, one that rapidly induces a dream state. The physical effort, the calories burned, the time, measured not in minutes like most sports, but in days, weeks and even months, requires the greatest commitment in an environment of real risk. Compare this to any team game where the action takes place over ninety minutes and where the level of commitment is paying for a round of drinks afterwards.

I came to skiing late, after I had turned twenty. As a teenager I heard friends talking about it. I would denigrate them, calling it an activity for the soft, an expensive way to go on holiday. The reality was I knew my parents could not afford for me to go on the school trips when I was at Abbotsholme, so I never asked – but I wanted to go. My first ski holiday was in Austria. At the end of my year in India, I flew from Delhi to Athens and on to Rome where I caught a train to Solden to join the Longland family. I soon managed to run the metal edge of my left ski down my right shin and spent the rest of the week nursing a deep cut and watching the others. Despite the injury I knew I wanted to be a skier. I wanted to weave my way down a steep snow slope, to hear the brittle chatter of metal edges on ice, to float through powder.

My next try was on Cairn Gorm. On the first run, down Coire Cas, I fell and cut my head on a rock that was hiding under the snow. I skied down to the car park dripping blood and caught the bus back to Aviemore, got cleaned up, had thirteen stiches, and went straight back up to the slopes. I learned by watching others and I learned quickly. By the end of the week I was able to ski quite fast, but with no room for errors, and with absolutely no style. While skiing down the White Lady I stopped at a hillock at the side of the piste. A fit-looking bloke came to a halt next to me. He suggested that rather than bend forward from the waist to get my weight over the skis, I should 'lean' forwards. That was my first ski lesson. My instructor, I found out the following week, was Eric Beard, record-holder for just about every fell-running challenge in Britain at the time and working at Glenmore Lodge. He would die tragically young in a car crash in 1969.

Two years in Antarctica gave me the opportunity to become proficient in an idiosyncratic sort of way. I learned to ski in *mukluks*, Inuit boots made from sealskin, though ours were made from canvas. They gave little by way of support, but encouraged good technique, and that was where, at last, I felt I was a skier. After starting Wild Country, I was too busy during the summer months to take any time off for a holiday so skiing filled the gap. Jan found she liked it too and we soon found skiing to be a habit. We took Jody, aged three, to the Austrian resort of Brand in 1980.

In 1981, Julian Mills, an ex-Alpine Sports employee now resident in Chamonix, and Jean-Jacques Blanc, a *Chamoniard* and one time son-in-law of Alan Blackshaw, were trying to get a specialist skiing and outdoor shop going in Chamonix. In an attempt to raise capital, they asked Dick Turnbull and I if we would be interested in becoming shareholders. Chamonix had twenty-three outdoor shops at that time, so this was always going to be a challenge. But if the shop was not my most sensible investment I still wanted to do it. The idea of being an owner of a shop in Chamonix appealed to me. I purchased a package of shares in Eurotunnel so I could get the best Channel Tunnel deals and Dick and I chipped in £10,000 for a quarter shareholding each. The important thing was that it was done frivolously. I could afford to spend the money and if it all went wrong it would be a shame but not a disaster.

We called the shop Sport Extreme and opened for business. The shop was part of a new build on the main street of Chamonix, Rue du Dr Paccard, almost opposite the Patagonia shop. Had we felt so inclined, we could have thrown an ice axe through the window from our front door. Over a period of twelve years we made little more on the investment than if we had put the cash into a building society but I revelled in the feeling that this was all part of The Dream. I got to use the latest skis and boots and expenses took care of most of the transport. I usually went out with the family for New Year. We'd have an excellent New Year dinner with friends at Le National and then spend a week in somewhere like Val d'Isère. I would have the same argument with the accountant at the tax office every time we met. If I drove out to Chamonix he would say that I was going on holiday. I would say that I needed to keep abreast of whatever was going on in the skiing and climbing market and attend board meetings of Sport Extreme.

'But you're just going on holiday.'

'No,' I would reply, 'you're just objecting to the fact that I enjoy my work.'

From time to time I have heard I am a millionaire, sometimes directly, more often from second-hand gossip. Sometimes it would be said jokingly, sometimes accusingly. Bill Supple made me smile when he introduced my daughter Jody as 'the Wild Country heiress'. The more important question was this: is what I'm doing the thing I want to be doing?

It's possible that I might have come close to being a millionaire for a brief period in the late eighties and early nineties. I didn't have a big bag of money, but given the criteria by which a company is valued, its track record and in particular its potential for future growth, I may have had assets that exceeded my liabilities by as much as a million pounds. If I had sold Wild Country in the early nineties I could have made a lot more than I did eventually. There are many things I would like to have accomplished, but being filthy rich was not one of them. Averagely rich was quite good enough. I could afford to do the things I wanted to do and live where I wanted. If it sounds a little materialistic, then a dose of materialism is damn nice every now and then.

Unlike The Dream, some of the wealth Wild Country created was tangible: buildings, machinery, materials, work in process and finished stock. More difficult is assessing the value of the work force. How does one calculate the value of the skill and motivation of the workforce?

Motivation can be a function of the wage packet, but working conditions and a friendly, supportive environment are more a reflection of the knowledge, judgement and wisdom of the management.

I used to pay the shop-floor staff at Wild Country about five per cent more than they would get if they worked anywhere else in the surrounding area. This was not out of any sense of altruism; it was the most efficient way of managing the team. In addition there was a productivity deal. When I started Wild Country, the average wage was about £2 an hour. If a trained operator could make more than two-thirds as many units as I could in an hour, fifty to my seventy-five, then they got paid for them at the same rate. If they made a hundred units, they got £3. This worked well for the first few years because I was the fastest, but after a time the girls on the Friends and Rocks assembly overhauled me.

The cost of advertising for staff or trainees is high, but if you have a reputation for being a good employer who pays well, there is no need to advertise. All you have to do is put the word out on the street and you will have the pick of the bunch. Ben & Jerry's, whose ice cream I used to get for free at our offices in New Hampshire, had a pay policy stipulating that the highest paid people in the business could not be paid more than seven times the wage of the lowest-paid worker. You may argue with the detail, but the principle is worthwhile.

Wild Country established a strong, worldwide reputation in a remarkably short time. Visitors to the factory, expecting a much bigger facility, would ask where the rest of it was. In 2012, when Salewa purchased Wild Country from DMM, it valued the brand very highly. The name still had good international recognition. The logo was still strong. The catalogues, workbooks, DVDs and other brand support added depth to the company. Despite my antipathy to hired guns, the decision to sponsor the Wide Boyz, Tom Randall and Pete Whittaker, for their campaign on *Century Crack* in Canyonlands was inspired. That was some dream.

After all the commitment and effort, at the end of that long struggle to achieve something, you realise, later rather than sooner, that you were for a time living what you imagined. But if you want to continue you have to go out and do it again. Like I said, it's ephemeral. It soon slips through your fingers.

In my case The Dream became a nightmare and wasn't in the least ephemeral. The nightmare is called Parkinson's. For the first eight years I was in control. For the last eight or so it has been slowly stopping my body from doing the things that make it possible to climb. I lost the ability to stand on small footholds some time ago. For the last two years it has been having a go at my balance. Parkinson's is like that. It goes for the things you prize most. At present it is having a go at my voice, which is starting to sound thin and dry. I still occasionally dream as I used to do, though the colours are beginning to fade. But I'm also still fighting gravity – and always will.

ACKNOWLEDGEMENTS

Thanks...

To my wife Jan for lots of things, including a valiant attempt to reconcile my imaginative spelling with something more conventional.

Special thanks to my daughter Jody for making me proud.

To Nick Longland, Dick Turnbull, Al Edmonds, Roger Briggs, Peter Freeman and Graham Hoyland for all the climbing, and to Mike Browell for lending me his bike.

To Terry Gifford, Adele Long, Angus Stokes, Geoff and Sue Douglas, and Martin Sinker for encouragement.

To Johnny Dawes, for telling me I should write a book, and Jerry Moffatt for the work he did and the fun we had on our trips to Spain.

To Steve Bean for a remarkable eight-year partnership. To Russell Brice for helping me to go high, and to Iain Peter who gave me good advice when I asked for it, but never when I didn't.

To Ed Douglas, for undertaking the editing of the final manuscript. I wrote the words, but Ed put them in the right order.

Finally, to Ray Jardine, who should take some of the blame.

Mark Vallance
22 February 2016